Language Education in the National Curriculum

Language in Education

Series Editor
Michael Stubbs

Language is central to education. Yet very little writing about language is presented in a way that is suitable for teachers to help and guide them in their classroom practice. This series aims to explore, in a non-technical way, aspects of language immediately relevant to practising and trainee teachers.

Learning about Writing: The Early Years
Pam Czerniewska

Teaching Grammar: A Guide for the National Curriculum
Richard Hudson

Girls, Boys, and Language
Joan Swann

Language Education in the National Curriculum
edited by Christopher Brumfit

Language Education in the National Curriculum

Edited by Christopher Brumfit

With contributions from

Kate Armes   Michael Benton
George Blue   Christopher Brumfit
Michael Grenfell   Andrew Hart
Janet Hooper   Virginia Kelly
Rosamond Mitchell   Melanie Smith

BLACKWELL
Oxford UK & Cambridge USA

Copyright © Basil Blackwell Ltd 1995

First published 1995

Blackwell Publishers, the publishing imprint of
Basil Blackwell Ltd
108 Cowley Road
Oxford OX4 1JF
UK

Basil Blackwell Inc.
238 Main Street
Cambridge, Massachusetts 02142
USA

British Library Cataloguing in Publication Data

A CIP catalogue record for this book is available from the British Library.

Library of Congress Cataloging-in-Publication Data

Language education in the national curriculum/edited by Christopher
    Brumfit: with contributions from Kate Armes . . . [et al.].
        p.   cm. — (Language in education)
    Includes bibliographical references and index.
    ISBN 0–631–18899–1 (alk. paper). — ISBN 0–631–18901–7 (pbk.
: alk. paper)
        1. Language and languages — Study and teaching — Great Britain.
    2. Language policy — Great Britain.   I. Brumfit, Christopher.
    II. Armes, Kate.   III. Series: Language in education (Oxford, England)
    P57.G7L35   1995
    407'.041 — dc20   94–31609
                                                                        CIP

Typeset in 11 on 13 pt Palatino by Best-set Typesetter Ltd., Hong Kong
Printed in Great Britain by Hartnolls Ltd, Bodmin, Cornwall

This book is printed on acid-free paper.

Contents

Editor's Foreword

This series contains short books on language in education, on topics where practical knowledge is urgently needed in schools. The books aim to help with daily practice in schools and classrooms in principled ways. They should be of interest to practising teachers and student teachers, to teacher trainers, advisors and inspectors, and to those involved in educational administration, for example at the level of head of department or head of school.

The books follow several important guidelines:

- their main purpose is to make knowledge about language accessible to those who need it.
- they therefore avoid jargon and presuppose no knowledge at all about linguistics.
- they are not, in fact, books about linguistics: but books about language, informed by current linguistic thinking
- they discuss topics which teachers and parents themselves think are important: What *is* grammar and why doesn't it seem to be taught these days? How do children learn to write? What is normal and abnormal in language development? Why is there so much debate about English teaching?

A great deal of knowledge has been gained about many linguistic topics which are important in education. For practical purposes, such knowledge can be accepted as widely agreed and factual – at least it is the best which we have available in areas where it is badly needed by teachers, advisors and administrators. However, this knowledge is often not in an appropriate form: it is often in journal articles or in relatively technical books.

It is therefore the responsibility of linguistics to present it to teachers, clearly and in an accessible form. If this is not done, then practical decisions will still be taken by individual teachers and others but possibly they will be uninformed by the best in current thinking about language in education.

There have recently been very large changes in the British education system, particularly centred on the Education Reform Act and the National Curriculum. In a longer-term perspective, the changes which this legislation has brought about are part of a long struggle around the forms and purposes of education. But debates about teaching English as a mother tongue and teaching foreign languages have certainly been very sharp in recent years. And there is no doubt that 'knowledge about language' has been given particular prominence (and has received a great deal of publicity in the mass media) via the curriculum proposals for English and modern languages. 'Standard English' and related topics carry a heavy symbolic load, and much of the discussion, sometimes fuelled by statements by prominent politicians and other public figures, has been confused and even hysterical. An aim of this series is to encourage considered and rational debate in an area where deeply-felt emotions are often at stake.

The books in the series have been written with British teachers in mind, though the issues they discuss are clearly also of relevance in other countries. Due to rapid changes in the school system, British teachers are currently under considerable pressures, and are under particular pressures in areas of the curriculum which concern language.

This book has been written by a well-known group of scholars in language in education. Several of the authors are individually very well known in their own right, and as a group they are uniquely qualified to tackle directly the range of topics, concerning language in schools, which are raised by the recent flood of legislation around the National Curriculum. It is the only book I know which provides a coherent criticism of all the major areas of interest to language teachers: English as a mother tongue and second language, foreign languages, bilingual children and community languages, drama, literature, literacy, media studies and knowledge about language.

The legislation around the National Curriculum has been (deliberately?) piecemeal, and not based on a coherent language policy. (Indeed, it is doubtful if the Ministers involved could make much sense of the concept of 'language policy'.) Different committees have been made to work at great speed, and in an uncoordinated fashion. The authors of this book have done teachers a great service by providing both an overview and a detailed explanation of this legislation, discussing it critically in the light of important educational and linguistic principles, and drawing out of it practical implications for teaching. The book is an important interpretation of these debates and deserves to be widely read by teachers and other educationalists. I hope it will also be carefully read at the Department for Education!

Series editor, Michael Stubbs

A Note on Curriculum Legislation

The Education Act of 1988 has 238 clauses and gave the Secretary of State for Education more than 400 new powers. Proposals for the National Curriculum (which formally applies only to England and Wales, though Scotland and Northern Ireland follow similar patterns) formed only a small part of the total legislative package, which was substantially concerned with many other contentious matters: enabling schools to opt out of local authority control, changing the funding of higher education and the conditions of academics, and establishing local financial management of schools, for example. Much of the legislation was not debated by parliament in detail, and subsequent education acts have tidied up unsatisfactory legislation, and enabled government second thoughts to be added to the major changes which had been rushed through parliament. The changes in the curriculum accompanied changes in almost every aspect of the structure and practice of education, so it was scarcely surprising that many teachers felt that they were reeling under constant attack on almost all the beliefs they had acquired in their professional careers and inherited from the past.

The curriculum changes were preceded by a large number of official working papers hinting at the direction of possible change.

The basic design of the Curriculum, as foreseen in the 1988 legislation, was as follows:

There were to be ten subjects; three were *core* – English, mathematics and science; seven further *foundation* subjects were to be taught – art, geography, history, modern languages (though only from ages 11–16), music, physical education and technology. In Wales Welsh could be either a *core* or a *foundation* subject.

The Secretary of State for Education's responsibilities include establishment of programmes of study for each of these, and definition of attainment targets, so that pupils' performance could be assessed in relation to these at the ages of seven, eleven, fourteen and sixteen.

It was expected that the demands of this curriculum would take up a minimum of 70 per cent and not more than 90 per cent of school teaching time. Cross-curricular activity was expected in areas like health education and information technology, and the schools' obligation to provide religious education would account for much of the remaining time.

Initially, particular areas of the curriculum were entrusted to government-selected working parties who made recommendations in the form of reports (usually known by the name of the Chair of each group: 'The Cox Report' for English, 'The Harris Report' for Modern Foreign Languages, etc.). These reports went directly to the Secretary of State, who then advised the National Curriculum Council (NCC) on how to convert them into NCC Consultation Reports, which in turn were converted to Draft Orders, which eventually passed through parliament and became legislation. In general, the curriculum became starker and less professionally contextualized with each refinement. With politically contentious areas of the curriculum, like English and History, this process might be extended by subsequent revisions (accompanied by much assertion and debate in the press) to the parliamentary Orders. This enabled lobbying groups (in practice most effectively new right pressure groups) to encourage change in directions they desired at each point in the revising process. Thus, for example, the debate about the role of spoken 'Standard English' resurfaces regularly, with demands to 'slim down' the curriculum enabling a narrower and narrower focus on a limited number of concepts to be the centre of political and journalistic attention.

The initial plans for assessment arose from the 'TGAT' (Task Group on Assessment and Testing) Report, presented in 1988. This recommended a ten-level scale for each subject, each level consisting of a number of *attainment targets*, and each attainment target containing a set of *statements of attainment*. The approaches to the major assessment ages of seven, eleven, fourteen and sixteen became known as the four *key stages*. Thus at any given moment, a teacher could be interested in a particular statement of attainment for a particular attainment target within a particular level as part of a particular key stage, for a particular subject.

In practice, the administrative load of this structure proved unworkable. It led to major unrest among all sectors concerned with education, culminating in the 1993 boycott of the national tests, led by teachers of English, but supported by many teachers, head teachers, governors and parents' groups. The review of National Curriculum Provision, conducted by Sir Ron Dearing, has been published as this book goes to press, and recommends a substantial reduction in complexity by slimming down the curricular provision. The precise impact of these proposals on the language curriculum remains to be seen.

To help the uninitiated reader, a list of the major recent government reports referred to follows. The most significant of these have been annotated.

Annotated List of Recent Government Reports Cited

1975 *A Language for Life (The Bullock Report)*. London: HMSO

An extended statement of the liberal consensus on English teaching and its role in education: to a considerable extent this represents the views that are under pressure from new right critics of educational values in the recent past.

1977 *Modern Languages in Comprehensive Schools*. London, HMSO

1983 *Foreign Languages in the School Curriculum: a consultative paper*. London: DES/WO

1984 *English 5–16*. Curriculum Matters 1. London: HMSO

The first of a series of papers from Her Majesty's Inspectorate (HMI) which tentatively put forward detailed curriculum principles, many of which were subsequently incorporated into National Curriculum guidelines.

1985 *Education for All (The Swann Report)*. London: HMSO

A major report on the education of ethnic minorities, with some discussion of language matters, but a refusal to recommend state support for community languages or bilingual education, and a view that independent teaching of English as a Second Language could be racist in effect.

1986 *English from 5–16, The Responses to Curriculum Matters 1*. London: HMSO

Contains a summary of responses to the 1984 paper in the last

xiv   List of Recent Government Reports Cited

officially supported public debate between teachers and the DES on substantive curriculum matters relating to language.

1986 *Foreign Languages in the School Curriculum: a draft statement of policy*. London: DES/WO

The beginnings of a recognition of increasing importance for modern languages in a European context.

1987 *Modern Foreign Languages 11 to 16*. Curriculum Matters 8. London: HMSO

HMIs' first proposals towards a new modern languages curriculum.

1988 *Languages in the School Curriculum: a Statement of Policy*. London: DES/WO

1988 *Report of the Committee of Inquiry into the Teaching of English Language (The Kingman Report)*. London: HMSO

The most substantial official attempt to address the issue of teachers' and learners' knowledge about language. Although directed to look at 'English', the Committee produced a check-list of general language categories that teachers and learners should be aware of.

1988 *Advancing A Levels: Report of a Committee appointed by the Secretary of State for Education and Science and the Secretary of State for Wales (The Higginson Report)*, London: HMSO

Recommended a diversification of advanced examination provision, but the proposals, though receiving widespread support in industry and education, have been consistently rejected by the government.

1988 *National Curriculum: Task Group on Assessment and Testing: A Report*, London: DES/WO

The 'TGAT' Report: the beginnings of the ten-level assessment structure for the whole curriculum.

1989 *English for Ages 5 to 16 (The Cox Report)*. London: DES

In spite of widespread fears of a narrowly-focused utilitarianism, this report of the national curriculum working group on English gained general support from the English teaching profession. However, the elements that link it most closely with the tradition of the Bullock Report (1975 above) have been gradually removed with successive revisions.

1989 *Drama from 5–16*. Curriculum Matters 17. London: HMSO

1989 *Welsh for Ages 5 to 16*. Cardiff: Welsh Office Education Department

National Curriculum proposals for Welsh, offering the only bilingual education available under National Curriculum legislation.

1990 *National Curriculum Modern Foreign Languages Working Group: Initial Advice. (The Harris Report)*. Darlington: DES

Performs the same role for Foreign Languages as the 1989 Cox Report does for English. But it is a broader brush document, since it has to address all the languages of the European Union, plus a range of others for which there is potential demand in Britain. Although generally welcomed, the implementation of its proposals for languages other than French remain difficult to predict, and its recommendations are being severely limited by the general slimming down of the National Curriculum expected from 1994 onwards.

1990 *English in the National Curriculum (No. 2)*. London: HMSO

The official proposals, reducing the Cox Report's discussion to a form thought to be administratively and legislatively manageable.

1990 *A Survey of Language Awareness and Foreign Language Taster Courses*. London: HMSO

1991 *Art for Ages 5 to 14*. York: National Curriculum Council

1991 *Music for Ages 5 to 14*. York: National Curriculum Council

1991 *Drama in the National Curriculum, Wall Chart*. York: National Curriculum Council

1991 *Modern Foreign Languages in the National Curriculum*. London: HMSO

The official proposals arising from the recommendations of the Harris Report, but turning them into an administratively and legislatively workable shape.

1992 *Modern Foreign Languages Non-statutory Guidance*. York: National Curriculum Council

1992 *National Curriculum English: The Case for Revising the Order*. York: National Curriculum Council

1993 *English for Ages 5–16: Proposals for the Revised Order*. London: HMSO

Further modifications and revisions.

1993 *The National Curriculum and its Assessment: Final Report (The Dearing Report)*. London: School Curriculum and Assessment Authority

Recommendations for a 'slimmed-down' curriculum in all areas, to reduce the workload, and return some freedom of manoeuvre to schools.

Centre for Language in Education, University of Southampton

The Centre was established in 1986–7 to bring together staff across the university in order to promote research and development work, in-service contacts, teaching, and other academic activities. 'Language in Education' is interpreted broadly, and staff have expertise in educational aspects of Drama, English as a Mother Tongue, EFL/ESL, Modern Languages, Language Awareness, Applied Linguistics, Literature, Media Studies, Multilingual and Multicultural Education, Reading, Research Methods, Television Studies, Linguistics, Sociolinguistics, Critical Theory, and Psycholinguistics.

There are about 30 academic staff members from the Faculties of Arts, Social Sciences and Educational Studies, and over 100 associate members from outside the university across southern England. Links have been established with 20 national and international centres of excellence in this field. There is a steady stream of overseas visitors to the Centre. Regular volumes of Working Papers, and less formal Occasional Papers, are produced to disseminate research, scholarship and development work. Some of this feeds in to the regular seminars and conferences held by the CLE (on average there has been an event for teachers and researchers, usually involving outside speakers, once every three weeks since 1987). The Centre also provides a base for networks of researchers in a range of language-related areas (for example Foreign Language Classroom Research, Media Education, Language Teacher Education, and Specific Learning Difficulties). Staff in the Centre have published widely, and edit a number of international journals; students working in the Centre are encouraged to participate in national and international conferences to present their work or to make contact with other researchers.

Acknowledgements

I am very grateful to George Blue for help in revising the final text, and to Michael Stubbs for helpful comments on the first draft of the book. We would all like to thank Rita Corbidge and Hazel Paul for substantial clerical support at various stages during the project.

Introduction

This book started out in 1989 as an attempt to summarize our understanding of the practice of language teaching. Although the arguments for and against the National Curriculum were at that time raging around us, it appeared that we should before long have documents outlining the expectations of teachers and learners in both English and Foreign Languages. We hoped, therefore, to illustrate from our experience as teachers, teacher educators and researchers the ways in which a coherent approach to linguistic and literary development could be established. In the Centre for Language in Education at Southampton University we had formulated an approach which saw language development as part of a single process of learning and maturation, a process which in contemporary society benefits from the guidance of professionally informed teachers. We saw this book as a contribution to a continuing debate, and a practical source of guidance for teachers, both those new to the profession, and those who were looking for refreshment and updating.

At the time we expected that there would be a period of consolidation, while publishers, writers, administrators and teachers could relate the new requirements to the best practices of the past and the most exciting proposals for the future. Instead, we found ourselves, along with all other teachers, responding to a bewildering set of improvizations, policy changes and reversals. Consequently, we have had to abandon our original plan, and attempt to interpret current policy directions in the light of the best available professional practice, backed up by understanding from empirical research and theoretical analysis. This means that the book has developed into an analysis and critique of current ideas and current practice in all the major areas of interest to language teachers. Where appropriate, we have referred to recent developments in curriculum policy, but we have not tried to tie ourselves to any specific pieces of legislation because the situation has become too unstable.

Nonetheless, we discuss legislation in some detail. To help the reader, an outline of main National Curriculum requirements and an annotated list of recent government reports can be found on p. xiii, and it is hoped that a brief skim through those will enable the inexperienced reader to clarify the general pattern of government intervention in school language activity.

Enthusiasm for National Curriculum legislation varies in different parts of our field. For Modern Linguists, there appears to be an increased recognition of foreign language needs (at least for Europe), and a belief in the necessity of languages for all. For those concerned with creativity, personal response and aesthetic issues, the National Curriculum has sometimes looked like an assault on almost everything that serious teachers have learnt in years of professional commitment and development. For those interested in languages other than the official languages of European states, or in bilingual learners, the emptiness at the centre of curricular discussion has been educationally and morally shocking. For those who believe that a concern for effective literacy (including media literacy) is a necessary base for all other learning, the National Curriculum may offer an opportunity to address issues that have been less central in some discussion than they might have been.

It would be reasonable to ask why we are addressing these issues now, when the shape of the curriculum is still emerging. The answer is that the education profession cannot afford to allow serious debate and discussion to be hijacked by the needs of legislators and subsequent press reporting. Neither of these promotes careful or considered response. At the same time, we should not equate care and consideration with an unwillingness to take up a position. This book reflects a range of deeply-felt responses to the curriculum as it is emerging, some positive, some negative. In spite of our opposition in some chapters to positions we believe to be educationally indefensible, in others we show that we believe there are opportunities for valuable development created by recent legislation. We have not hesitated to engage directly with political pronouncements on occasions (sometimes because they have been helpful, sometimes because they have been misguided or confused), but most of the book is concerned with making *educational* sense of official pronouncements preceding or following the 1988 legislation. By the time the book is published, the ground rules will again have been changed, and the financial or curricular goalposts will have retreated still further from the players. Such permanent revolution (which may be temporarily interrupted by Dearing's slimmed down curriculum and – for the first time – an official request for stability in the system) makes a detailed exploration of fundamental principles all the more important.

So much of the response to national curriculum legislation has been reaction to the assessment-driven and bureaucratic structure surrounding the changes, that less attention has been given to straight pedagogic principles than they deserve. Although we do refer to assessment issues on occasions, our prime concern is to make sense of the educational process implied by the curriculum debates, and to learning and teaching procedures within that process, in relation to research and theoretical debate from the past thirty or so years.

One effect of the speed of change (and even more of the speed of subsequent revision) was the removal from professional teachers of any time for taking stock. Not only were new teaching, assessment, administrative, and professional training arrangements all being imposed at once in an atmosphere of public criticism and political distrust, but each change was followed by adjustments, revisions and U-turns that made it difficult to examine what was happening because it kept changing. Consequently, there has been little book-length, considered analysis of the curricular changes, in relation to what is known of the theory and practice of teaching. Because change now occurs through the exercise of direct political power, opportunities to explore curricular issues with professional care and sophistication are liable to disappear. Any attempt to predict problems in proposed legislation risks accusations of reflecting 'professional vested interests refusing to change with the times'. And, indeed, knowledge does give a vested interest; but so too does ignorance accompanied by the power to intervene. If we have to learn to live with permanent change, as a result of government ministers now having more direct control of the detailed day-to-day practice of schools than at any time since compulsory education was established, we can only do so rationally within a clearly articulated set of beliefs about the major curriculum areas. So it is high time that professionals started detailed and scholarly public debate on what is happening in each curriculum area.

The discussion in this book attempts to raise some of the questions that are shown to be important by professional knowledge (based on experience, reflection, empirical research, knowledge of what happened in the past and what happens in other countries, as well as on commitment and 'interest'). As with any serious debate, it is an invitation to participate, a series of questions with partial answers, not a set of dogmatic assertions. In looking closely at the various language arts in school, we hope to provide a perspective which is at the same time engaged, critical, and analytical, while reflecting a considered position on the relations between the various language groups represented in schools, and on their roles in an overall education philosophy.

Within this common aim, our perspectives will inevitably differ. The national curriculum affects Drama, Literacy, Foreign Languages and Bilingual Learners in different ways. The responses of teachers concerned with these and other professional groupings have varied according to their own needs at the time of the legislation. But all our responses share a commitment to the integrity of language-based work, and to a high quality, demanding, honest and equal education system. We try to test the proposition that all language development is part of an overall maturation process that schools can guide, but cannot entirely control. Consequently, the totality of language intervention in schools is best seen as part of a single policy, in which teachers of English and modern languages (for historical reasons) will inevitably play central roles. We have not felt able to address the implications of this position for teachers of other subjects (who of course also contribute substantially to language development), but we have tried to locate our discussion within a broad social and educational context. Consequently, all of us have referred outwards to general issues of social policy when appropriate, all of us have been concerned with languages as expressions of individual and social wishes and needs, and all of us see 'language' as inevitably embracing literary and creative needs, mass communication, social confidence, and personal identity. The extent to which each of these aspects is significant in a particular sphere of language teaching varies, of course, according to the level and experience of learners, but each chapter in this book reflects a different dimension of language use.

We toyed with the idea of calling this book 'From Babble to Babel'; although it is not as all-embracing as that title suggests, it certainly attempts to recognize the development of language as a life-long process, and one which does not necessarily lead to world peace and mass communication. The Babel myth is a salutary reminder that language is a double-edged asset, one that can be used to facilitate incomprehension as much as comprehension. Because of that, teachers should not separate the development of linguistic competences from concerns about the values they are – and will be – used to express. That, in a nutshell, is the basis of our analysis. We hope that it contributes to the development and improvement of the curriculum, and that others will feel able to take up the challenges posed by these arguments and suggestions.

The book is the result of years of collaboration between the authors, as staff (and/or as students) in the Faculty of Educational Studies, University of Southampton, which has made a unique commitment to 'Language in Education' in the broadest sense by encouraging the cross-Faculty Centre for Language in Education. There is a sense, therefore, in which we can take collective responsibility for the book. At the same time, it would be unfair not to identify the individuals who were the original writers of each chapter. I have edited all the material, and attempted to make our styles reasonably consistent. Nonetheless, because we have tried to address all topics that we feel are central to a serious curriculum policy in this area, some chapters cannot relate closely to the legislation or government recommendation, either because they do not exist, or because they are vague or ill-formed. Consequently, we have not tried to address the topics in exactly the same way in each chapter. The organization and style reflects the approach felt by the main author to be most appropriate to the issue being addressed.

Main authors by chapter are as follows: 1 Christopher Brumfit, 2 Rosamond Mitchell, 3 Christopher Brumfit, 4 Virginia Kelly, 5 Michael Benton, 6 Kate Armes, 7 Andrew Hart, 8 Christopher Brumfit and Rosamond Mitchell, 9 Michael Grenfell, 10 Melanie Smith, 11 Janet Hooper, 12 George Blue.

References appear at the end of the book, followed by suggestions of a few sources of useful further reading for each chapter. These are provided for readers who wish to take the argument further.

We hope, then, that this will provide both teachers and students with a serious, coherent (but not schematic) approach to the language curriculum. We would welcome comments from readers, at the Centre for Language in Education, University of Southampton, Southampton SO17 1BJ.

Christopher Brumfit

Part I

General Issues

1

Language in the Curriculum

Introduction

This book attempts to lay the basis for implementing a coherent language curriculum in schools at a time of rapid change. It draws upon experience of research and teaching at primary, secondary and tertiary levels, and in English (including language, literature, media and drama work), foreign language and second language classes. This chapter will outline the rationale for our approach, and relate this to the social context of British education. It will also refer to what is known about language development and language use, for teachers of language must necessarily guide a process which will take place, for all normal human beings, whether or not schools intervene. Unlike many other subject areas, language work involves guidance of processes that do not depend mainly on schools.

Everyone both learns language in a conscious and organised way, and acquires it in an unconscious and accidental way. Parents and carers of children expose them to language and guide their progress. They correct misuse of words, and often correct pronunciation and grammar. Children themselves ask questions about language, and guide the ways in which adults and other children talk to them. Sometimes even quite young children 'correct' adults when they hear them using language differently from their friends or other adults. We grow up conscious of language variety just as we grow up conscious of human variety.

We also become increasingly aware that language variation has social significance. Going to school (for all children, even the children of teachers!), exposes us to a new and different linguistic environment. We meet other children whose language varies from ours (sometimes slightly, sometimes substantially, when they may speak other languages which we have never heard before). We learn early in our school careers that if a teacher says 'Would you like to read now?' that this is a polite order, rather than a genuine request. We learn, even if we do not make this explicit to ourselves, that the style of speech appropriate for the playground is not used in more formal moments in class, that speech to large groups like school assemblies differs from speech in small groups in class, and that some of the private language used at home (taboo words, terms of endearment, private family jokes and references) is inappropriate for school. For some, the shift from home to school may mean moving from one language to another; for everyone, it will mean a shift in dialect.

In addition, for almost everyone, school means moving from a substantially oral culture to a strongly literate one. Even though many homes have many books, even though television and computer games expose most children to written language, even though some children's religious classes may demand literacy at an early age, the jump to school is a jump into a world where you are expected to read and write, and where your teachers will use these as a major means of communication for the next ten years at least. You will be surrounded by books, and pictures with text; you will be asked to write, both words and numbers; you will be expected to read and produce material for other people to read. And your own spoken language will inevitably change because of this exposure to the written word. So, too, will your expectations and your ways of thinking.

What is more, these processes will continue for the whole of your life. We never stop learning language, though our memory becomes more fallible as we grow older. Any of us could list words that we have acquired in the last five years – perhaps because they are new coinages for new ideas, perhaps because we have moved to a new environment and encountered someone else's dialect for the first time, perhaps because we are learning a new subject and new terms to go with it, perhaps even because we have invented new terms for new private ideas. When we learn a new language, or move into a new and difficult subject area, we become self-conscious about this process of language development. But it is going on all the time, for all of us. Our pronunciation changes gradually in response to the speech of those around us (people moving to the United States soon acquire some features of the American accent); our vocabulary expands; our grammar changes. Perhaps we say 'gotten' from contact with Americans, or 'different to' instead of 'different from' because we live with people who do this, or avoid the generic 'he' and opt for 'they' because we are convinced by feminist arguments. Whatever the causes, our language shifts according to who we speak to, and adapts to the expectations of our hearers. And of course it also changes according to context. Written language differs from spoken, formal from informal; speech to strangers is different from speech to people whose ideas we know well.

So life is a constant process of linguistic adaptation and development, which is partly within our control and partly not. We may not want to acquire the pronunciation of our neighbours when we move to live in a new area – but most of us will to some degree. Much of the unconscious language change we shall not notice or bother about, for we have more important things to concern us. But sometimes language becomes a major factor in social activity. Then we may try to make conscious choices, even to prevent other people from behaving linguistically in certain ways. We may believe, for example, that to be illiterate is to be excluded from democratic politics and we may decide that therefore literacy is a necessary goal for all children, whether they want it or not, and enforce teaching to read through a national curriculum. (We could also, less desirably, enforce literacy in a totalitarian state from a desire to control all reading and thus increase state control – literacy is not in itself either good or bad.) We may, as we saw earlier, make language choices out of a wish to support feminist beliefs about language and equality. Parents may forbid their children to use certain language because it is felt to be vulgar or obscene or inappropriately posh, or just because they do not like difference from the way they talk. All of these cause intervention into unconscious language development for social reasons.

And schools unavoidably participate in this intervention. They are there, among other purposes, to promote literacy – as well as creativity, critical competence, clear-thinking, empathy, self-confidence, and other qualities closely connected with language use. The procedures teachers adopt, the curriculum within which they work, the kinds of assessment that are imposed on schools by the demands of politicians, employers and parents, all reflect systematic attempts to intervene in the language acquisition process for social purposes. What role we personally see for creativity, for literary understanding, for international communication, for media awareness, to name only a few potential concerns, will directly affect the attitude we take to the learning of language.

Because we all acquire language, it is closely bound up with our personal identity. Because of its social role, we need it for participation in a world of different identities and different social goals from our own. Schooling has to mediate between individual needs and social ambitions, and language development is central to this process. In the next section, we shall outline a Charter for language development which we believe to be defensible as a basis for a just, sensitive and liberating approach to language in schools.

What Should We Be Entitled To?

The Charter outlined below was originally proposed, before charters became fashionable political devices, in a lecture in 1986 (published as Brumfit, 1989) and attempted to use work in language learning to underpin language policies for schools in the British context. The purpose of the Charter was to define provision in national terms: to formulate language policy for education in such a way that all learners, whatever the linguistic knowledge and capacities they brought to their schooling, would be equally addressed, and equally included in the formal provision.

The argument for a 'charter' concept is that this enables us to define what is desirable, and to express a commitment to realising those goals, insofar as resources and circumstances permit. The charter would provide a frame of reference against which the commitment of each school or education authority could be measured.

The intention is that this Charter should be:

- equally beneficial to each individual entitled to education (and thus it would not in principle advantage English speakers at the expense of others);
- sensitive to the most authoritative reseach on language acquisition and education;
- realizable, at least to some degree, for every learner; and
- responsive to the linguistic needs of British-educated learners for the foreseeable future.

Language Charter

It is the policy of _____

(insert name of institution or authority)

to enable all learners, to the maximum extent possible within available legislation and resources

(i)   to develop their own mother tongue or dialect to maximum confident and effective use;

(ii)   to develop competence in a range of styles of English for educational, work-based, social and public-life purposes;

(iii)   to develop their knowledge of how language operates in a multilingual society, including basic experience of languages other than their own that are significant either in education or the local community;

(iv)   to develop as extensive as possible a practical competence in at least one language other than their own.

It is our belief that the development of these four strands in combination will contribute to an effective language

---

curriculum for Britain in the twenty-first century more than emphasis on any one of them separately at the expense of the others.

Signed: _____

Date: _____

The major unusual feature of this Charter is a determination to see the home dialect of English, or other community language *plus* access to English as the language of education and public life *plus* foreign and classical language development as part of a single coherent strategy. It is not incompatible with a sensitive working out of national curriculum requirements, but it is also defensible as a coherent strategy which reflects the ways in which individuals and social groups use language themselves.

It also links language development with broader social goals. British education has to be responsive to linguistic and cultural diversity. The Charter is couched in terms which apply to every single learner resident in Britain. Thus it does not diminish some people's rights at the expense of others. Because it is responsive to the latest current research, it is intellectually defensible. Because each element is being addressed to some extent already by teachers and community leaders, it is realizable, at least in part. But above all, it provides an agenda for agreement on what effective language development consists of.

Such a Charter should prevent the rigidity of the National Curriculum from becoming stultifying, enabling it to be effective in ways that motivate teachers and learners. It will guide implementation, while at the same time enabling a sensitive and well-informed extension of understanding to be developed as change inevitably takes place.

This proposal also enables us to build on the practice of teachers of language throughout the school system. Effective development of language, whether a personal language or dialect, or a public and national one, requires awareness of literary traditions and practices, of the nature of the media through which much external communication passes, of what it is to be a reader, and of how to be a confident user of language. These involve processes as much as they involve knowledge. Literature is something we participate in, as well as something we know about; improvization and story-telling are practices that have social and therapeutic value; communication is too complex a phenomenon to be reduced to merely knowing, merely expressing, or merely performing to specified competences. In the chapters that follow, we attempt to offer critical and sympathetic comment on the many dimensions of language activity that constitute the language curriculum in education.

2

The National Curriculum as a Language Policy

Although there is no indication that the government's intentions with the National Curriculum legislation were to move towards a language policy, there is undoubtedly such a policy implicit in the changes, at least for England and Wales. Because of the speed of implementation, work in individual subjects was piecemeal between 1988 and 1993, with the National Curriculum Council attempting to add retrospective consistency while engaged in its prime task of converting recommendations from subject panels into legislatively convenient packages, and subsequently into effective guidelines for teachers. The language area followed this pattern, with separate working parties for English, Welsh and Modern Foreign Languages, defined as separate subjects, and no single group responsible for 'language' overall (DES/WO, 1989, 1990c; WO, 1989).

Language provision for languages other than English distinguishes clearly between the Celtic languages (which have long-standing historical claims and established political 'territory' of their own), and all other languages. Welsh has achieved a range of National Curriculum provision, not only for those who positively want it, though they must be living in Wales, but also for all children at school in Wales (WO, 1989), whether they or their parents want it or not. It is compulsory to teach Welsh to all, and a range of differentiated Programmes of Study and Attainment Targets has been proposed, so that children in Welsh medium schools are accommodated, as well as those starting from scratch to learn it as a subject, with adaptation to the differing needs of individuals starting at primary or at secondary levels. In Scotland, although the demarcation is not so clear, and the National Curriculum legislation is not directly applicable, a similar pattern is appearing in the Western Isles for Gaelic. In contrast, language in the primary curriculum for England, as Mitchell (1991: 107) points out, has been decisively redefined as English:

> Ignoring many recent, local initiatives to promote the all-sided development of bilingual children's language skills (documented for example in Bourne, 1989), the final, statutory version of the English curriculum document (DES/WO, 1990d) contains *one* single statutory sentence regarding other languages: 'Pupils should be encouraged to respect their own language(s) or dialect(s) and those of others'. (DES/WO, 1990d: 25)

Nor is the situation different at secondary level in England. It is true that a number of community/heritage languages have been included among those which may be taught as 'modern foreign languages' (Arabic, Bengali, Chinese, Greek, Gujerati, Modern Hebrew, Hindi, Italian, Panjabi, Turkish, and Urdu). But the report of the National Curriculum Modern Foreign Languages Working Group makes it clear that these are targeted primarily at beginners with no prior knowledge – they are regarded as foreign languages, not as heritage languages (DES/WO, 1990c, chs 3 and 4; DES/WO, 1991). There is no sense in which such provision is seen as maintaining the language of already proficient users; nor is the need for flexibility of interpretation of work in these areas (necessary for circumstances in which there will be wide differentiation between the expectations and attainment of individual learners) emphasized in any way.

There are a number of implicit principles in this conceptualization of language work, particularly territory and political power. We shall return to these issues later. For the moment let us simply note that two major areas of potentially valuable research to support the development of an effective curriculum remain unexploited. First, there has been no systematic account of actual attainment levels in language introduced into the discussion: the kind of evidence required from the Assessment of Performance Unit (APU) studies, or called for in

academic conferences has not been forthcoming. Second, possible comparisons with national curriculum requirements for
other countries have not been made at all. Nor indeed is there
serious evidence of careful consideration of research literature
from any major professional sources.

Principles behind Curricular Assumptions

The history of the debate about teaching English is instructive in
attempting to perceive consistency in the National Curriculum
on language questions. The HMI Report, *English 5–16* (DES,
1984) attempted to move 'English' away from the generally literary focus of the liberal tradition that had culminated in the
'Bullock Report' (DES, 1975), and included a specific (though
somewhat crudely presented) section on knowledge about
language. This provoked a variety of largely negative responses
which were summarised in a later report in the same series (DES,
1986). At the same time, political and journalistic concern about
the language issue led to the establishment of the 'Kingman
Inquiry', which fed in to the eventual reports on English specifically aimed at the National Curriculum itself.

What is striking about the original *English 5–16*, though, and
also about the Kingman Report (DES, 1988b), is that both of them
have pre-empted to 'English' the whole business of language
development, without serious acknowledgement that this has
any implications, either for other first languages than English,
or for the development of competence at school in foreign
languages (or – indeed – classics). 'Language development' was
simply assumed to be 'English development'. For a policy of any
kind on other languages, it was necessary to look at the implications of a quite different report, whose recommendations were
substantially ignored by National Curriculum discussion: the
Swann Report (DES, 1985) on the education of ethnic minority
children. Here, it is claimed that any potential benefits from the
establishment of community languages as a regular part of the
curriculum in schools (except as single subjects at secondary

level), are outweighed by possible negative social consequences. They argued that systematic in-school community language provision, particularly the use of these languages as media of instruction, could prove socially divisive, and contribute to the educational 'ghettoization' of ethnic minorities. The sole exception to this principle recognised by the report's authors was induction into the school at the very beginning.

The desire of non-English-using speech communities to transmit community/heritage languages to their children was recognized, but seen as something which communities themselves should take responsibility for. This should not, the Report argued, be the concern of mainstream schooling. The arguments in favour of bilingual schooling are summarized, focusing on individual psychological, social and educational benefits. Cognitive development, confidence and motivation, and linguistic skills will all be improved. Then there are benefits to the child's speech community. Use of the community/heritage language in school is seen as having symbolic value, enhancing the status of the language both among community members and others, practical value, contributing to the vitality of the speech community through language maintenance, and cultural value in maintaining and transmitting the community's tradition. Finally, support for multilingualism is seen as important for society as a whole, both culturally and economically. Even though Swann ultimately rejects these arguments, they provide an interesting parallel with those found in the National Curriculum Welsh consultative report, with the title 'The advantages of bilingualism' (WO, 1989: 6). Here, in contrast to the initial focus of the previous list on individual children's claimed 'needs', the Welsh list begins with the social and cultural argument that language maintenance/transmission is the 'responsibility of educators today' – on the grounds of linguistic antiquity and present-day vitality, as well as nationhood/territoriality (para 2.18). In paragraphs 2.19 and 2.20, arguments are advanced which have no close parallel in the former list. These refer to Welsh as a necessary precondition for full participation in linguistic/cultural life (much as English National Curriculum documentation presumes an essential role for standard English in the political and democratic process). It is also argued in the final paragraph (2.24) that a knowledge of Welsh is vocationally advantageous.

Only at the end (paragraph 2.23) does the document address the personal development of the individual, which came first for Swann's list. And the claims are much more muted; it is argued more that cognitive development, and control of English, will not be adversely affected by bilingual Welsh/English schooling, rather than that this may be helped by such experience.

One explanation for the differences between these two lists may be the different social prestige, and differing extent of existing institutionalisation (both in education and the wider society), of the so-called 'indigenous' language on the one hand, and the newer community/heritage languages of England on the other.

For the low status languages with limited institutionalization, the prime emphasis has been placed on the individual child's presumed 'needs'. Moreover, for these children, a key argument advanced is that that bilingual/heritage language school experience will enhance achievement in terms of 'mainstream' norms and goals (i.e. overall school success), as well as promoting a sense of identity and providing access to the culture and life of their local speech community. The goals of language and cultural maintenance or transmission are mentioned only tentatively in comparison. The speech community is not territorially defined, as it is with Welsh, even in the sense of local school decision making; there is clearly no expectation that the wider society could adopt the minority language as a means of wider communication beyond the group, even in localities with thriving speech communities.

But for Welsh language maintenance arguments take pride of place. There is a clear territorial claim that all children in Wales study Welsh, not only those from currently Welsh-using communities. This is necessary, it is claimed, for full participation in the public life of Wales, while arguments about possible enhancement of individual children's cognitive and academic achievement are much less central to the Welsh case, and are played down. This 'territorial' view is further supported by the fact that Welsh speakers outside Wales have no opportunities whatsoever to learn Welsh within the National Curriculum.

The arguments being currently advanced for bilingual education involving the new community/heritage languages are thus primarily educational; the arguments involving the 'indigenous' language are primarily social and cultural.

Whatever the merits of the respective sets of arguments, however, it is clear that Welsh has done very substantially better out of the National Curriculum policy than any other minority language.

So far, then, we have identified two elements in the National Curriculum policy in England and Wales. First there is what we might call a 'lingual' role for English in England: that is the claim that English is not so much a particular language, as the source of language development in general. Second, there is a territorial claim for Welsh, and implicitly for English, that within a particular political territory, all inhabitants should have access to the language of claimed political power. Note also that this claim is not dependent on demonstration of the effectiveness or otherwise of such language use. As recent protests by parents show, not all inhabitants of Wales perceive their linguistic needs to coincide with those defined in National Curriculum documentation, while in contrast the Swann Report's chapters on minority language speaking groups (DES, 1985: chs 10–14) make it clear that access to English certainly does carry the support of minority communities.

Other countries, for example Australia, Canada, and New Zealand, have adopted less territorial views of language provision within multilingual communities. For Britain, though, if we follow our argument so far, the choice seems to be 'lingualism' through English and 'multilingualism' outside schools (unless you live in Welsh territory).

But that is not the whole story. Modern languages, as we noted at the beginning, introduce the final element in National Curriculum provision. The current official position about 'Modern Foreign Languages' is defined in DES, 1991, published in November. The relevant clause of the statutory instrument (39) reads as follows:

Schools *must* offer one or more of the official languages of the EC (Danish, Dutch, French, German, Modern Greek, Italian,

Portugese, Spanish). *Schools may in addition offer* one or more of the non-EC languages listed (Arabic, Bengali, Gujerati, Hindi, Japanese, Mandarin or Cantonese Chinese, Modern Hebrew, Panjabi, Russian, Turkish, Urdu). Pupils choosing to do one of the non-EC languages do not have to study one of the official languages of the EC as well. But the non-EC language will not count as the foundation subject *unless* the school offers all pupils concerned the possibility of studying an official language of the EC to meet the National Curriculum requirements.

The rationale behind this statement (which offers a stronger role for community languages than earlier consultation documents did) is difficult to interpret, but appears to be something along these lines. Within school, learners should have the option of learning languages which have a political and territorial base in the European community. If they refuse this option they may if they choose learn languages that have an official and/or territorial status in certain other parts of the world, some of which (like Russian) have no sizeable language community in UK, others of which (like Panjabi) do have such a community. But some sizeable UK language groups (like Polish, Irish, or Welsh unless you live in Wales) may not choose their language as an option.

Further, as the Statements of Attainment make clear, all languages are to be treated in the same way (with minor exceptions for the learning of Chinese and Japanese characters). So that learners of all these languages are learning, as beginners, a 'modern, foreign language' – and not a mother tongue, not a community language, but a foreign language for use in school. Languages of community or family use are sometimes ignored, as Polish and Irish are, or are presumed to be learnt as school languages with the levels of attainment suitable for German or Italian as a foreign language. It is difficult to find a term for this policy – perhaps 'scholingual'?

Since the second list contains twelve languages, it is a little difficult to see why an entirely open choice, negotiated locally but perhaps requiring DES (now DFE) approval, could not have been suggested. However, to do that would imply that the prime issue is student (or parent) individual choice. In fact, as we have seen, other considerations appear to be the prime ones.

To summarize, then. The underlying linguistic principles of the National Curriculum for England and Wales appear to be the following:

1. An assumption that language development in general must take place through the medium of English: English lingualism.

2. An assumption that bilingualism in state education is territorially based, so that only Welsh may be an entitlement as an alternative language of development, or as a community language option: territorial multilingualism.

3. An assumption that *all* other language provision in school derives from a centrally determined list, with all learners being expected to take routes appropriate for school-based foreign language learning: scholingualism.

These principles were originally proposed in a lecture in February 1992 (to the National Congress on Languages in Education). However, debates between 1992 and 1994 about the place of Standard English in speech and writing in school do little to change the summary above. The development of a rich and just linguistic curriculum, incorporating all aspects of language use, has to take place within these constraints. Fortunately, as we show in later chapters, the National Curriculum enables us to develop effective work in at least some of these key areas.

Note

The argument of this chapter was presented in part in Mitchell (1991), and at the presentation on which that was based (Annual Meeting of the British Association for Applied Linguistics in Swansea, September 1990); and in part at the meeting of the National Congress on Languages in Education, London, February 1992.

Part II

Language in School

3

English Teaching: Language, Literacy and Learning

The purpose of this chapter is to consider the role of language in English teaching in relation to other major aims. It is divided into four sections: 'Cultural Heritage', 'Growth', 'Functional Literacy' and 'Critical Awareness'. A fifth approach, which draws on several of these, is discussed in more detail in chapter 5. Each of these sections examines a general approach for English teachers and for teachers of language in British schools which has been influential in recent years, and which implies specific ways of organizing language development. However, it is important to recognize that these approaches cannot sensibly be completely separated. All four are appropriate goals for development of language in schools, because anybody who is moving through the school system will have to develop:

- some awareness of their cultural inheritance in language and literature through the years;
- an understanding, as they grow and mature, of this inheritance and what it means to them, and how they relate to it;
- an ability to function effectively with spoken and written language and to understand both of them for normal activities as a citizen; and
- a critical perspective on the whole process.

In relation to the Language Charter, all of these factors will be important in each of the four elements, though the emphasis will vary with different sets of learners and different social contexts. Indeed, teachers who orientate themselves towards one or other of these particular models will only rarely ignore aspects of the others. A well-rounded development of language will necessarily involve recognition of all of them.

Cultural Heritage

The tradition of cultural heritage derives ultimately from the teaching of classics. It can be epitomized by Hollindale (1972: 335) saying 'the English teacher's province . . . includes the transmission of a great literature, together with some sense of the wider culture from which that literature sprang; the custody of a great language'. Throughout the 1970s this concern, being somewhat unfashionable, especially when it concentrated on simple acquisition of knowledge, was probably voiced less often than it was felt. Nonetheless, in recent years developments in national curriculum procedures have made it clear that for many people outside the teaching profession an awareness of the major writers and their works is felt to be a necessary part of the inheritance for learners of English.

This model can have several different aspects to it and may be seen as containing the following elements:

Knowledge about the tradition of English literature.
Knowledge about how literature operates.
Knowledge about the history of the English language.

Although this tradition embraces a concern for knowledge, it also expects there to be direct experience of effective language use through valued writing from the past. At the same time, though, the concept of 'good writing' is not entirely straightforward. At different times in history there have been very distinct traditions. In the eighteenth century, for example, the successful literary artist was expected to produce a carefully crafted prose with balanced clauses, and even to derive the rhythms of the English language from a tradition of writing that went back ultimately to the style of effective Latin writers. The selection of vocabulary was expected to distinguish literary language from the normal spoken language, and there was constant emphasis on classical reference. An example of this tradition would be the works of Samuel Johnson. In the period after the French Revolution, there was a desire to bring literary language back to a close relationship to the spoken language of ordinary people, illustrated by Wordsworth and Coleridge's preface to the *Lyrical Ballads* in 1799. In the twentieth century it has been most frequent for people to demand plain, clear English (plainness being identified with honesty), particularly under the influence of such polemicists as George Orwell. Because of the way different periods value different styles, it makes sense to introduce an element of critical awareness into discussions both of literature and of styles for learners to imitate in their own writing. It is clear that literary style, like other linguistic choices, reflects particular personal, social and political positions taken up by the people who advocate them.

Knowledge of the tradition of English literature is also problematic in some respects. There may not be major disagreement about the need for professional literary critics to know about the various traditions they reflect on. Clearly, to write with authority they require an understanding of the history of English literature in all its aspects, with an awareness of the social context in which each writer was active. But whether a version of such understanding is desirable for all learners, and if so what is the best way of leading people towards this understanding, is less clear. There is a substantial debate about the extent to which learners should be introduced to literary texts which are immediately accessible, or whether they should be introduced to the classics regardless of accessibility. In its strongest form this boils down to an argument that if you are only going to read three or four books in your life these should be three or four classics. Such a view is difficult to defend if we are interested in the quality of reading, but those who believe that exposure to major tokens of our culture is important will defend even this position.

This debate becomes educationally more defensible if there is an intention to locate any contact with the classics into an understanding of the role which literature plays in society, in order that people can understand what they are doing when they are reading. But even this will require some degree of understanding of the social development of the English language, and of the concerns of particular writers. Because the concerns of particular writers inevitably reflect the periods in which they operate, the whole business of the nature of the tradition, and the so-called 'canon' of English literature, is seen by many as repressive and serving the interests of an elite minority. It is not necessary to agree with this view to see that the 'canon' is undoubtedly a reflection of the particular interests of particular readers, writers, publishers and teachers, usually university teachers. Nonetheless, it is perfectly possible to see the 'canon' as those major works from the past which – for whatever reason – enable us to enrich our discussion of present concerns. In this sense the list of books which are part of the 'canon' varies from time to time, though there are many works, such as those of Shakespeare or Homer, which will in practice be found in everybody's list. Such books are works which we enjoy discussing, which we feel have some relevance to the different situations of different individuals and different periods of history, and which we feel contribute to our understanding of the human condition. Such a weak version of the tradition enables us to value works for themselves, as well as see how they contribute to a developing series of themes which make some contribution towards our national awareness.

However, we have to recognize that our national awareness is a product of the people who live in the country at a particular moment. The British Isles have never been peopled by individuals all of whom were born and bred here. Throughout the last 2000 years there have been successions of immigrations and invasions, and all of these have contributed to contemporary culture. Consequently, the development of the English language, both in the way in which it has spread outwards with the British and American Empires, and in the way in which it has received input from writers from other countries, has never been straightforward. The strong desire of some critics to have a centrist notion of the tradition of English literature runs counter to the internationalism which is implicit in almost all major writers. To mention only a few areas, much of English literature has been heavily dependent on influx from Irish writers. Recent writers in English of note contain a very large number of people who originally were from areas of the British Commonwealth. It is only necessary to mention Nobel Prize winners like Wole Soyinka, or Booker Prize winners like Kazuo Ishiguro, or Ben Okri, or the most famous of contemporary novelists (for reasons which are nothing to do with literature) Salman Rushdie.

Finally, we should refer to the issue of knowledge of the history of the English language. We have already mentioned this as an inevitable part of the development of literary understanding, but it is also an ideal way of understanding the ways in which the language has had to respond to changing historical events.

All in all, the cultural heritage model is valuable as establishing a historical base for our understanding of language or literature. However, English teachers do not see their role as primarily historical. They see themselves as contributing to understanding the processes of reading so that people can become skilled and competent readers. For this purpose the cultural heritage model is merely providing the tokens for playing a game, but it does not provide the game itself.

Growth Model

The growth model is most clearly described in John Dixon's book *Growth through English* originally published in 1967. This picked up a metaphor which was increasingly associated with a group of commentators around Professor Jimmy Britton, who were concerned with the 'naturalness' of English development. It emphasizes the extent to which maturation inevitably leads children to develop their own language and to move it in directions which enable them to acquire literary understanding as well as acquire competence in all uses of language for normal purposes.

However, there are considerable dangers in producing a metaphor associated with growth, without any reference to the goals to which this growth should be directed. It would be correctly seen that English teachers were avoiding their responsibilities if they were merely to refer to undifferentiated maturation as a desirable language teaching goal. It is one thing to say that children should be enabled to make maximally effective use of the language and reading abilities that they develop; it is another to say that they should simply be allowed to develop and be given the opportunities to flower in any direction that they wish. This would be refusing to make any definition whatsoever of 'maximally effective'. Growth and change are not in themselves valuable unless they are directed to defensible ends. Nonetheless, the value of this image is that it enables us to see that English teaching is in certain respects quite distinct from the teaching of other subjects. English language development will take place even if learners never go to school at all, providing they are socialized and have widespread contact with other English language speakers.Consequently, the English teacher is in certain important respects guiding a process which is there anyway, rather than providing access to a body of understanding which might be entirely avoided by learners if they did not go to school at all.

Functional Literacy

This approach (defined as 'Adult needs', DES/WO, 1989: 2–23) derives directly from concerns about the social needs of the present-day world. Ultimately it relates back to needs analysis and to a society-based set of goals. In English teaching it has been most powerful in the past in Further Education, but it nonetheless has major implications for schools and in recent debates has been prominent as part of the criticism of the liberal, allegedly wishy-washy traditions of recent English teaching in schools. The argument that is made most strongly is that democracy depends upon individuals being able to participate fully in the language of their community, and that access to written (and in many people's views spoken) standard English is necessary for full participation. Insofar as schools provide access to the literacy which is necessary for achievement in almost any subject in British education, this is undoubtedly a very strong case. Recent developments in the National Curriculum in 1992–3 make it clear that there is just as much concern about spoken English, in the eyes of some commentators including those most influential on government policies, as there is for written English. The arguments for this are less straightforward, but the general view is that people who cannot express themselves in the dialect used for most advanced professional work throughout the nation are likely to be both ineffective and disadvantaged in work.

Underlying the notion of functional literacy is a concept of needs analysis. The so-called needs of learners are analyzed, and these needs are then defined as the bases for the English curriculum. It would be difficult to argue that large numbers of English teachers have ever been against the achievement of basic literacy, and in most cases teachers have accepted the view that competent spoken language is an essential prerequisite for participation in adult life also. However, there is very considerable argument about the most effective *means* towards these ends. Many people would feel that the most important means of developing skilled speech is confident use of your own dialect, which will move towards standard English as it is increasingly exposed to standard English, and as individuals are motivated to make use of the dialect of wider communication. Not everybody is happy about the view that there should be explicit, let alone dogmatic instruction in standard English as if it is a second dialect. In contrast with the heritage model, the functional literacy model concentrates on the current social needs of learners, and is orientated towards skills rather than knowledge. The risk is that learners' needs may be perceived as relatively impoverished; certainly the needs are specifically defined by the curriculum, so that there is a danger of over-direction. The expectations that are attributed to learners may be so reduced as to be patronising, or they may bear little relation to learners' own wants. On the other hand, to neglect such needs is to neglect the minimum requirement for participation in a democracy, and many people would argue that some English teachers have tended to concentrate too much on higher needs, even with learners who have not fulfilled the basic requirements of such participation. Whatever view we take, we clearly cannot be satisfied if there are substantial numbers of learners whose English competence is less than they want themselves to compete for jobs, or participate in normal social and political activities.

Critical Awareness

To some extent the movement towards critical awareness (or 'Cultural analysis', DES/WO, 1989: 2.25) has tried to redress the imbalances caused by too exclusive adherence to some of the goals discussed above, particularly in the functional literacy approach. Awareness of language, and of the ways in which readers and listeners may be manipulated, is held to be liberating for learners. This movement encompasses a political attitude with concerns wider than language (though its proponents would argue that the other approaches also incorporate concerns beyond language). It takes up some strands of earlier discussion associated with the tradition following the literary critic F. R. Leavis, using critical techniques refined on literary texts to examine non-literary use of language. Leavis undoubtedly had a general social programme in mind, and saw literature as central to the development of subtle and sensitive reading and interpretation of everything around us. But the critical language awareness movement takes its inspiration from sociology and linguistics, through the analysis of all types of communicative discourse, more than from literary criticism. Nonetheless, it has the advantage over functional literacy of providing some motivation for needing to understand how language operates, and a possible rationale for linking aspects of all these major approaches. The critical awareness that is required under this model involves understanding the principles which are exemplified in constructing 'texts' (a term used to cover both spoken and written language), and seeing them as either conscious or unconscious choices by those who make the 'texts'. 'Texts' are viewed as necessarily serving the interests of particular groups of people (because we all produce language to serve our own interests in communicating), and, because there are many competing interests, they reflect the conflicts within any society. Consequently this is not a model which is attractive to people who wish to see society as essentially harmonious and stable.

The proponents of a critical awareness view would argue that society has never been stable, and that the contention for position and power is something which anybody looking at the development of either literature or language needs to understand. It is possible, as with the other models, to accept a strong or a weak position. The strong position may be attacked by many who feel that underlying it is essentially a desire to use language learning for political and social indoctrination, Whether or not one accepts this view, it is difficult to see how any education can object to the notion that the key concepts underlying such terms as 'literature', 'classical texts', 'language', or 'dialect', should be problematized, analysed and questioned. Anybody who considers these terms in contemporary society will inevitably realize that they are concepts which reflect categories that have been to some degree created by such powerful social and economic factors as educational institutions, particularly higher education, publishing houses, dictionary makers, government policies (including such policies as the imposition of a national curriculum) and similar agencies. Contemporary philosophy makes it impossible for anyone not to see such major manifestations of power as of interest and significance in themselves, and cutting English teaching off from the awareness of this would be to isolate it quite unnecessarily from much-debated contemporary ideas.

Conclusion

It will be clear from the way in which we have reported on these different traditions that we do not believe them to be entirely separate. English teachers who are concerned that their learners should develop as intelligent, humane and knowledgeable members of society will inevitably draw upon all of these. It is essential that anybody who is going to participate in the late twentieth century world should be able to communicate as effectively as possible. Consequently, any English teacher must have among their aims those of the Language Charter (pp. 13–14). They would expect all learners to have confidence in standard English for all work, public life, and educational purposes, as well as the confidence and competence to express themselves if they wished totally fluently in their own dialect or their own mother tongue.

At the same time, they would expect that anybody would be able to recognize and respond to the major literary tradition within English, recognizing that this tradition is one that is rich and diverse and constantly being renewed. However, to be able to respond to this tradition does require considerable knowledge of the writers and texts that operate within this tradition, and of those that challenge it. Further, we would expect that the process by which people acquire this is a process which is compatible with the maturation process of learners as they go through the school system, and we would expect that any intelligent person would look at these categories recognizing that they are not categories that should be taken for granted as simple, straightforward and uncontentious facts.

Within this rich and diverse range of traditions, it should be possible for effective English teaching to operate. It should furthermore be possible for modern language teaching to develop out of this tradition and to reinforce the secure base in working with English as a first language or a national language towards the understanding of other traditions in other languages through that work.

4

Reading to Learn

Introduction

The development of pupils' reading skills has a vital place within the National Curriculum and within our Language Charter alike. Reading forms a separate attainment target within the English requirements, where it is given a wide definition as 'the development of the ability to read accurately, widely and fluently, encountering texts of increasing complexity' (DFE, 1993a: 25). Although initial reading skills are covered by Level 3, the strands for comprehension, response to literature and information handling continue to be elaborated through to Level 10. Moreover, reading is one of the areas where National Curriculum documents have from the beginning most strongly emphasised a need for a whole school policy and cross-curricular planning and activities. The development of reading is not to be left just to teachers of English; within specific subject material there is a recognition that it will be impossible to separate success in mastering the subject content from a need to read and understand written materials. History, for example, with its emphasis on source material, acknowledges its dependence 'on an ability to understand and use language . . . [including] Reading (AT2)' (Non-statutory Guidance, C10).

It is interesting to remember the origins of the word 'read' (Wolf, 1980: 109) were to do with taking charge or explaining the obscure, rather than decoding texts. We still talk about reading the weather from looking at the sky or reading maps or even reading a person's palm. This is a wide view of reading as collecting and interpreting information, and it is well represented in the National Curriculum. Tables, graphs and other displays of numerical and statistical data, sources in History such as posters, parish records, census data or photographs, maps in Geography and plans in Design and Technology, for example, all need to be 'read' accurately. In this chapter, where we are concerned mainly with reading words, one should not ignore this breadth. Even within English, reading specifically includes 'meaning beyond the literal' (DFE, 1993a: Key Stages 3 and 4: 40) and 'the language of advertising' and 'the language of poetry' are given as examples pupils might consider. And it is clearly vital to their success as readers that pupils learn to cope with a wide range of text types across all their subjects.

Our thinking about reading within the National Curriculum, then, must not be focused just on how children first learn to recognise individual words in print, important as that is, but much more widely on the process of how they can become expert readers and on the factors we must consider as teachers if we are to facilitate this process for them. Under such a curriculum, the teaching of reading cannot be the province of a select group of specialists designated as Reading Teachers or even English Teachers. Where would they find the time, or indeed the expertise, to instruct pupils in the finer points of reading in Science, History, Geography and Technology, each of which has, to some extent at least, its own special vocabulary and forms of text organisation? On the other hand, this is not to deny that there is a domain of expertise involved in the teaching of reading, particularly in helping beginning readers and those who find progress difficult to achieve. Somehow, relevant parts of this expertise must be shared among a wide group of subject teachers at all levels.

To take this view of what makes a reader involves an acknowledgement of the importance of both reading skill and reading development when setting almost all work for pupils. Planning for the second of these is more unusual than considering the first, especially in subject work other than English. But a groundwork of good practice exists in both individual classrooms and published studies. Teachers at Key Stage 1 are often adept at seeing most lessons as having double focus: improving reading *and* conveying subject content. Pupils are actively taught both medium and message via well-planned and deliberate strategies. This duality is not always carried forward by teachers of older age groups. They may assume pupils will advance in reading skill simply by exposure to more complex reading situations and texts; and indeed this does happen for many readers but equally it does not for others. Or teachers may see the difficulties pupils are having but not have the expertise to deal with them. Paradoxically, it may be hard for many teachers to help with reading because they are such good readers themselves. For them, the complexity of what is going on is lost in the fluency of automatic performance. They are expert readers, living in a world of words, seldom needing to isolate and think about 'what to do when in difficulty' and perhaps with little to call on in designing help for pupils except random memories of their own learning experiences. The distinction between being a good reader oneself and being adept at helping poorer readers progress is analogous to being a competent driver or computer-user and being able to teach someone else; a good deal of reflection and some acquisition of technical skill lies between. It is the purpose of this chapter to suggest promising pathways for the reflection and some of the technical skills which we need both for ourselves and our pupils.

Learning to read

There is much that we do not know about how people learn to read, and attempting to unweave the threads led at one time to a focus on separate and isolated skills. If only we can check that the child has all the component skills, ran the argument, then we can train him or her in any that are missing and then all children will learn to read. For initial reading this led to structured practice in decoding skills and word attack, the era of flash cards and the cat on the mat. At a higher level of competence, there was a similar focus on something called 'higher order skills': formal practice in techniques such as outlining. Although there is an appealing tidiness about the idea of systematically finding and training component skills until a whole is achieved, it did not prove a magic answer at either initial or higher levels (Brown, 1982: 47ff). Certainly there *are* skills involved in the learning of all stages of reading, but it seems that it is the putting together of these skills which is crucial. Successful reading is automatic and integrative. Realizing this, some researchers swung strongly in the other direction (e.g. Smith, 1982). They focused on the natural, social way children learn to speak and suggested this could be applied to reading. If we help children concentrate on finding meaning in text, they argued, and give them plenty of practice, the skills will develop naturally, just as they do with speech. This became quite a popular view, but unfortunately not all children made clear progress under this regime either.

The extremes of these positions are not tenable for real teachers of real learners today. But we can learn something by reflecting on their opposition. They express the tension caused by shifting one's focus between the obvious technical skill with which good readers cope with difficult new words or complicated, unfamiliar text (Brown, 1982), and the automatic, integrative nature of fluent reading displayed by those same performers when everything is going along smoothly. Focusing constantly on one or other aspect of reading, and deriving an entire theory of reading instruction from it, would lead to an apparent split between analytical and naturalistic approaches. What we need to do instead is look at how good readers read, including how they sort out difficulties, and learn from that study how to help our less successful pupils improve.

An important question to ask ourselves is how we know if our pupils are becoming 'expert' or even 'good' readers? In other contexts an answer might be that they can read well enough for what they want to do with reading. But National Curriculum reading is 'school' reading and in school we have a number of purposes which we impose on pupils. Reading for personal enjoyment is a specific goal, but so too are learning for subject work, gathering knowledge and appreciation of written works which are part of our national cultural heritage, and being able to comprehend and respond to a number of forms of writing which are commonly used by adults in Britain (such as letters, reports, news and magazine articles). Ambitious target skills for information handling are outlined at the higher levels of English, such as selecting and collating information from a variety of sources, and the major material for this must be expected to come from other subject areas. There is a strong emphasis in all of this on the link between reading and learning. Enjoyment and personal response are valued, but with texts of 'increasing complexity' as the focus, and an emphasis on 'the quality and depth of what they read' (Key Stage 2, pt. 5), reading for learning is the purpose of most reading in school.

The goals set by the National Curriculum for our readers are ambitious: reading with 'fluency, accuracy and understanding' (Key Stage 1), 'enthusiastic and reflective' (Key Stage 2), and eventually 'independent' reading (Key Stages 3 and 4). Indeed, we are trying to produce an expert at learning from and about text by reading! A model highlighting four sets of factors taken into account by expert learners, including learners of reading, may help us organize some thoughts about how we can help our readers learn (Campione and Armbruster, 1985). Expert learners, setting out to master new material, would decide how they were going to deal with it by considering four general areas: the nature of the material to be learnt, the learning activities (techniques) which might be employed to learn with, the goal or 'criterial task' (what they may have to do later to demonstrate mastery of the learning), and their own characteristics and preferences as a learner. No one of these domains is more important than the others, although the way they interact may be different in different learning situations.

In the centre of Figure 1 is the learner. Each domain, or set of factors, interacts through the learner with all the others. Although for convenience we may consider them separately, in the end the model will help us remember that everything works

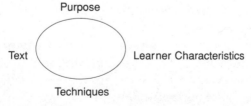

Figure 1   Reading to learn – some areas to guide our thinking.
Source: Adapted from Campione and Armbruster, 1985 and Jenkins, 1979.

– or does not work – together. But something else is important: a good learner exercises control within each of these domains and brings them together to develop a plan for learning. So they might consider what has to be read (the text) and think about how it needs to be mastered, perhaps for a test in Geography. This involves recall of key points (the criterial task) and note-making, techniques that might have proved useful in a similar situation in the past. Because this learner likes diagrams (a characteristic of the learner) and recognizes that the text shows a process (analysis of the material), they may then translate the text into a drawing with labels for the different stages. Then to get ready for the test, they may self-test by trying to reconstruct the notes from memory the next day. The expertise of the learner *as a learner* (not their mastery of the content) is measured by the control they can exert over this whole process and the way the different aspects can be brought together to serve their ends.

Suppose we were able to watch a pupil at work on this reading and learning task. As teachers, we can think about what we observed at two different levels. Firstly, we might consider it diagnostically. How good a learner is our pupil? How well did they 'read' the text in relation to the end task of being ready for the test? And if the learning was not effective, where did the problems arise? Was the text hard to read because its words were difficult? or because the learner did not recognize it as a description of a process? or because the steps were not clearly explained in the passage? Perhaps the learner was trying to remember everything rather than making suitable notes? or did not know a technique to match this style of material? And so on. There are many points at which we might notice a breakdown in learning control more specific, and therefore more helpful to our future teaching, than a generalized 'They didn't read it very well.'

A second way of reflecting on our observation of this pupil at work is to ask how we could intervene, not only to help the pupil do better at this task but to leave him or her in a better position to tackle a similar task another time. As we think specifically about this, let us go around the four domains of the model and reflect on how they may affect the teaching and learning of reading.

Text

There is a view of reading that says it is merely turning printed symbols into spoken sounds, but one would be unlikely to find a thoughtful reader who would agree with this for long, if at all. Reading is making sense of written language; without the sense, we have what is sometimes called 'barking at print' – the ability to say the words but not comprehend, which misses the entire point of reading. This is not to say we can never read things without being mystified by the content or the language of the text, but we should know when we are mystified and react appropriately to this mystification. This is as much a part of reading as being able to speak a particular word we see in print. It follows from this that *what* learning readers are given to read is vitally important. As Margaret Meek says, we cannot 'treat all text as the neutral substance on which the process works, as if the reader did the same things with a poem, a timetable, a warning notice' (Meek, 1988: 5). Real reading is a varied and complex activity which children master only if they practice with a wide variety of texts, read in a supportive context.

Margaret Donaldson (1978), writing about the development of children's thinking, gives learning to read an important place in the development of thinking skills. She begins with what she calls the dramatic differences between the spoken and the written word.

> The spoken word (unless recorded, which is another thing again) exists for a brief moment as one element in a tangle of shifting events . . . The written word endures. It is there on the page, distinct, lasting. We may return to it tomorrow. By its very nature it can be quite free of non-linguistic context. (p. 90)

Written language has to stand alone. There are no gestures or expressions, no tone of voice and often no context of action to support it. It can be moved away from the situation in which it began, and leave the reader to make sense of just the words. It is this 'disembedding' of written language from non-linguistic contexts that provides both the opportunity and the difficulty of reading. In providing opportunity, the persistence of the written text allows a reader to come at it again and again, not to decode the sound (although that too may be important for early readers) but to establish meaning. These written words can be revisited and thought about without risk of memory failure. They can touch off thought which can wander freely without fear of losing the starting point. Written words can also be shared. Two readers can begin from the same text, make separate thought-journeys and return to compare their experiences.

Some of the difficulty of reading also comes from its stand alone, disembedded quality. There is a widespread awareness that some children arrive in school with spoken language not matched to the demands of group-based learning. They need help from teachers in bridging the gap from the immediate, familiar language they use at home to a somewhat specialized, more formal language used in school. This bridging must extend into reading, guiding us to choose texts which are close enough to the child's personal spoken language to be naturally meaningful to the new reader (Clay, 1979, ch. 5).

Donaldson argues that beginning to read is a critical opportunity to begin to recognize language as something that exists in its own right, not just as an adjunct of actions or immediate situations, and that from this awareness in turn flows the beginnings of the kind of controlled thinking which is at the heart of problem-solving behaviour. Children with this sort of awareness learn, for instance, that the exact wording of a question or problem may be critical. They therefore examine the language for its exact meaning, checking the meanings and relationships of terms against an initial impression of what is being asked or required. Donaldson's view is that this reflective approach to language is a major part of children's development of the ability to attend to relevant aspects of a situation and hence to focus on developing relevant solutions to problems.

> Those very features of the written word which encourage awareness of language may also encourage awareness of one's own thinking and be relevant to the development of intellectual self-control, with incalculable consequences for the development of

the kinds of thinking which are characteristic of logic, mathematics and the sciences. (p. 95)

This is to look at reading through the other end of the telescope from a 'crack the code' view. Making the 'right' sound for a set of written squiggles is an external sign that one necessary part of learning to read is being mastered, but the interaction of reader with coherent text is the heart of the matter. Even in reading a list of individual words, language resonances are touched off in the reader which are critical to understanding. Carried to its conclusion we could surmise that for older pupils, even a question about what a certain word *means* will be more difficult for children who do not read well, because the 'stand alone' idea of language will be so much less familiar to them than to a reader. This way of thinking about language and reading may help explain a difficulty encountered in some older children: the persistent 'mis-reading' of the questions teachers use to set essays or for examinations. How often do we hear, 'They just don't read the question!' Citing work with young pre-readers, Donaldson found a tendency for them to 'substitute a more natural question' (p. 89) for that asked by the experimenter, rather than to focus on the exact words as used by the task-setter. Is this not what our older pupils do? They, like their young counterparts, are adopting a meaning without checking the words.

We need to be conscious of the extent to which older pupils also depend on shared contexts of classroom experience and discourse to help them find meaning in the kinds of texts we ask them to read (Edwards and Mercer, 1986). This is not true only for less successful readers. Those 'more demanding texts' suggested by the National Curriculum as the goal of our best readers will be in part the formal, academic style of more advanced subject texts. This is far removed from the speech and early reading experience which our pupils are generally likely to have met, just that sort of written word which is most disembedded from social context and related to abstract and logical thinking, and we should not assume they will find meaning accessible without definite assistance from us.

The emphasis on familiarity with and ability to use a wide range of texts within the National Curriculum is striking, both in English and in considering reading in other subjects. Davies has suggested (1990) that one way to help make planning the teaching of reading manageable is to begin by classifying the genres with which pupils need to become familiar according to primary social function and reader purpose. Such a classification could be used to help bring the mass of reading material under control and link it to the individual needs of pupils at any given point, as well as to pedagogical aims of extending and broadening the reading experiences pupils might have if left to themselves. She argues a case for our need as teachers to have deliberate methods of arriving at an understanding of what pupils select for themselves to read and to link this to a broad, rationally defined view of the pattern of texts we propose for them to read. Particularly important, she stresses involving pupils in seeing the overview of this classification system – the character and function of different types of text and how this influences the different reading strategies which might be used in reading them. This is an important idea, remembering the control element in our four-point model, because it could begin to help our learners explicitly link things about the text with techniques for reading and learning.

Goal, Purpose and Criterial Tasks

Goals have already appeared in this discussion in the form of National Curriculum goals and teaching goals. Here let us think about the purposes which learners have when they are reading particular texts, which are on the whole much narrower. Readers in school might be reading a story, searching for particular bits of information for topic work, filling in background before writing an essay, or going back over notes to revise for a test. Any of us, in doing any of these, might say we were using a different 'style' of reading. Effective readers can vary the speed and attention of reading, reading swiftly or slowly, concentrating on confirming previous expectation or discovering new ideas. They can also vary the *focus* of their attention, thinking as they go about the organization of the material, for example, or about how an author uses language. It is this ability to control reading to make it effective which is picked up when the English Programme of Study says (Key Stage 2) that pupils should differentiate their reading style for different purposes.

We need some care, however, not to oversimplify the very complex analysis and controls which come into this quadrant of our model of what a learner does. The two examples of reading purpose mentioned at Key Stage 2 are gaining an overall impression of the text and locating a specific piece of information and they are linked to two specific techniques: skimming and scanning. The danger is that we might think these two purposes and techniques for reading are most of what we need to cover, rather than a quick sample. In fact, purpose interacts with all the other areas – the text, the reader's characteristics, and the range of reading strategies controlled by the learner – to define a style of reading which a particular reader may adopt. In the very next paragraph, for example, are two purposes for reading which are common in school: distinguish between fact and opinion, and make succinct notes (4 ii of Key Stage 2). Just how a good reader would go about either of these tasks would vary with, among other things, the familiarity of the content, the complexity of how it was expressed, the surface features of the text (headings or lack of them, for example) and the note-making techniques known to the reader.

This is not to suggest that for teachers to help readers focus on the purpose of their reading or develop the self-control to adjust their reading style is anything except a worthwhile enterprise. On the contrary, both are vital to mature reading and studying, but they will not be helped by missing the complexity of what either reader or teacher is trying to do. For learners to adjust their reading style to help themselves achieve defined goals is the heart of strategic behaviour. Technique and strategy are often used as interchangeable terms, but the difference in their meaning highlights an important step in learning. A technique is a mechanical skill based on expert knowledge. A strategy is a plan of action to reach a goal. We can teach techniques, and even encourage practice, but it is the learner independently deciding to use a particular technique to reach a goal that turns it into a strategy.

There is considerable evidence that this transition to purposeful strategy use is difficult, and particularly that it is difficult for poorer readers. Children may know a lot of relevant things, including specifically how to skim text, for example, and yet still not be aware that they could put their knowledge to work to help them learn. Even at college, some students may read everything in the same way and at the same rate. Clearly this area of being explicitly aware of a purpose for reading and learning to choose from a range of possible ways to read, one which is suitable to the current text, task and situation, is one to reflect on.

In school the immediate purpose of reading is frequently set by a teacher. 'Read this and answer the questions.' 'Learn that section for a test.' 'Go to the library and find out about frogs.' Answering the questions, knowing the answers for the test, or making notes about frogs can be called 'criterial tasks', that is, they set the criteria by which the success or failure of the reader's learning will be judged. There are two things that all teachers could do that would at the very least provide a facilitating context for pupils to learn about purpose and reading. The first is to be sure they make both task and purpose explicit before pupils begin reading. This is not as trivial an undertaking as it might sound, since it is easy, especially with older children, to slip into instructions such as 'just read it and make a few notes', where the focus of the notes (and hence the learning) may be anything but clear to the pupil. The second is to spend a few minutes discussing purpose and reading style with the class whenever an opportunity presents itself in the course of normal classroom work. This regular re-visiting of the issue in a practical context will make clear its importance and help pupils clarify their ideas by discussion with both teacher and peers.

Some kinds of reading (and writing) tasks allow pupils to develop highly effective strategies for meeting the immediate requirement but thereby by-pass the teacher's underlying purpose. An example is the 'comprehension' question which a pupil can answer in neat sentences without understanding the content. Try reading this short passage and answering the question which follows:

It must be admitted, however, that there is an occasional pumtumference of a diseased condition in wild animals which seems like a giky martable. Let us return to the retites.

1.   What does this remarkable case seem like?

(From C. Sutton, *Communicating in the Classroom*, cited in Bulman, 1985, p. 91)

This is a constructed example; the real version can be much more difficult to detect, which accounts for the fact that some pupils who have missed out almost wholly on the reality of reading comprehension still survive their classroom assignments with an appearance of success. The short-term purpose of 'finish the assignment neatly' has over-ridden the longer term goal of understanding the topic. Thinking in terms of purpose served by this reading task helps make explicit the interweaving of language knowledge which underlies effective teaching of reading at the higher levels. A pupil satisfied with the answer, 'It seems like a giky martable,' has correctly manipulated the sentences in the text but has not advanced in either subject knowledge or reading skill; and the criterial task, which should be monitoring both, has revealed neither failure. Understanding terminology is the issue here, whether it is counted as a reading or a curriculum issue. A group task focused on 'find and clarify any terms you do not understand' would have fostered more learning than the apparently rigorous list of questions to answer, both about the subject and about what is involved in mature reading.

A moral for teachers from the above example is that there is a good deal of technical skill in detecting how well our pupils use their reading and also in setting 'double purpose' tasks and activities, covering content and reading. A useful starting point can be books on reading intended for teachers of English as a foreign language, since they often explicitly target purposeful reading of complex text in an analytical way (for example, Grellet, 1981). Not every pupil will need this detailed teaching, but teachers need to be aware for the sake of those that do.

Techniques and Strategies

Good readers have a stock of specific ways of approaching and managing texts; this goes hand-in-hand with varying reading style for differing purposes. For expert learners, techniques are fun. It is interesting to learn new ones, challenging to try them out, satisfying when they work. But we have already seen in the case of reading for specific purposes that for less expert pupils, the mastering of when to use techniques is not straightforward. This can apply throughout the learning-to-read process, from its very beginnings to the reading-to-learn applications more common with older pupils. For example, it is recognized that many expert readers find it useful to underline or highlight key sections of texts to help them understand and remember what they are reading. However, many attempts to train pupils to use the techniques of underlining or highlighting to improve their reading effectiveness appear to be successful during the training period, but produce little improvement in how well the pupils do on tests of content comprehension. (A number of such studies are reviewed in Brown, 1982.) For these learners, techniques are not fun, or even effective.

The problem seems to lie in the amount of control the reader exercises over the technique, which shows up in two ways: one is in how securely the technique is mastered in itself and the other how confidently the learner can then deploy it as a method of achieving his or her purpose. To master the use of highlighting or underlining as an aid to study, for example, readers need first to see how and why it might be helpful (roughly, it enables the reader to glance back and quickly focus on points which are particularly important in the text). Then they need to practise, first how to choose which parts to highlight and later using the highlighted text to aid recall. It must prove successful in helping learning before our new learner will believe in it! Feeling comfortable with the technique of highlighting may take quite a lot of practice, since every text is a little different and therefore presents slightly different problems of choice. And then there is still the second stage to go, that of moving to using highlighting as a strategy. Here the learner takes full control, able to decide in a complex learning situation that highlighting is the technique to use, and confident of being able to select the relevant things to highlight.

The difficulty in teaching techniques to do with reading is that they take a long time to learn. To be useful, they need to be flexible and powerful, which means learners need both an introductory teaching period and opportunities to practise with sufficient support to ensure they gradually master the complexities of using the technique in many varied situations. One way of arranging this is through what is called scaffolded teaching (Wood et al., 1976; Beed et al., 1991). This is a supportive style of teaching in which a learner works with a more experienced person to achieve a goal together. As they work, the expert exposes not only the actions which need to be learned but the thinking behind them; points of decision and making choices are particularly attended to. As the learner gains knowledge and confidence over a number of joint experiences, the expert gradually hands over control until the learner becomes independent. Discussion of the thinking behind the practice is a crucial part of this style of teaching, and so is expectation of success. It is particularly appropriate to learning complex activities, since it provides support while the learner internalizes the decision-making skills needed for success.

A scaffolded approach to teaching is not new to sensitive teachers, of course. But recently there has been specific attention to applying it to reading instruction, to the role of dialogue and social interaction in the learning, and to incorporating it specifically into programmes which teachers can use in classrooms. A widely successful approach to rescuing early failing readers, Marie Clay's 'Reading Recovery', is essentially a scaffolded learning approach (Clay, 1985). Clay's emphasis is not on devising specific materials for the children but training the teacher in detailed analytical observation of the children's reading behaviour as a basis for deciding which reading strategies to foster in a child as they share reading activities together. It is a blending of a very precise technical knowledge on the part of the teacher with a supportive, task-based environment for the child. Dialogue between them mediates the transfer of expertise from one to the other.

Also based on scaffolded teaching, the 'Reciprocal Teaching' programme was developed in the USA to improve reading comprehension (Brown and Palincsar, 1987). The programme was developed for 12-year olds but has since been used successfully with much younger as well as much older pupils. It is based on four techniques used by good readers when they are reading text they find difficult:

- summarizing;
- clarifying terminology or language structures which are unclear;
- formulating a good 'test' question based on sections of the text; and
- predicting what the next section will be about.

The methodology of Reciprocal Teaching is critical. Pupils are not only taught the techniques, using a variety of texts at their intellectual (not reading comprehension) level; they also practise in groups on shared texts, taking turns to be the group manager. The role of the manager is to choose people for the various activities but also, and crucially, to provide feedback to the participants. A teacher participates in each group and initially is the manager, providing a model of how the techniques should be used and giving feedback to pupils to help them improve their techniques. As pupils become more skillful, the teacher hands over control to them and they help each other decide which are good questions and what points need clarification. In learning to foster correct use of a technique in others, pupils acting as 'manager' significantly advance their own ability to apply the techniques strategically. In later parts of the research project, varying conditions were used to establish that this pupil-into-teacher element and its encouragement of reflective learning was a key factor in the significantly increased comprehension of text shown by most of the participants. Two other important findings, both relevant to the National Curriculum reading context, are:

1. that pupils did best when the reading texts were directly related to their subject work; and

2. that the period of instruction before the strategies were assimilated and transferred to pupils' own reading was substantial (generally of the order of 20 hours).

Similar findings came from Sharon Markless' work for NFER on students acquiring information handling skills (Markless and Morrison, 1992). Her team found that selection and retrieval skills were best learned through working on subject assignments rather than separated 'study skills' lessons. An important concomitant finding was that activities needed to be explicitly structured to facilitate this learning; pupils did not gain from merely practising things they did not clearly know how to do. Teachers needed a clear scheme of what skills were being taught, practised and assessed with each assignment. Selectivity and targeting are important, rather than trying to cover too many skills within one activity.

The Schools Council project *Reading for Learning in the Secondary School* produced materials based on actual classroom experience to help teachers encourage reflective reading among pupils. In particular *Learning from the Written Word* (Lunzer and Gardner, 1984) introduced the idea of DARTS (Directed Activities Related to Texts). This is just the sort of dual-purpose activity implied by the National Curriculum criteria: activities which both increase pupil knowledge of subject material and at the same time are explicitly designed to advance pupils' knowledge about text – in this case, text structure. Such activities are being used in some classrooms and several publishers have produced materials directly available for class use in the middle years of schooling (the original DARTS are exemplars for teachers to use in designing their own work). However the full benefit will not be felt by pupils unless they are not only doing the activities but also being encouraged to reflect on what they are doing and why it helps them understand the text. Without this element of 'stand back and think about what we have been doing', pupils may be left with the relevant knowledge and experience (technique) but not able to apply it to help themselves in other learning situations.

Characteristics of the Learner

And so to our fourth consideration: the characteristics of the learner-reader. Teachers observe a huge variety of characteristics in their pupils which are relevant to learning; it can be a problem to know which ones to attend to at any particular time. Much of this book is about how and why individuals vary in their language, and some of the implications for reading of this variation have already been mentioned. Where pupils are unsuccessful readers, in particular, a lack of 'match' between their individual characteristics and the reading situations, methods of teaching or materials which they encounter may be implicated, and there is a large literature about this. But if we think of learning to read as an on-going growth of technical skills applied to purposeful tasks, then patterns of individual strengths and weaknesses will affect *all* pupils' reading long beyond the initial reading stages. Variations in language background and previous experience of genre and register will be factors in pupils' ability to learn from text in the same way as variations in the previous knowledge they have of the subject matter.

Every learner has strengths and weaknesses and every learner has preferences for certain learning activities. Success in a learning task depends partly on matching the choice of learning activity both to the material to be learned and to the learner's strongest channels of learning. If we think about how we learn, most of us could say whether we remember best what we see, what we hear, or what we do. Expert learners build on this; they develop strategies for turning difficult material into a form which is easier to learn and to remember. Learning by reading is no exception. Presentation which is eye-catching to one reader will be visually confusing to another. Note-making based on words will suit one reader, while another will be happier with diagrams or charts.

There are two problems here for novice learners. One is that they may not have sufficient reflective experience to know how they learn best. A second is that school may present material in a way that does not match the learner's strengths but may convey – intentionally or by accident – that this is the right way to learn. The learner may then abandon the sensible searching behaviour which leads to control, try to do everything the teacher's way, and become a less effective learner. Either of these difficulties can affect pupils' control over learning to read or using reading as a tool for other learning.

Fortunately teachers who are aware can help forestall problems. By being alert to the ways reading material is presented and the difficulties some pupils may have, they can make opportunities to discuss, in passing, features such as headings, captions, and placement of text related to pictures or diagrams. They can discuss different ways to make notes and let pupils air preferences and suggest reasons why they like particular methods. Many small references, in the context of what pupils see as 'real work' in the classroom, will help make explicit not only the variety of possibilities but also the acceptability of variation. Some teachers are very word-based and find it difficult to even think of note structures which use few words. Pupils who process and remember best by other methods will gain from exchanging ideas. And, of course, it can work the other way around!

There is growing evidence that even quite young children can learn to reflect on the state of their own knowledge, including how they learn and what they need to do to learn better. The name *metacognition* has been given to this self-knowledge, because it is 'knowing about knowing' or having an overview of oneself as a learner. Reading has been a particular subject for investigation, partly because of the problem-solving view that is now being taken by many about the process of learning to read. Particularly for study reading, or higher order reading-related activities such as note making, there have been studies which show gains in reading control when an element of guided reflection aimed at improving self-knowledge is added to reading instruction (see Paris et al., 1988 for a review, and Currie, 1993, for specific references to National Curriculum reading). This is a fairly new area of research, where the links between theory and practice have yet to be fully explored, but it is particularly likely to be useful for children over the age of about twelve, helping to foster just that searching behaviour which we have said is necessary to find a match between learner, technique and text when the goal is understanding and control.

Assessing where we are

One essential aspect of reading in the National Curriculum has been largely ignored in this chapter so far: it is arranged in levels defined by Attainment Targets which are intended to be assessed in a cumulative order. There are understandable reasons for this, including a climate of opinion that is concerned about measurable standards and a decision to arrange all curriculum goals in this way. As a major skill underlying so much of what and how pupils learn in school, it may even seem particularly appropriate to define such levels for reading. However, we would like to suggest that there are potential hazards in uncritically accepting this outlook.

Looking back at the variety of factors our young 'model reader' will be trying to control, they support the idea of establishing definite criteria for what we want pupils to learn about reading and for thinking carefully about specific techniques which support successful reading. Suggesting that these must or even can be mastered only in a particular order, however, is a far more tenuous proposition. Many of the skill targets, such as extracting main points or relating information from different sources, can be implemented on texts of many different degrees of complexity. Pupils who are introduced early to consulting a variety of sources will undoubtedly be on the road to better reading, as long as those sources are not beyond their understanding. Deciding the 'level' of readers, however, depends not only on checking sources against each other, but on the vocabulary, sentence structure and content of the text they can understand. And this in turn is partly a function of life experience and linguistic background. We are back to the highly integrative nature of reading with which we began; success is not just technique and not just meaning but putting it all together.

Thinking about pupils who do *not* move smoothly forward with reading can make us cautious also. Will we have a problem of denying access to 'higher' levels to pupils who have difficulty with decoding? This is not just a matter of content – giving a simple language version of a literary classic to children who cannot read the big words. 'Access to literature appropriate to their age range and maturity' can be arranged by reading aloud, through drama, film and discussion. Fortunately, most children can learn in a variety of ways. But how will they be marked? And can any but the most sensitive of teachers resist plugging away at 'lower' goals in favour of giving pupils opportunities to explore 'aspects of [text] language, structure and main themes' (Level 6, Response to Literature)?

In practice, as the levels move upward, the criteria become less explicit about what evidence will indicate adequate achievement. The difference between a pupil who can 'synthesize complex information from a wide range of materials' (English Level 7, Information Handling) and one who can 'make effective use of complex information drawn from many sources' (Level 8) will come back to the professional judgement of a teacher who has seen many examples of pupil work. In the outside world, Level 7 to Level 8 may be the divide between admission to further education or not, or a job interview or not. The situation is not very different from the 'C' grade watershed of old; but this may not be clear in public expectations.

Finally, care should be taken about the relationship between assessment levels and pupils' view of themselves. Learning to read well is a challenge, as indeed reading to learn may also be! Some pupils respond to challenges happily, adjusting their behaviour until they have solved the problems before them. Psychologists call this a 'mastery-oriented' response to problem solving. Others develop what is called a 'helpless' pattern, and seek to avoid challenge for fear of failure. Developing one or other of these patterns is not related to ability, nor to previous history of failure. Instead, there is evidence that it is related to whether they see themselves as pursuing learning goals, steps along a road to self-improvement, or as undergoing evaluation against a set standard to which their relationship is already fixed (Dweck and Leggett, 1988). The effect of adopting one or the other stance is profound. While the mastery-oriented children see hard work as a sign of progress and failure as an indication to change their learning strategy, the 'helpless' children see even expenditure of effort as a sign that their intelligence is insufficient to deal with the challenge facing them. The relevance to reading, and particularly to study reading or other challenging texts is clear. If we are to work with levels, we must be very careful that they are used diagnostically and to foster progress; and our pupils must see them this way too. Otherwise the very guidelines which are intended to promote higher standards will contribute to the behaviours least likely to achieve this goal.

5

Literature Teaching and the National Curriculum

The requirements of our Language Charter include 'maximum confident and effective use', 'competence', and 'knowledge of how language operates'. None of these can exclude understanding of traditional concerns of English teachers which move beyond the language code itself. Consequently, Literature, Drama and Media Studies all have a deservedly important place in the curriculum. Particularly, Literature is a prime source of aesthetic awareness and personal linguistic development. Few teachers of Literature are happy about recent developments, so in this chapter we sketch the basis for an alternative perspective, constituting an additional approach to English teaching to those already outlined in chapter 3.

The 'AND' of this chapter's title links two concepts in an uncomfortable *appositional* relationship. The first part of the chapter therefore explains the source of this uneasiness through a brief account of the shift of ideas about teaching literature in recent decades. This acts, in turn, as a context for then considering the provision for literature *in* the National Curriculum; the second part of the chapter is thus concerned with the *institutional* view of literature teaching as laid down in the official documentation. The final part reads this official description *against* the developments in good practice of the last twenty-five years and offers an *oppositional*, pragmatic view of the teaching of literature in schools.

'AND'

The nationalization of the literature curriculum has all the characteristics one expects when politicians, of whatever colour, interfere in the details of professional matters: in particular, the assumption that there is consensus about the nature of the subject and how it should be taught; the desire for a socially and culturally unifying curriculum; and the need to describe the subject as existing in a stable state, including an edifice of books which everyone recognises. Literature, like all the arts, thrives upon risk, upon unpredictable outcomes, sudden insights; upon 'How do I know what I think till I see what I say?' This is as true for the child in the classroom as for the professional writer. To specify in detail a national curriculum in literature is, to say the least, a questionable act. What and who is it for? Are we falling behind our competitors in the production of poets? Is there a national outcry at the feebleness of literature classes which prepare students to go on to study this consistently popular subject in higher education? The characteristics of this nationalization are, in fact, nothing to do with good practice and everything to do with centralized control of the curriculum.

The gravest risk is stagnation: the pressure for consensus blunts the desire to challenge, to include new texts and new ways of teaching them; the wish for a curriculum reflecting cultural unity ignores the multi-cultural diversity of our society or, at least, reduces it to mere tokenism; and the desire to define a list of contents for literature lessons is driven partly by a nostalgia for that which is familiar and partly by the expediency of that which can be centrally tested. National Curriculum literature has already been subject to a succession of revisions and adaptations. Such has been the ostentation of recent public debate about English teaching, in which the role of literature has been central, that the steadily changing face of the literature classroom over the preceding decades has often been overlooked. This contrast between recent noisy debate and empirically researched developments in schools indicates the apposition: essentially, it is between the *imposition* of a literature curriculum and the *evolution* of professional practice. Before considering the details of literature in the National Curriculum, the context against which they are set needs to be outlined.

Forty years ago, English teaching in schools and universities was operating within a liberal humanist ideology influenced directly or indirectly by the work of F. R. Leavis. Literature teaching, in particular, was driven by two imperatives: a moral imperative that stemmed from the Arnold–Leavis belief in the civilizing effect of good literature; and an artistic imperative that followed from the New Criticism idea of aesthetic totalities, that minute textual scrutiny could establish conclusively how a work of art functioned. To the pupil in secondary school, these emphases showed themselves by the stress placed upon (and given by!) comprehension and criticism, both effectively buttressed by the examination system. Literature lessons for the pre-16 year olds were dominated by comprehension exercises; for sixth formers, 'practical criticism' or 'critical appreciation' were phrases that implied an approach to literature that elevated a method of detailed analysis over an individual's personal reading of a text.

Authorship both did and did not matter: it depended upon use. If the purpose was comprehension, a variety of passages from minor essayists or novelists would serve; a selection of unattributed poems, for students to assign to poets and periods could provide an academic game of 'blind date' for the upper sixth as a throwback to I. A. Richards. On the other hand, authorship was important – and some authors more important than others. If the purpose was 'critical appreciation' then it was necessary to know where the names stood in the literary class system so that the two parts of the exercise could be suitably counterpointed. For, essentially, the student was working to someone else's agenda of literary worth. Most A-level students soon discovered whose:

> The great English novelists are Jane Austen, George Eliot, Henry James and Joseph Conrad – to stop for the moment at that comparatively safe point in history. (Leavis, 1948: 1)

Those were the novels of the great tradition; and *Revaluation* (1936), with a little help from T. S. Eliot, had already given us the poets. Shelley and Tennyson were 'out'; Donne and Herbert were 'in'. More recently, a post-Leavisite critic has done a similar job for children's literature, deliberately aping his master:

> The great children's novelists are Lewis Carroll, Rudyard Kipling, Frances Hodgson Burnett, Arthur Ransome, William Mayne and

Philippa Pearce – to stop for the moment at that comparatively
safe point on an uncertain list. (Inglis, 1981: 1)

So far no one has done the same for children's poets but no
doubt Edward Lear, Eleanor Farjeon and Walter de la Mare
would be canonized. Nowadays, presumably, the champions of
both adults' and children's lists would each want to claim Blake.
One of the many oddities of canons is that they are heavily
context-bound. While the academic literary canon might be as
described above, the school literary canon might be quite other.
Brian Cox has described his own from the 1930s and 1940s as
including 'Kinglake's *Eothen*, Thomas Hughes's *Tom Brown's
Schooldays*, Charles Kingsley's *The Water Babies* and the essays
of Charles Lamb, all little read by the young of today' (Cox
1991: 69). Another from the 1940s and 1950s included Helen
Bannerman's *Little Black Sambo*, John Buchan's *Prester John*, much
Victorian poetry, including 'Horatius' from Macaulay's *Lays of
Ancient Rome*; masses of Sherlock Holmes' stories; and for O-
level, Charles Reade's *The Cloister and the Hearth*. Some are still
successfully read in school forty years on; others clearly reflect
out-of-date literary and social opinions that now rule them out of
the classroom.

Beyond this, there are two significant features relevant to the
current debate. First, that the school canon has always contained
much that apologists for the academic canon would regard as
second or third-rate literature. Canons are always variable 'constructs' according to time, place and function (in schools they
have to contribute to learning, for example). Thus, to allow
people other than professional English teachers (such as Ministers or their advisers) to define the school canon completely
misunderstands its purpose. Secondly, there is the necessity of
rubbish, or, at least, the young reader's need for a mixed diet
including plenty of roughage as well as the plums. Setting aside
the question of who decides something is rubbish, the fact is that
readers use reading for different purposes and this applies to
school reading as much as any other. If the teacher's aims include the wish to captivate the class with the mystery and sus-
pense of a developing plot, or with the heroism and adventure of
a story in rhyme, then Conan Doyle and Macaulay's *Horatius* are

good material – yet few would place these authors high in the academic canon. Where fiction is concerned, young readers need to be 'hooked' by a compelling story well told; with verse there is the enchantment of the fiction and the form in which the appeal of rhyme and rhythm are basic. On these criteria, 'minor' writers are arguably more likely to capture young readers than the more sophisticated members of the academic canon.

Traditional literature teaching also placed a high premium on formal essay writing. For those going into higher education this remains an important type of writing to master; but the problem in the past was that this was the *only* type of writing about literature required of pupils. Indeed, as Widdowson (1982) has argued, teaching literature to post-16 students was largely a matter of teaching essay writing; and, in many schools, this emphasis started earlier. It took some years before teachers re-alized that there is nothing sacrosanct, or even particularly ap-propriate, about the essay as a mode of response to literature. It is a form descended from *belles-lettres*, appropriated by literary criticism, and bolstered by an examination system geared to assessing verbal chunks of timed virtuosity. In many respects it is a curiously inhibiting form of writing in which to require pupils to express their reactions to literature. It is given to detached argument rather than personal response, to evaluation rather than exploration. As such, it is a sophisticated form, suitable for those aspiring to study literature in Higher Education, but which needs to be developed from a basis of the more varied and informal writing agenda that is appropriate for *all* pupils.

In all these areas – criticism, reading, the canon, writing about literature – the past 25 years have seen the steady evolution of good practice. With Leavisite cultural elitism discredited and the explosion in modern literary theory producing at best exciting new ways of reading and at worst a new intellectual elitism, literature teachers have increasingly tended to find a sense of direction in the area of reader-response theory and practice. This development is, as we argue in the last section of this chapter, the evolutionary successor to Leavisite liberal humanism and has provided a framework of now familiar ideas which are widely accepted among literature teachers and to which other lines of critical activity often make reference: the plurality of meanings within a literary work; the creative participation of the reader; the acknowledgement that the reader is not a *tabula rasa* but brings idiosyncratic knowledge and personal style to the act of reading; and the awareness that interpretation is socially, historically and culturally formed. Just as the stable state of post-war literary criticism has shattered, and the reader has returned to challenge the dominance of the text, so, too, have the traditional canons been exploded. Revaluations of academic and school lists have been brought about notably by feminist critics, the development of media studies, and the increasingly multi-cultural character of literature written in English. Pupils' writing about literature has focused more upon process, upon using writing as an aid to thinking. 'Creative' responses, genre transformation, informal jotting around texts, journal writing are just some of the ways that teachers have sought to encourage pupils to explore and refine their responses to literature.

This rich agenda in the main areas of literature teaching, developed and classroom-tested by teachers for 25 years, has now been subjected to bureaucratic reductiveness in a revised National Curriculum that, as Joan Clanchy remarked shortly after resigning from the National Curriculum Council over the proposals for the new English order, 'has been constructed for tests, as if the Highway Code had been narrowed down to instructions on the three-point turn' (*The Independent*, 22 April 1993).

'IN'

By contrast, The Cox Report (DES/WO, 1989) had acknowledged complexity. It did so in five fundamental aspects of literature teaching: teachers' differing constructs of its status and role; pupils' literary development; text choice and the canon; approaches to classroom teaching, and assessment. Little of the complexity of the arguments around these issues survived in the bland summaries and anodyne prose of the Attainment Targets in the Order (DES, 1990d); and it is only occasionally hinted at in the non-statutory guidance that followed (for example, para 1.5 on the importance of individual response to literature). For this reason, the Cox Report (DES/WO, 1989) and the author's own commentary upon it (Cox, 1991) together make the most comprehensive and reliable statement of principles for National Curriculum English – one which the majority of teachers have been operating with successfully for the past few years and which we will take as the composite basic text before considering the Proposals for the Revised Order (DFE, 1993b).

Cox begins from a position that stresses the unitary nature of the subject and the teacher's traditional concern 'to increase children's understanding of how texts convey multiple layers of meaning and meanings expressed from different points of view' (2.16). The status of literature and its role in school are explicitly included in the discussion of three of 'the famous five' views of English in the curriculum. The 'personal growth' view emphasises 'the role of literature in developing children's imaginative and aesthetic lives' (2.21); the 'cultural heritage' view emphasizes the need 'to lead children to an appreciation of those works of literature that have been widely regarded as amongst the finest in the language' (2.24); and the 'cultural analysis' or 'critical awareness' view emphasizes 'helping children towards a critical understanding of the world and cultural environment in which they live' (2.25). (For our more detailed discussion of these, see chapter 3.) Cox's chapter 7, on Literature, explores these points, acknowledging the fun and the challenge of developing young children's 'natural enthusiasms for story structures and role-play'. It begins by affirming support for the fundamental importance of narrative both as a means of organising individual consciousness and as a form of literature (cf. Harding, 1962; Hardy, 1975); and, in recognizing that 'children construct the world through story', it stresses the teacher's role in developing 'interest in the act of reading' (7.1). The terms in which this interest should be furthered are significant. They include: the 'development of an ear for language' and 'knowledge of the range of possible patterns of thought and feeling made accessible by the power and range of language' (7.2); the belief that 'literature and language are inseparably intertwined' (7.7); and the conviction that 'learning to read and learning to write are intimately related', and that 'literature has an important role to play . . . in improving abilities in speaking and listening and in

writing, as well as in reading' (7.8). 'Creative responses' to literature are encouraged as means to understanding the craft and
construction of literary texts (7.9). This whole emphasis upon the
act of reading is visualized both as appropriate in itself and as
the most fruitful preparation for the development of abilities in
literary critical analysis with older pupils (7.10). The significance
of this description lies in the interdependency of all these
elements.

Secondly, Cox stresses pupils' literary development. The hope
(and presumably the aim) is expressed that pupils will
'... "grow" through literature – both emotionally and aesthet-
ically, both morally and socially...' (7.3). Literature is seen as
enabling in all these spheres, and the vicarious experiences it
offers are regarded as means to a better understanding of self
and society. Again, the issue is complex and cross-hatches two
ideas: the notion that literary progress is non-linear, uneven,
sometimes regressive; and the notion of how learning through
literary experiences relates to maturation and behaviour in the
real world. The purpose of the Report is to make teachers aware
of the issues and give guidance from a principled standpoint.
Rather than expounding these notions *per se*, the Report settles
for a pragmatic statement about the need for pupils 'to make
progress as readers and to master increasingly demanding written material' (7.17). The account of the likely sources of textual
difficulty (7.17) shows a subtle understanding of the ways that
subject matter, structure, language and length interrelate in the
practice of working on poems and stories with children of different ages.

Thirdly, on the question of text choice and the canon, Cox
eschews lists of books in favour of guidelines to inform teachers'
own judgements, and stresses two main points: the need to draw
upon the vast range of literature in English, both current and
from past centuries (7.4 and 7.5); and the importance of trusting
the teachers' professional knowledge and judgement in the selection of texts for their classes (7.14). 'Formulations of "literary
tradition", "our literary heritage" or lists of "great works", however influential their proponents, may change radically during
the course of time' (7.14). Prescription would, therefore, not only
be perverse but also an unjustifiable restriction upon pro-

fessional freedom. The only exception is Shakespeare, whose plays are 'so rich that in every age they can produce fresh meanings and even those who deny his universality agree on his cultural importance' (7.16). It was in this area that, with the benefit of hindsight, Cox accepted the criticism that his Report had taken for granted major assumptions about the value of great literature in the curriculum (Cox, 1991: 70). This led him to expand on three central issues: the desire for an English national tradition; the Leavisite belief that the study of literature promotes moral sensitivity; and the criticism that 'great literature' enjoys a privileged and unacceptable status (Cox, 1991: 70–8). Essentially, his responses are, respectively, that schools should now be teaching literature in English, not English Literature, to reflect the internationalism that characterizes the language and the literature in both contemporary and historical respects. Secondly, quoting Kermode in support, he agrees that literary study makes better readers, not better people; nevertheless, better readers are better equipped to be questioning individuals. Thirdly, without engaging with the nature of the canon as Kermode (1990: 13–18) has done, Cox counters the issue of privilege by arguing for as wide a range of texts as possible. While his post-structuralist critics would scarcely be persuaded by his arguments (any more than they are by Kermode's), Cox's emphases upon the *range* of texts and the *responsibilities* of teachers are the points, among others, that united the majority of literature teachers behind his Report.

Fourthly, on the issue of approaches to literature, Cox stresses two key words: 'active' and 'response'. Approaches which actively engage pupils working on texts are far more likely to lead to enjoyment and understanding than those relying upon the passive acceptance of the teacher's knowledge and views. This, in turn, implies that the individual response to literature is fundamental. The Report quotes Benton's words to support this stance:

As Michael Benton puts it: 'The development of a methodology that is based upon informed concepts of *reading* and *response* rather than upon conventional, narrowly-conceived ideas of *comprehension* and *criticism* is now the priority'. (7.22)

While there is little discussion of the notion of literary response in the Report (something that the final section of this
chapter attempts to give), there is a clear indication in the 'Ap-
pendix: Approaches to the Class Novel' that the practical implications have been accepted.

Finally, Cox indicates that the already complex issue of assessment was made impossible by the Task Group on Assessment
and Testing (TGAT)'s requirement to fall in line with a criterion-
referenced set of levels of attainment. We can now see the *naiveté*
of Cox's statement that his working group took to heart TGAT's
comment that 'The assessment process itself should not determine what is to be taught and learned. It should be the servant,
not the master, of the curriculum' (14.3). Cox acknowledges the
recursive nature of language learning and the inappropriateness
of a linear sequence of attainment descriptions to monitor development (14.5 and 14.6). This is especially so where literary
progress is concerned. Hence, in Attainment Target 2, Reading,
Cox is driven to repeat the same description at levels 8, 9 and 10
in strand (i), on the range of literature (16.19 and 16.20); and to do
all but the same in strand (ii) on response where development
hinges on fine distinctions between 'perceptive' (Level 9) and
'sophisticated' (Level 10). Cox makes a brave effort at compromise but the exercise of fitting a reader's literary progress neatly
into ten levels is absurd and one suspects Cox knows it. This is
not to say that development cannot be monitored, but a much
broader brush is needed both to describe the phases and to paint
a fuller picture of the evidence on a more inclusive basis. The
analogy with Art is helpful, as we argue presently.

In this, as in the other areas we have outlined, there is the
sense of complex issues having been debated, advice heeded,
and careful judgements explained. How do the Proposals for the
Revised Order (PRO) (April 1993) compare?

The *remit* of the review includes the perceived need to 'be
more explicit about how pupils could develop the habit of reading widely, and be introduced to great literature'. The *result* of
the review is a disagreement between the English and the Welsh
Councils over one of the main issues that Cox had discussed:
prescribed texts. Specifically, the Welsh Council stays close to the
spirit of the Cox Report and recommends 'that the requirements

in the programmes of study for KS 3 and 4 covering the range of literature that pupils should read should be less prescriptive' (p. iii). Undeterred, the National Curriculum Council (NCC) proposed to keep a tight corset on English Literature and its promotion. It labelled Attainment Target 2 clumsily as 'Reading (including Literature)' and, far from discussing the rationale for its judgements, simply asserted what it took to be self-evident truths.

The regression to Leavisite principles in the PRO is obvious in its ideas and vocabulary. Not satisfied with the inclusion of lists of 'required reading', the Secretary of State is to ask the Councils 'whether the programme of study for the reading of fiction for KS 3 and 4 could be better designed to ensure a study of the great tradition of the novel . . .' (p. v, para 18). Back to set books, to prescribed lists of approved texts, and to the assumption that NCC can 'out-Leavis' Leavis and 'define the criteria for good literature' (6.13). Indeed, the frequency with which the phrases 'good quality literature', 'literary heritage', 'classic fiction and verse' (or variants on these) appear indicates that the anonymous writers of PRO see as unproblematic the very areas where Cox had acknowledged complexity.

A further example of its limited horizons is the parochialism with which PRO describes the canon. After acknowledging the difficulties of defining it, the main problem turns out to be as follows:

> . . . it will be important to consider the nature of the balance which needs to be struck between the reading of, on the one hand, English and, on the other, commonwealth and world literature . . . (2.1)

Such was the remit; and the result? Under Attainment Target 2 we are told that Council has sought to ensure that pupils

> are introduced to those writers and texts which are of central importance to our literary heritage whilst also introducing pupils to other traditions and cultures. (6.6)

'Our' and 'other'; 'us' and 'them'. In an embarrassingly inept attempt to justify this division, Council states that it distinguishes 'between reading literature produced in the British Isles and Commonwealth and world literature' (6.15). So, it is the production site that matters, not the book, let alone its author.

This attempt at an unsustainable distinction between 'our' and 'other' is irrelevant to the practice of literature teaching: it is one of the more blatant examples of the desire to use literature to express notions of a national heritage when, in fact, 'writing has always consisted of a mosaic of international traditions and forms' (Letter to *The Guardian*, 19 May 1993).

The above quotation is from a letter signed by 18 authors whose names or works have been put on the lists in the PRO and who wish to dissociate themselves from this exercise. Their objections range widely but they identify some specific deficiencies of the lists which can be summarized as follows:

1. the lists are authoritarian in that they come without either debate or commentary;

2. they have a negative effect upon teachers' understanding of and enthusiasm for literature through delimiting and dictating choice;

3. they are unrepresentative of many cultural traditions that have prevailed in the past and are important today; and, as they trenchantly state;

4. 'If we are "approved" authors, then by implication other writers are "not approved". We do not wish to be part of such a blanket, uncritical rejection of fellow writers'.

The new proposals attempt to fudge such issues by making two disingenuous points in their four brief paragraphs explaining the Council's views on 'Understanding and Appreciating Literature'. First, they claim to make 'a careful distinction . . . between the *reading* of novels, poems and plays and the *study* of them' (6.12). Secondly, they claim to have 'struck a pragmatic balance between prescription and flexibility' (6.13). In fact, they achieve neither.

Wide reading is invariably linked with introducing the literary heritage and Council sees 'no conflict between these two objectives' (6.12); and the lists of books are explicitly to 'provide a clearer definition of what pupils' wide reading should look like'

(6.14). Reading is, thus, only as wide as NCC says it should be. Their understanding of the *study* of literature is even more seriously flawed, as is clear from the descriptions of the strands on 'Comprehension' and 'Response to Literature' under Attainment Target 2. There is no rationale for the relationship between the two; indeed, the one is sometimes defined in terms of the other. Thus, at Level 10, comprehension involves pupils' abilities to 'articulate a detailed, critical response to a complex and challenging passage from a text . . .'; and in the next column, response requires that pupils show 'a detailed understanding of [the] themes' of a text. Through the ten levels, comprehension is defined in respect of hidden meanings (Level 6) or authorial intentions (Level 7), with words like 'subtle', 'complex' and 'difficult' finding particular favour, and without any sense that, in literary reading particularly, what the reader brings to the task of making meaning is at least as important as what the text says. Nor is this omission catered for in the adjacent columns, where response is defined by reference to 'the language, structure and themes' of a text (Level 9), and where there is a marked emphasis upon the final draft, considered response and no concern for the actual process of responding to literature. 'Response to literature' is, clearly, a most convenient umbrella term for the NCC to put up: it allows them to parade examples of activities for levels 6–10, all of which read like examination essay questions, while sheltering under cover of a virtuous title.

The 'balance between prescription and flexibility' is also meant to beguile – this time with its appealing pragmatism; yet, its purpose, too, is to narrow the literature curriculum to make it easily testable. This 'balance' is defined in weasel words:

> Council has chosen not to prescribe rigidly, but to require a choice
> of authors from a defined list. (6.13)

What does 'require' mean if not 'prescribe'? This required reading is then curiously justified as a more sensible approach than 'to introduce pupils to authors' work by using extracts in anthologies'. Does this mean that we have only just escaped a national anthology, compiled in an office in York and obligatory for all schools: Pascall's *Golden Treasury*? Whatever it means, the confused fumbling with 'prescribe', 'require' and 'defined' indicates not balance but a feeble attempt to disguise NCC's real intentions to dictate to English teachers which texts should be taught in schools.

The institutional view of literature in the National Curriculum shows a dramatic belittlement in its revised version. It lacks a coherent literary or pedagogic rationale and substitutes a functional one in which over-simplification purports to be clarification. The institution is primarily concerned to define an English literary heritage; it is more interested in control than in curriculum. For this reason, the issues of literature and learning are ignored; tests of levels of attainment are the levers of control.

Against

The oppositional view expressed here focuses upon three basic issues that have been the subject of advances in our understanding in the past 25 years and are either neglected or misunderstood in the PRO:

1. The act of reading and, in particular, what has been learned about the process of literary response;

2. Reading development and its assessment; and

3. The nature of literary canons and the associated question of value.

Reader-response writings

Reader-response writings during the 1970s and 80s have increasingly forged a new relationship between the act of reading and the act of teaching literature. In the literature classroom, reader response has become the new orthodoxy. Theoretical writings of the 1970s in this area were succeeded by a rash of publications on the methodology of literature teaching (Protherough, 1983; Benton and Fox, 1985; Scholes, 1985; Cooper, 1985; Dias and Hayhoe, 1988; Benton et al., 1988) culminating in Britain in the high profile given to the reader's response to literature in the Cox Report (DES/WO, 1989), which still survives in skeletal form despite Government interference in 1993. Such has been what one standard book on modern literary theory calls 'the vertiginous rise of reader-response criticism' (Jefferson and Robey, 1986: 142), that its authors see it as threatening to engulf all other approaches. What the PRO fail to understand is that reader-response theory and practice operate from a philosophical basis that displaces the notion of an autonomous text to be examined in and on its own terms from the centre of critical discussion and substitutes the reader's re-creation of that text. (A clear exposition of this phenomenon is in the opening two pages of Freund's *The Return of the Reader* (1987).) Reading is not the discovering of meaning, like some sort of archaelogical 'dig', but the creation of it. The central concerns of response-oriented approaches focus upon (a) what constitutes the source of literary meaning; and (b) what is the nature of the interpretative process that creates it. Both issues are fundamental to classroom action. Iser's theory of aesthetic response (1978) and Rosenblatt's transactional theory of the literary work (1978; 1985) have been seminal in changing the culture of the classroom to one which, as John Lucas notes in the *Times Literary Supplement*, November 1987, operates on the principle that the text cannot be said to have a meaningful existence outside the relationship between itself and its reader(s). This transfer of power represents a sea-change in critical emphasis and in pedagogical practice from the assumptions most critics and teachers held even a generation ago. Yet it is evolutionary change, not sudden revolution – a progressive re-thinking of the way readers create literary experiences for themselves with poems and stories, which is concerned to honour both the integrity of the text and of the reader. The concern with pedagogy, most clearly seen in Rosenblatt's work, goes back to Richards but without the debilitating effect that his notorious 'ten difficulties' produced in the literature teaching that derived from *Practical Criticism* (1929). In Rosenblatt's transactional theory the relationship between the nature of reading and the teaching of literature is central and her portrait of the reader has an altogether more human face than others to be found in modern criticism (Rosenblatt, 1970: 30–1). Each 'reading' is to be understood in the context of the whole literary and life experience of an individual. A reader's personality, needs, interests and so on are significant mediators in any response. This fuller role preserves the participatory reader from being merely an intellectual cipher that is implied, for example, by Wayne Booth, without consigning the reader to the analyst's couch as a transformational theorist like Holland is tempted to do; and it derives directly from Rosenblatt's belief that literature stands in a unique relationship with knowledge. Literature does not provide information as much as experience. 'Literature provides a *living-through*, not simply *knowledge about*' (Rosenblatt, 1970: 38).

Learning through literature is different from other learning experiences because of its grounding in an aesthetic process. There are plentiful examples in modern literary theory and in reading theory of approaches and techniques which reduce the reading process to a ready-made system of analysis, or give what Richard Rorty has called 'methodical readings' (Eco, 1992: 106–7). These are ones which, far from offering a sense of fresh encounter of new vital experience, settle instead for the utilitarian opportunity to use a text as a specimen reiterating a type, or an example on which to exercise particular skills or techniques. Sadly, there are many instances, too, where classroom method reduces what should be the experience of literature to the arid inquisition of just another sort of textbook. In theory and practice, in literary and educational studies, there is the constant danger of dealing with aesthetic experiences in reductive ways. As Rosenblatt (1985: 39) says: '. . . keeping the aesthetic transaction central (has) important implications for questions raised and methods used in both teaching and research.'

Reader-response in the past two decades has sought to avoid this reductiveness through the use of exploratory talk and informal writing to help pupils monitor, record and share their thinking with that of others. Such activities follow from a theoretical position which can live comfortably with the idea of resisting closure, with meanings not fixed, with the infinitely renewable quality of literary experience. By starting where the readers are and thus avoiding the twin tendencies to *explication de texte* and to premature value judgements – the Scylla and Charybdis of classroom methods between which many a poem and story has been crushed – response-oriented approaches claim to hold the reader's initial engagement with a text and develop it in ways that are both valid and valued by pupils as interpretive acts. It is highly unlikely that the next generation of pupils will see either the validity or the value of their work in literature in these terms, given the PRO's functional, exam-style examples of classroom activities mentioned earlier and the banalities of the SATs.

In an article in the *Times Educational Supplement* (5 March 1993), Sue Hackman makes the pedagogical point succinctly:

> Consider reading. In the tests, reading is presented as a comprehension exercise of the most literal kind. The pupil is confined to 'fill-in-the-gaps' type of answers. This is because the ideology which underpins the tests sees textual meanings as fixed, and demands conformity of interpretation. In this model, a good teacher is able to put pupils in touch with accepted readings.
>
> English teachers are committed to another view of reading, in which meanings are more volatile and diverse, each reading formed by the interaction of reader, text and cultural context, and modified when it is shared and challenged among the wider reading community. Critical interpretation is encouraged, and pupils are asked to account for their views by close reference to the text. In this model, the teacher is helping the pupil towards independent literacy.
>
> Despite some overlaps, the pedagogies are quite different. Teachers who now see themselves as guiding and intervening in individual development are being required to convert to a transmission style of teaching, seeing themselves much more as custodians of, and inductors into, established knowledge.

Reading development and its assessment

Development in reading is a notoriously tricky area which has been approached from various directions: attempts to match the child's literary capabilities and interests with his or her psychological development (Applebee, 1978; Tucker, 1981); studies of children as readers, where individual and age group needs dictate appropriate books (Fisher, 1964; Meek, 1982); deductions drawn from surveys of children's reading habits (Whitehead et al., 1977); and even personal reminiscences of bookish child-hoods (Sampson, 1947; Inglis, 1981). In their different ways, all these approaches indicate that, while there are noticeable phases in reading development – and even crucial stages around the age of seven and at the beginning of the teens – there are also many variables. The amount and type of reading a child does is likely to be uneven, to reflect gender preferences, and to be subject to many cultural, personal and peer influences. Reading behaviour, especially that of young people, owes as much to serendipity as anything else. Any literature policy that imposes artificial limits on choice, that predicts or prejudges children's preferences, that conceptualises development by numbers, is at odds with the evidence. As Benton and Fox argued some years ago, it is necess-ary to ask how development actually operates.

> At any point, children have a past, present and future to their reading development. In other words, they need books they *have read* already – familiar favourites, easy to relate to, predictable and secure; books they *are reading* – a catholic selection of books ap-propriate for their current stage of development; and books they *are growing into*, ones that are mentally and emotionally stretching and which we may judge to have some elements that are beyond them. Development does not mean leaving one sort of literature behind for ever as one moves on to another. Certainly, children who become habitual readers do experience the feeling of grow-ing out of childish things that no longer satisfy ('growing out' of the series books, for example, is common in early adolescence); but, generally, development operates in a less clearly defined manner than this. For children, like their parents and teachers, use books for various purposes and to satisfy diverse needs. Depending upon a host of variables in a child's life at any one moment, he or she may turn to books that are known to be undemanding because they are familiar, exciting because they are new and unknown, or challenging because they are known to be rather 'old' or 'difficult' for someone of his or her age. When this stage has been reached, children have begun to see them-selves as readers. When a thirteen year old is reading in rapid succession – or even concurrently – a Famous Five story, a new book by Jan Mark, and a novel by Hardy after seeing it on TV, then the past, present and future are in a reassuring and often amusing relationship.

If the growth of literary competence and satisfaction are most likely to be nourished by wide and catholic reading and by respecting the individuality of each child's development, it nevertheless remains true that literature teachers have a special responsibility for widening and deepening children's knowledge and experience of stories and poems. (Benton and Fox, 1985: 34–5)

To fix the template of a 10-level development and assessment scale upon this growth is profoundly irresponsible. The weight of professional evidence – particularly at GCSE – is that assessment is most valuable to pupils' progress when it is carefully integrated into their day-to-day work. A substantial element of externally moderated coursework assessment has enabled teachers to plan for individual needs and pupils to show what they know, understand and can do. Forms of assessment which reflect literature as one of the arts are essential. Course work folders, akin to an Art portfolio, go some way to meeting this need in providing for varied types of writing, creative responses, the pursuit of individual enthusiasms for particular books or themes and so on. It is little wonder that what has angered English teachers most in recent times has been the undermining of GCSE course work and its intended substitution by the requirement to enter pupils for separate levels of a hierarchical examination, involving different types of text, paper or question. Together with the SATs and the requirement to study an Anthology that no publisher would choose to print nor any informed teacher choose to teach, the reading development of the next generation of pupils is likely to be seriously eroded.

Literary canons and the question of value

The Key Stage 3 Anthology introduced in 1993 reflects neither the academic canon nor the school canon; it reflects a bureaucratic compromise canon calculated to appease particular interests and, therefore, satisfies no-one. Extracts from the 'classics', popular classroom literature, some writing by Caribbean authors, even four women out of 27 writers: the inclusions emphasize the exclusions; the choices draw attention not so much to the implied values but to the sense of expediency. Yet the question of value is clearly central to the NCC's argument, as can be seen in the Proposals for the Revised Order. The Council's ignorance of reader-response theory and practice has, in fact, denied it the opportunity to present the issue of the canon in a coherent way which, while any definition is unlikely to meet the objections of those who regard the very notion as cultural oppression, does nonetheless follow from the view of literary reading that we have advocated above.

For, by asserting the importance of the individual's 'reading' of a text, response-oriented approaches are in tune with contemporary thinking which has preferred to define value in transitive terms (texts have value for given people in particular contexts) rather than to locate value as an inherent quality of the text itself.

One way of translating such a definition into practice is to see the classroom as a micro-version of Fish's (1980) interpretive community where the value students find in literary works is an attribute discovered over time through the exercise of common interpretive strategies rather than a judgement on one or other occasion. Valuing literature is a process of coming to know, of growing personal ownership.

This view of literary value has implications for the concept of the canon. Over time, the aggregate of readings by particular people in particular contexts grows into a collection of what a society deems to be highly valued texts.

In this way our work with pupils plays its part in the 'historical evolution of art' which, as Kundera, one of those 'other' novelists, reminds us, is not a mere succession of events but an essential pursuit of values. He remarks:

> If we reject the question of value and settle for a description (thematic, sociological, formalist) of a work (of a historical period, culture, etc.); if we equate all cultures and all cultural activities (Bach and rock, comic strips and Proust); if the criticism of art (meditation on value) can no longer find room for expression, then the 'historical evolution of art' will lose its meaning, will crumble, will turn into a vast and absurd storehouse of works. (Kundera, 1988: 152)

The relationship between response and responsibility (to self and text) is reader-response criticism's counter to such a

Dunciadical vision. Instead it offers an alternative picture of a constantly revalued anthology of texts which renews itself both by the inclusion of new works from diverse sources and by the reappraisal of older, existing works. This prospect of a continuously revisable canon goes some way towards meeting the well-known arguments levelled at the traditional canon that it is male-dominated, culturally unrepresentative, resistant to change, and both exclusive and narrow in its definition of what constitutes a 'text'. The shift from the 'heritage model' to this 'evolutionary model' is scarcely a dramatic one for NCC to make and excludes only those who see literature as a collection of classic texts like national monuments, stamped with preservation orders, there to be revered with uncritical praise.

Pragmatically, though, the teacher still has to select: the books on the syllabus, from whatever source they derive, are never a matter of indifference. Choices have to be made in schools and choices are a declaration of values just as much for the individual teacher as for the NCC. So, when faced with the pupil's not infrequent question: 'Why do we have to read this book?', the honest answer (assuming freedom from prescribed lists) is: 'Because I judged you'd like it and because it forms one part of the reading programme I envisage for you and the class this year.' The values are enjoyment and progress in literary studies. But these depend upon trusting the professional knowledge and judgements of teachers – two things the NCC consistently fails to do, which is why we urge an oppositional view of literature teaching against the current provisions laid down so rigidly for National Curriculum English.

6

Drama in Education

This chapter examines the current state of Drama in schools and the various directions in which it can be taken, bearing in mind the implications of the National Curriculum.

Drama as a subject in its own right does not feature in the National Curriculum and the demands on time that teaching the statutory subjects takes mean that Drama, together with other non-statutory subjects, is squeezed into a small time slot. When this first became known there was concern in the ranks of Drama teachers, for Art and Music received honourable mentions and their places in the grand scheme of educational reform was assured.

In the Cox report on English, *English for Ages 5 to 16* (DES/WO, 1989), Drama was given an important place within English teaching (although not exclusively within English: 'We would stress, however, that the inclusion of drama methods in English should not in any way replace drama as a subject for specialist study' (section 8.2). However, realistically its future in most schools appears to be as a part of English rather than a subject in its own right. The fact that the report supported Drama as a separate subject was lost when the National Curriculum documents were drawn up. Following an invited submission by a small group of Drama specialists, the NCC set up a Drama Task Group. Their brief was to cover four areas: to look at existing references to Drama within the National Curriculum; to provide guidance to teachers and Headteachers on the contribution that Drama makes to the curriculum; to consider and advise Council on the elements of Drama beyond Level 6 which the English Working Group did not define; to provide examples of how schemes of work derived from programmes of study can include Drama across shared attainment targets.

This seemed to be quite a promising development, and although the brief was quite restrictive the final document that was produced was more wide ranging and quite substantial. The NCC assured the team that it would be published as 'Curriculum Guidance Number 9' in February 1991. However, this was delayed and it was decided by the NCC that it would publish a circular, which would very briefly outline areas of attainment, in the Spring of 1991 and follow this with the guidance document.

In fact what has been published so far is a *Poster* (DES, 1991): a poster entitled 'Drama in the National Curriculum', identifying references to Drama in the Orders for English, science, technology and history and in the proposals for modern foreign languages. As all these references can be read in the relevant documents anyway, this is certainly not an adequate substitute for the guidance document written by the Drama specialists.

So what exactly do we have of Drama in the National Curriculum? As one would expect, as it has no place of its own, Drama is seen as a tool and service subject. The references to 'role-play' found in Technology, History, and Modern Foreign Languages are intended to facilitate knowledge development for those particular subjects. They have nothing to do with learning the processes or forms of Drama that might be the purpose if the role-plays were part of a Drama lesson.

O'Neill's (1983) 'essentialist' quality of Drama as a 'way of knowing' could be employed particularly in a subject like history. But this is something the teacher will have to create independently if the stated intention of a role-play is set out in terms of whether by the end of it a pupil can ask for a kilo of onions, or knows how medieval people bartered grain for land.

As one would expect, the most extensive references to Drama come within the English Order. However, they relate, in the most part, to a very narrow interpretation of Drama and one which many Drama specialists would argue is not Drama at all. The references can be grouped under the headings: Performance; Text Study/Knowledge; Role-play; Improvisation. As they stand they seem to be reasonable expressions of Drama. However, when we look closely at the intended learning outcomes we find that once again Drama is being relegated to a position as a tool for achieving particular learning and not as a subject in its own right.

Here is a closer look at some specific references.

Text study/knowledge

At Key Stage 1 pupils should 'write in response to a full range of well chosen . . . plays'.

At Key Stage 2 pupils 'should listen and respond to an increasing range of plays' and 'write in response to a wide range of stimuli, including . . . plays'.

At Key Stage 3 'Literary texts (including drama scripts) . . . might furnish many of the materials and topics for discussion for which planned outcomes, e.g. in written work or presentations, might emerge'.

At Key Stage 4 pupils should 'write in a wider range of forms, including . . . reviews of . . . plays, . . . playscripts' and recognize and describe some of the 'lexical, grammatical and organis-ational characteristics of different types of written text, e.g. . . . playscripts'.

The Statements of Attainment list a number of activities that arise from text, such as writing about characters and development of plot, reading a range of fiction and non-fiction including drama, listening and responding to stories and poems.

Although some of these activities purport to be Drama, many of them are standard English Literature exercises masquerading as Drama. For example dramatic text has always featured on English Literature syllabuses and been read, analyzed and treated exactly like any other form of text. Few English teachers have really got to grips with dramatic text as 'notation' for per-formance (Hornbrook, 1991: 49), which is the way in which it would be treated in a Drama classroom. The references here continue to treat playscripts in the same way; that is texts for study and for learning based firmly in the Literature mode. Although 'presentation' is mentioned once, there is no mention of the facets of text that would be of vital importance to the Drama teacher; staging, design, how to make a text work on stage, bringing the text to life. There is considerable room under this heading to make all this work related to text and more Drama orientated and therefore a much stronger and more relevant learning experience: even the most ardent and traditional Literature teacher must agree that at some stage the study of dramatic text has to take performance into account.

Performance

At Key Stage 1 pupils should be guided to 'develop the capacity to convey, when reading aloud, the meaning of the text clearly to the listener through intonation and phrasing'.

At Key Stage 2 pupils should 'recite and read aloud in a variety of contexts, with increasing fluency and awareness of audience'.

At Key Stage 3 pupils should be encouraged to work in a 'wider range of situations in which their individual contributions are given greater emphasis, e.g., . . . planning and taking part in a group presentation, which . . . might include performance of a playscript for a school production'.

What becomes apparent here is the emphasis on 'performance' which many Drama teachers would avoid in Drama altogether. While teachers debate the philosophies of Drama in Education and the place of performance in it, for Drama in English they are being asked to return to something that has more than a hint of traditional 'speech and drama' about it.

Role-play

At Key Stage 1 activities should ensure that pupils 'read in the context of role-play and dramatic play e.g. in the home corner, class shop, . . .' pupils should be able to participate 'as speakers and listeners in group activities, including imaginative play, e.g. play the role of shop-keeper . . . in the class shop'.

At Key Stage 2 pupils should have the opportunity to learn how to 'use, and understand the use of, role-play in teaching and learning, e.g. to explore an aspect of history'.

All these opportunities for role-play are a means to an end: to teach language skills, to further reading ability, as a means of packaging content, e.g. in exploring history. None is first and foremost about Drama and the learning that Drama can provide.

Improvisation

At Key Stage 1 the range of activities should be designed 'to develop pupils' ability to speak and listen, should include imaginative play and improvised drama'.

At Key Stage 2 activities should include 'simulations and group drama' and pupils should 'be helped to make more extended contributions to group or class discussions and to informal or formal presentation, e.g. dramatic improvisation'.

In the Statements of Attainment pupils are expected to: 'produce well-structured pieces of writing, some of which handle demanding subject matter . . . e.g., . . . develop a playscript from an improvisation'.

Of all the categories, this looks the most promising as Drama in Education. But once again the learning aims limit this category. At Key Stage 1 the 'imaginative play and improvised drama has been given the role of promoting speaking and listening and while that is the aim, the other learning experiences that could be available are relegated or lost altogether'. At Key Stage 2 there is mention of 'simulation and group drama' but it comes in the context of the reference to KS2 under 'Role-play', that is as a means of exploring history or a piece of literature, so the content becomes the learning aim, rather than the process itself. At Key Stages 3 and 4 references to improvisation are virtually lost, with the exception of one statement of attainment which uses it only as a stimulus for formal writing. All the many other learning experiences that improvisation can offer, most importantly, those which are unique to Drama, are not considered at all.

So the National Curriculum is offering very little to the Drama teacher who believes that the value of Drama in Education is the individual and unique learning it can offer children in schools. What it does is pay lip service to an outdated, ill-defined view of what non-specialists think Drama is about and offer Drama as a service subject for the Foundation subjects. It is certainly not a very satisfactory position for the future of Drama in Education or for its practitioners.

In 1989, HM Inspectorate published a paper in the Curriculum Matters series, entitled *Drama from 5 to 16* (DES, 1989). It was hoped that the paper would 'contribute to the continuing debate about the nature of drama in our schools' and set out a framework 'to help schools formulate policies and practices for the teaching and learning of drama appropriate to their pupils' (p. v). This was a much more positive document for Drama than anything that has come since from government departments.

Although it has some shortcomings (for example it is rather pedestrian in its examination of Drama and fails to deal adequately with the unique qualities that Drama offers learning), it is a useful starting point for debate. It offers some sense of the range of activities that make up classroom Drama and formulates a set of aims and objectives in learning through Drama, with the objectives being set out like the Statements of Attainment in the National Curriculum.

For example, by the age of seven, the end of Key Stage 1, children should 'understand and take pleasure in the difference between pretence and reality' (p. 4). At eleven, the end of Key Stage 2, pupils should 'know how to structure dramatic sequences in order to convey meaning' (p. 4). While at sixteen, the end of Key Stage 4, pupils should be able to 'try out different ideas or unorthodox approaches in experimenting with improvisation and text' (p. 5). Thus in this document we are for the first time given some clear guidelines about what the content of

Drama lessons should be, because we have a set of aims and objectives.

Given the state of the present legislation, what are our own experts telling us now? The debates within Drama in Education continue to follow 'Drama versus Theatre' lines, as they have for the past decade; despite the two schools of thought becoming less rigid and aspects of the two merging more readily, there is a continued friction:

> We had wrongly assumed that there was now a generally held understanding of theatre as a process which calls on many art forms to create meaning, resulting in a recognition of the sym-biotic relationship between theatre and drama, drawing as both do, on dramatic form. That theatre in educational contexts was now widely utilised, not simply as the play or production end goal of process orientated drama, but as an integral feature of such work; and that the choice of the appropriate way of working was fundamentally tied to an assessment of learning needs rather than any allegiance to process, product or any other camp.
>
> However, it would appear that while the shrillness of debate centred on the supposed dichotomy between drama and theatre has abated, fundamental differences of intent still underlie the surface agreement on mutuality we seem to have achieved. (Clark and Goode, 1991: 10)

We have quoted this passage in full because not only does it voice succinctly the underlying friction that exists despite sur-face appearances, but it also expresses most succinctly the re-lationship between Drama and Theatre. It also reminds us once again of the importance of learning aims for the teacher, because it is the aims that will determine the methods, structures and ways of working within the Drama lesson.

As Clark and Goode are prominent practitioners it is also worth looking at their definition of Drama. They seek to redirect teachers towards Drama in Education, an Arts subject that re-cognizes and uses the 'symbiotic relationship between theatre and drama'. This is the definition they use:

> An essential form of behaviour in all cultures which allows for the exploration of issues and problems central to the human con-

dition and offers the individual the opportunity to define and clarify their own culture. It is a creative group activity in which individuals behave in 'as if' situations as either themselves or as other people. This attitude of the participants in the drama process demands a response from others at a direct feeling level. Awareness of the make-believe situation allows them to reflect, make sense and give meaning to their experience . . . So drama occurs when a group agree to pretend and maintain that pretence in action through the imagined use of people, time and space. (Clark and Goode, 1991: 10)

This definition certainly points out more clearly the vast gulf that exists between Drama in the National Curriculum and the Drama of Clark and Goode. And it does not require any imagination to guess behind whom the majority of Drama teachers would line up if asked to show their allegiance.

Other influential Drama educators still show this underlying difference in approach to the subject in their writing. Neelands writes:

Drama (in the educational context) is not as concerned with the transmission of theatre-skills as it is with the construction of imagined experience. Imagined experience (controlled by the conventions of game and theatre) is seen as being a particularly efficient context for children to try out and experiment with new ideas, concepts, values, roles and language in action (i.e. in the situational context in which they would naturally occur). Drama is to do with the child experiencing rather than with the child performing. (Neelands, 1984: 6)

In this view of Drama Neelands is clearly rejecting any notion of Drama as encompassing Theatre Arts and even in a more recent publication *Structuring Drama Work* (1990), which acknowledges more readily the 'symbiotic' relationship between Theatre and Drama, he maintains a view of Drama that is removed from Theatre Arts and Theatre Skills. The book sets out very clearly ways of working in Drama lessons. He divides the structure into four sections: context-building; narrative; poetic; reflective. Each structure is described, given 'cultural connections', learning opportunities and examples.

In his rationale, Neelands describes the conventions he uses:

> The conventions and the examples emphasize interactive forms of interchange, even fusion, of the roles of spectator and actor, rather than those conventions associated with performance where the roles of spectator and actor tend to be more clearly defined. The conventions selected are mainly concerned with the process of theatre as a means of developing understanding about both human experience and Theatre itself. This may, or may not, later become translated and communicated through performance. The conventions have been chosen to emphasize theatre's traditional role as an educative form of entertainment which responds to a basic human need to interpret and express the world through symbolic form. The conventions recognize that theatre is not taught, rather that our own basic use of theatre in play and other forms of imitative behaviour become refined and developed by experiencing increasingly complex relationships of convention and content. The conventions selected, therefore, form a bridge between spontaneous and innate uses of theatre and the more poetic conventions of performance craft. They are consciously associated with other familiar youth culture forms in order to stress the familiarity and pervasiveness of theatre. (Neelands, 1990: 5)

Neelands is at pains to point out that although he is using Theatre in his methods and approaches, it is Theatre in its broadest sense and not Theatre Skills as such. This is emphasized in his view that 'theatre is not taught . . . (but) developed by experiencing'. Experiencing remains the central issue in this philosophy of Drama in Education.

This view is in marked contrast to that of David Hornbrook, who writes:

> I believe there is a real danger that our well-intentioned efforts to respond to the claims of children's sub-culture (their knowledge) we effectively deny them the knowledge through which they can effect change (our knowledge). Under such a scheme, we go to 'Hamlet' at the National Theatre while they must be content with role-playing and improvisation, not only because we designate these latter activities as more relevant to their needs, but also because professionally we are not prepared to make qualitative

judgements between the two experiences. Who are we (the argument goes) to impose our middle-class cultural values on work-
ing-class children, when their needs are so patently different?
(Hornbrook, 1989: 95)

Hornbrook goes on to advocate a syllabus that, in our present
understanding, most of us would call Theatre Arts, or at any rate
one containing a strong element of Theatre Arts:

> I shall have in mind not only the traditionally accepted and fam-
> iliar mainstream practices of drama-in-education, the creative
> improvisations and directed role-playing, but all those less
> publicised manifestations of drama in our schools, such as visits
> to the theatre and the school play, puppetry and mime, design,
> play study and theatre technology. All these, and many other
> aspects of dramatic art evident in schools, have been for too long
> submerged beneath the prolific advertising of certain favoured
> methodologies. Dramatic art is strictly non-sectarian. Nothing
> which can contribute to the making of dramas must be excluded
> from consideration. (Hornbrook, 1989: 104)

Hornbrook boldly takes a stand against the Whatever-you-do-
don't-mention-the-Theatre brigade. Other Drama teachers may
sympathize with the belief that there is no difference between
'Drama' and 'Theatre'. Hornbrook states that 'conceptually there
is nothing which differentiates the child acting in the classroom
from the actor on the stage in the theatre' (p. 104).

If he represents a future consensus (and Hornbrook writes
very convincingly), a great deal of time has been wasted over
internal wrangling about philosophies and methodologies for
Drama in Education. While readers are still reeling from that
thought, Hornbrook snakes another of the cornerstones of the
field:

> ... although it is true that both actor and child are involved in
> a process, dramatic art, the outcome of that process, is itself
> inescapably a product. In more complex forms of drama making,
> such as the performance of a play in the theatre, many partici-
> pants with a wide range of specialist skills are likely to have
> contributed to what we commonly know as the production
> process. But classroom improvisations also involve a production

process, even though, of course, there may never be a formal,
enacted presentation. Children experiment with a theme, they
rehearse, reject some aspects, try again, abandon the idea. The
teacher takes on a role and directs the action, the drama moves
forward. Like the artist beginning a painting or the writer a novel,
the possibility of arrival is implicit in the very act of starting the
journey. (Hornbrook, 1989: 105)

Drama teachers may find this rather startling view very re-
assuring. Having firmly believed that the process was the purpose, they will have felt very guilty when despite all planning
and guiding, classes show far too much interest in 'finishing
their play'. It is in fact a much more realistic position to take, to
acknowledge the product of Drama in this way, as we have yet to
meet a class that was not at some time or other excited by that
idea of 'arrival'.

So two of our most prominent Drama practitioners are not
yet reconciled in their view of what Drama in Education should
be about. This tends to leave classroom teachers doing exactly
what they have always done, that is, trying to do what they feel
to be right with a particular class at a particular time, employing
the methodologies and ideas of others when they seem to be
useful.

The problem that arises through this complete individualism
of teaching is that there is not necessarily any sense of progress
or even connection when a child moves from one Drama teacher
to the next or from one school to the next.

Alistair Black recognizes this problem in his interview with
Ken Taylor:

> ... we have gone wrong as Drama teachers in not being able to
> record how children have developed in their Drama work. The
> time has come when children have a right to expect to progress in
> their Drama work and to be able to identify that progression
> because of clearly laid out criteria and schemes of work that the
> teacher has at his or her disposal. (Black, 1991: 17)

A further recent development is the establishment of
'National Drama'. It was established in 1990 after several years
of discussion between the major Drama Associations in order to

be 'One Voice for Drama'. Then, instead of having a number of smaller organizations representing different areas of specialism, there would be one, much larger, and therefore stronger association embracing all those involved in Drama Education. It would include Drama teachers, Advisers, Inspectors, Lecturers, Theatre-in-Education performers and all others with an interest in the field.

The association was mooted on 11 November 1989, which as Armistice Day seems appropriate and symbolic for an attempt to achieve a united voice to speak for the cause of Drama. An inaugural conference took place at the end of March 1990, followed by a first major conference in the autumn of 1990, and the election of a committee. It was the intention of the association from the outset to provide not only courses, publications and a forum for discussion for Drama practitioners, but also a political voice for Drama in Education. John Boylan, on behalf of the Interim Committee for National Drama wrote in *London Drama* that 'With Art and Music named as foundation subjects in the National Curriculum, Drama needs a special voice – not several, as in the past – but one' (Boylan, 1990: 9).

In July 1990, *London Drama*, the journal of the London Drama Association, under the same Editorial Board, became *The Drama Magazine*, the journal of National Drama, and through the early 1990s Drama teachers have been uniting to defend their traditions. If Drama is to survive and the cut-backs in training be countered, substantial in-service provision will be necessary, as well as research in aspects of Drama, funding and support for international contact, and increased liaison with other beleaguered Arts groupings. Such work will require the strong and committed support of all those who believe in Drama in Education, whether as process or as performance.

Note

This chapter is developed from an unpublished MA (Ed.) dissertation, *Drama in Education in Contemporary Society*, by Kate Armes, Faculty of Educational Studies, University of Southampton, 1991.

7

Media Education and the Secondary English Curriculum

Introduction

Like Literature and Drama, Media Education has a place in contemporary language education, particularly as part of learners' 'knowledge of how language operates in a multilingual society' (Language Charter, iii, p. 13). This chapter focuses on the recent growth and current role of Media Education in the Secondary curriculum, drawing on debates about who should teach it and at what level it should be taught. It explores some of the strategic questions about media work raised by the most recent demands of the National Curriculum, especially *English 5–16* (DFE, 1993a). Initially, however, it is worth looking backwards for a moment.

In the days when 'SAT' was usually an intransitive verb and English teachers were not necessarily obliged to be aware of that fact, it was possible to think of 'the media' as just another topic within the English Curriculum. It could offer interesting examples of writing for a purpose, provide vivid images which could stimulate classroom talk and writing, or it could furnish examples of 'journalistic' writing which could be compared unfavourably with Literature.

A colleague who trains English teachers used to give students a list of activities commonly experienced in secondary English lessons as a starting-point for discussion of 'What is English?'. At the very end of a list of seven areas of study and processes was an eighth item (perhaps added most recently) which read: 'work on the mass media – TV, radio, film, video, newspapers . . .' Study of the mass media was an additional and, for many teachers, optional activity which might enhance English work.

Developments in Drama and Media since then have been validated by the Cox Report (DES/WO, 1989) in a way which commanded a broad consensus. As a result, it now seems odd to consider 'work on the mass media' as a process rather than as an area of content. Yet the latest revisions to the English National Curriculum ask teachers to envisage Drama and Media as instruments for delivering 'the fundamental objectives of the Order rather than to see them as distinctive areas of study' (DFE, 1993a: viii).

It now seems vital to reassert not only the central importance of studying the media, but also its appropriateness and relevance within the English curriculum. Of course English in secondary classrooms is by no means identical with what is prescribed in the Cox Report (DES/WO, 1989), in the Statutory Orders of 1990 (DES, 1990d), or in the 1993 revisions. Similarly, the Non-statutory Guidance which began to appear in 1990 may not have made a great deal of difference yet to what happens in classrooms. Without adequate training, how could it? Many teachers have had to rely on a mixture of self-development, panic measures and commercial publications.

Our recent research suggests that there are some secondary English classrooms, at least, in which teachers have embraced the systematic study of the media with enthusiasm and success (Hart and Benson, 1992, 1993). But it would be a mistake to assume a consensus amongst teachers about the importance of Media Education. It would certainly be wrong to expect any unanimity or uniformity as to the purposes and methods of Media Education.

Consider, for example, an article by a Hertfordshire teacher of English and Media Studies, Michael Casey, which appeared in *Teachers' Weekly* of 21 February 1991. The headline of the piece read:

WE MUST RETRIEVE THE IMAGINATIONS OF THE YOUNG FROM THE THIEF IN THE CORNER OF THE ROOM – SPARE THE TV OFF-SWITCH AND SPOIL THE CHILD

Casey blames the decline in reading standards firmly on early habits of passive television watching. He uses some of the derogatory labels applied to television, like 'electronic childminder' and 'the box', and complains that parental indulgence is responsible for declining literacy. But television has also begun to invade the classroom, he claims, for teachers now see television and video as an educational panacea which can quieten a normally noisy class. Films of literary texts have superseded the texts themselves, 'saturating (and) drowning thought and leaving the mind a sponge for all sorts of dubious ideas'.

We may be used to such rhetoric from politicians, but it is disturbing to hear it from a teacher of English and Media Studies. Where are the classrooms in which films have replaced written texts? In reality, it is about as hard to find an English teacher in a secondary school who frequently uses television and video as it is to find the equipment for doing so when it is needed.

Kenneth Baker shares this view of television watching as the enemy of imaginative engagement. Children, he argues, have an inner life which needs to tapped by teachers. He quotes Ted Hughes on the 'world of final reality, the world of memory, emotion, imagination, intelligence and natural common sense, which goes on all the time, consciously or unconsciously, like the heart-beat' (*Sunday Times*, 22 February 1988). We may all agree with the centrality of this inner life in education, but we may disagree about the means by which it can be developed in children.

Mr Baker starts from a position of cultural protectionism. The English language is 'one of the glories of western civilization' whose rich heritage is preserved in the classics in general and in Shakespeare in particular. He had already made such claims in his earlier Alan Palmer lecture when he first began to publicize the concern with language and literature teaching which led to the Kingman and Cox Reports. 'Next to our people,' he announced, 'our language is our greatest asset.' The theme was repeated in a later article along with extracts from the original lecture (*The Times*, 7 November 1986; *Sunday Times*, 22 February 1988).

It is clear what Mr Baker hopes for:

When I visit schools, I like to call in on English lessons and am particularly pleased if the children are being taught one of the classics. I believe passionately that the future of our language depends upon us bringing up children to appreciate its past.

It is equally clear what disappoints and depresses him.

Children watch too much television . . . I find this depressing. Literature, the reading of good books, is in many important ways a superior, richer and deeper experience than watching television. A particular feature of the written or spoken word is the unique demand it makes upon the imagination.

Yet Mr Baker's main concern is not so much with the quantity of television viewing as with the quality of the experience, with the psychology of the process. He claims that television watching bypasses the imagination. It is a predominantly visual medium (no 'spoken word'?) which makes life too easy for viewers. He acknowledges that television drama can be excellent, but that there is always something missing.

Even the best television adaptations are thin when compared with the books themselves.

Why is it that he should see television as too easy an experience? It seems to be because he sees it as merely a window on reality. Unlike Shakespeare himself, he prefers his plays to be *read*, because only books offer authors an 'engagement with language as they wrestle to create sense out of chaos and meaning out of absurdity'. Turning texts into performances on stage or television or radio does not, apparently, transform them. He concludes that 'the viewer must become a reader'.

Such a view fails to recognize one of the most basic differences which English, Drama and Media teachers have worked for many years to establish, that performances change texts and that the medium within which a text is realised helps to determine its significance. But it also fails to accept the possibility of badly written and unimaginative books, let alone well made and imaginative television programmes. Television is simply not seen as an art-form which is capable of imaginative expression. Yet we now spend more time watching drama on television than feeding ourselves and more total time in a week than most Elizabethan theatre-goers in a life-time.

Michael Holroyd, the distinguished biographer and literary critic, attacked television in similar vein a decade ago:

> Like travel, television narrows the mind . . . The difference between television and literature is fundamental. When we read a book we enter into a secret intimacy with the author, an intimacy . . . between strangers. We form our own images in our heads. But when we watch television we all plug ourselves into our sets and collectively receive identical images. (*Sunday Times*, 10 February 1982)

Holroyd's view ignores the way in which each viewer's experience brings a perspective to any programme which causes them to perceive and interpret it according to a personal dimension of meaning. But he makes more serious allegations. Television subverts individual visualisation and imagination, but it is not merely a form of visual valium. It will eventually displace, he argues, Literature and the other arts by its massive economic power, its domestic intrusiveness and its compulsion to drive all that it touches down-market. It is 'an eye that watches us and eventually controls the way we see ourselves'.

There is indeed plenty which is wrong with television. But it is a product of the cultural and economic environment which we have created around it. So it is not true that the medium itself is inherently inferior, nor that literature is necessarily superior. Still less that, because television viewing depends on a different process of signification from writing, it is therefore incapable of engaging the imagination.

No doubt the plethora of cheaply made continuous serials ('soap opera') which now dominate peak-time viewing would confirm him in his views. All three of Britain's major soaps are broadcast during family viewing hours before the 9 p.m. 'watershed'. They all (particularly *Neighbours*) have some appeal for children. Yet none of these facts has anything to do with the quality of viewing experience they offer.

They differ from each other and they all depend on the imaginative involvement of viewers. They are not typical of television drama as a whole, nor even television drama for children.

The first National Curriculum for English Order did at least recognize the value of non-literary texts and requires that they be given some attention. But whilst Prince Charles and others have complained about the threats to our literary heritage which National Curriculum English poses, many teachers are concerned, on the contrary, that its assumptions about reading are far too traditional (Hart, 1991, 1992). The controversial assessment processes introduced for Key Stage 3 in 1993 and the new English Order take these assumptions even further and threaten to produce a narrow and mechanical curriculum.

The Cox Report was initially very influential in defining the role of Media Education in National Curriculum English. It has also managed to define the framework within which other NC subjects like Art and Music have approached media work (NCC, 1991a,b). But as a relatively new subject, the study of the media remains problematic. It has only just established a foothold in training institutions and is fighting for survival in schools. It is most at risk at Secondary level, since primary and post-16 curricula allow for flexibility on the one hand and specialization on the other. In spite of these uncertainties, specialised GCSE and A-level Media Studies courses have flourished and many English departments have developed more general Media Education work in years 7–9.

The systematic study of the media has grown historically out of (and sometimes in opposition to) traditional 'Leavisite' approaches to English. Yet now it appears as a mandatory requirement at all levels in National Curriculum English. The Cox Report actually suggests that Media Education approaches to English (i.e. a concern with audiences, selection, production and institutions) should be adopted by all English teachers.

Media Education through the Curriculum

By contrast with the Cox Report, the strategy advocated in the influential BFI document *Secondary Media Education: a Curriculum*

Statement (Bowker, 1991) has been to argue primarily for a cross-curricular approach under the title Media Education rather than the more specialized subject of Media Studies. The model here has been the *Primary Curriculum Statement* (Bazalgette, 1989). But given the way in which the 'other' foundation subjects like Art and Music have latched on to central elements in a 'core' subject like English (especially in media work) it now looks as though a strategy of developing a strong specialism within an established subject is the key to ensuring the future of media work. Without such a strategy, we have to ask what will happen when GCSE Media Studies is 'rationalized'? How can its survival best be ensured? The danger of the BFI policy is that it ignores some of the ideological compromises and practical problems which cross-curricular Media Education entails.

The 'Key Concepts' of Agencies, Categories, Technologies, Languages, Audiences and Representations developed by the BFI in the *Primary Statement* are in danger of removing History altogether from work on the media. It may be that this is more appropriate to Primary Education than Secondary. But many teachers will feel that the social, political and historical dimensions of the media are equally important for younger children. They will also want to question the BFI's reliance on a 'progressive-liberal' model of the individual imagination engaging in a quasi-linguistic dialogue with media texts. It may also be the case that this avoidance of History explains the Primary Statement's reliance on a model of curriculum change which derives from the Bullock Report's recommendations on language or the Schools Council's hopes for Drama across the curriculum. The last twenty years or so have shown that, for all their desirability, these approaches are not workable in practice in Secondary Education.

There are certainly some problems, as Buckingham has pointed out, in incorporating work on the media within English (Buckingham, 1990a, 1990b). Redefining 'texts' to include non-literary ones was difficult enough for Cox and the NCC and may also be difficult for some English teachers. The Secondary Statement suggests that English teachers are ill equipped to deal with the issues which surround the production and circulation of media texts and that they harbour prejudices about media in relation to literacy.

> Media Education in its most developed sense will be more likely to happen only in conjunction with other subjects because of the limited frame of reference in the English Standing Order which gives preference to literary values and literary works over other media such as film, television and photography. (Bowker, 1991: 65)

This approach creates a dilemma within the Statement. It acknowledges the breadth and quality of media work within English but rejects it as a specialist base for Media Education.

> In our view, it is important that secondary schools do not leave full responsibility for Media Education to the English Department. All subject areas share the potential for a wider ranging use and study of media technologies, products and institutions. This means that schools will have to plan for whole school development. (Bowker, 1991: 3)

But if there really are problems in leaving the teaching of media to English teachers, there are even more problems in expecting teachers of other subjects to handle it. Since the Statement does not deal with these problems, we should like to examine some of them here.

It is relatively easy to quantify and show the presence of 'media' in many different subject areas. But what is meant by 'media' in these different contexts? What kind of teaching is going on? What kind of learning is happening? Without the kind of detailed research which no one has yet begun to undertake, these questions are impossible to answer. As a result, many accounts of whole school involvement in Media Education may have more to do with public relations profiles than a genuine curriculum. As the external pressures on schools, competition for staff and students and the need for school managements to present a corporate identity increase, the dangers of creating a nominal curriculum will also increase. Schools are no more immune than NASA from being taken in by their own public relations images.

National Curriculum technology and media

Take, for example, Technology. Media use technology, runs the familiar argument, so there must be common ground. As the Statement comments (Bowker, 1991: 10), 'the use of media technologies (in Media Education) raises exactly the same issues as technology in the NC'. This is unfortunately misleading. Media Education and Media Studies are essentially concerned with media in their social contexts. There is no place within Media Education for the use or study of technology without such contexts. As the Statement suggests, areas of media study within Technology could include:

- the impact of media technology in the work place, home and leisure spaces . . . ; [and]
- the ideas of audience and agency in relation to the production and marketing of products; how design constructs meaning . . . through the use of colour, shape, texture and material. (Bowker, 1991: 72)

We may feel that Technology ought to be concerned with the social and cultural contexts of techology. But does it actually make these demands? As it currently appears in the Standing Orders, it plainly does not. It recognises the relations between technology and human purposes. It also acknowledges the importance of media in the process of communication and presentation. There is certainly plenty of scope for use of media in project design processes. But none of this involves the study of media nor any recognition of media in a wider social context (i.e. as mass media). Not until Level 10 of Attainment Target 5 does the study of technology occur in any social context.

Quantity and quality

There is undoubtedly a need for Media Education across the curriculum at primary level, where the claims made in the *Primary Curriculum Statement* are convincing (Bazalgette, 1989).

There is a strong quantitative argument for permeating the curriculum with Media Education at secondary level and there are certainly opportunities for developing it in this way. Cross-curricular courses can reach the parts of the student body that specialist subjects cannot reach: the more cross-curricular Media Education on offer, the more students will experience it (Bowker, 1991: 4).

It is particularly necessary in a National Curriculum context to avoid duplication and to ensure progression. As the Statement acknowledges elsewhere, students may end up doing 'the same type of activity... in several subject areas in the same year' and there is therefore an urgent need for 'whole school policies to provide coherent learning programmes and experiences' (Bowker, 1991: 103).

But there is also a question of quality and depth. Coverage is no substitute for understanding. The dangers of this cross-curricular approach are similar to those which bedevilled Liberal Studies and General Studies in the past. We may all agree on the need for a strong cross-curricular form of Media Education, but there are many reasons to fear that, as with Liberal Studies, we might actually get a weak form. It may be seen by some teachers and students as a 'soft option', it may suffer from not being examined or it may suffer from ghetto timetabling.

Weak forms of Media Education: Science

Some of the examples reported in the BFI Statement unwittingly demonstrate this weak form acutely. The Science example (Bowker, 1991: 30–2) cites the potentially challenging Attainment Target 12 that 'Pupils should be able to select and group common features underlying various communication systems and interpret the economic and social implications' (Level 8, Statement of Attainment 2) and that they should 'understand and be able to discuss the implications of information and control technology for everyday life' (Level 10, Statement of Attainment 1). Yet when applied in practice in this example, these targets are reduced to using presentational techniques 'to produce their finished product' and using information technology 'in the portrayal of information' (Bowker, 1991: 31). Although this sequence of work also focused on images of scientists and selection skills which are basic to Science, what students learnt overall is not clear. One student's realization that Science is not just about atoms and chemicals, but about 'how we mess things up by using chemicals' (Bowker, 1991: 32) does not suggest that the attempt to integrate learning about the media with learning about Science has been worth the effort. The only other example of Science teaching referred to is reproduced from a previously published account (Buckingham, 1990c).

Weak forms of Media Education: Maths

The example of a Media Education approach to teaching Maths also shows this weak form in an extreme way. There is no doubt that these Year 9 students developed great enthusiasm for the study of mathematical co-ordinates through a television game-show format. But the focus was clearly on mathematical understanding rather than learning about media. As the teacher herself says:

> I had to address myself to teaching Maths, which was, after all, the main purpose of the project. I was more anxious about their understanding co-ordinates and their application than the media input. (Bowker, 1991: 52–3)

The discussion of stereotyping and representation which occurred in the planning of the game-show seems to have consisted of finding out who could best imitate the correct behaviour, facial expressions and tone of voice of a game-show host. The fact that the students 'used media language during their work in the studio' does not guarantee the development of 'critical and creative powers through analysis and production'. The final video-recording of *Pick a Square* was seen very much as an 'end of term . . . special treat' and it was the technician, not the teacher or students, who did the captioning and editing.

Media Education has been reduced here to an exciting audiovisual teaching method. There is no Media Education content.

From the point of view of the Maths teacher there is nothing wrong with that: understandably, Maths must take precedence. From a general point of view, too, teaching and learning methods which create enthusiasm, concentration, and understanding need to be encouraged. But this is only nominally Media Education since it makes no contribution to the creation of the 'more active and critical media users' envisaged in the Cox Report and both BFI Curriculum Statements.

There are, nevertheless, some good examples in the Statement of subject learning working alongside Media Education so that learning in both areas is enhanced. The Sarajevo news simulation in History is particularly promising (Bowker, 1991: 53–4). Similarly, there are rich opportunities in cross-curricular themes like Health Education for looking at specific advertising campaigns in relation to learning about health issues and changing behaviour patterns (Bowker, 1991: 59–61). But, in view of the problems noted above, we need to be clear as to whether we are talking about media work within other subject areas or as a cross-curricular theme outside and in addition to other subjects.

The central issue for the development of media work in the Secondary curriculum is not so much conceptual as strategic. The Statement acknowledges that the basic premises of Media Studies and Media Education are identical (Bowker, 1991: 3). We can all agree on the need for whole school policies. But there are some basic conflicts which need to be considered. How can the specialised study of media be reconciled with a cross-curricular process? They are radically different modes of delivering the curriculum in schools and colleges. In spite of the Statement's insistence on the need for Media Education throughout the curriculum, it also clearly acknowledges (as did the Cox Report) the role of Media Studies as a distinct subject and the need for a specialist base as a resource for other subjects (Bowker, 1991: 101).

The immediate need is for pragmatism and flexibility rather than conceptual rigidity and orthodoxy. Our concern should be with preserving and developing the distinctiveness of the subject in a National Curriculum context, rather than merely ensuring its survival at any price, in some sort of watered-down form. The strategic question is therefore how this distinctiveness can be preserved.

English and Media

The answer to this question may be that only National Curriculum English, in spite of its acknowledged differences from Media Studies and in spite of the 1993 revision, can provide the appropriate curricular context for the growth of Media Studies as a subject. There is also an important issue of stability here. We have to recognize that there is a heavy financial investment in English staff in schools and that English commands high ground as one of the three core foundation subjects in the National Curriculum. There is a need for an important political alliance here. We need a powerful base of understanding and commitment within a subject department as well as through cross-curricular approaches. English teachers occupy a privileged position in school timetables. They have an undisputed power base within the curriculum and are therefore well positioned to deliver specialized media courses. At tertiary level, with the dynamic growth of A-level Media Studies courses on top of existing Communication Studies ones and the continued offering of GCSE Media Studies, there can be no doubt about this.

To acknowledge the potential for both quantitative and qualitative development of media work within English is not to question or diminish the contributions which can be made by other subject areas like Art and Sociology. Nor is it to deny access to media work to all but a small minority. It is simply to recognize a genuine disciplinary linkage of Media with literary and linguistic studies. The training, experience and interests of English teachers are a sound basis for approaching the study of the media. Our concerns with the business of communication and our familiarity with methodologies which seek to integrate practice and analysis in the study and production of texts offer a solid platform for Media Education.

In fact, the inevitability of developing Media Education through English is unconsciously recognized in the BFI Statement. It devotes a whole chapter (Bowker, 1991: ch. 5) to media work though English/Welsh. When it comes to illustrating basic principles through classroom practice, it constantly draws on examples from English. It is clear that, despite the emphasis on cross-curricular initiatives, the BFI obviously had difficulty finding actual examples of media work outside English. Nearly half of the eleven examples of teaching approaches described in the lengthy chapter 4 are from English lessons or teachers.

Family cartoons

The Statement contains some excellent examples of the special approaches and insights which English teachers can bring to the study of media in the classroom. One five-week unit within a specialized GCSE course at Latymer School used a single episode of *The Flintstones* for exploring how the family is represented on television. This involved an examination of sex-role stereotyping implicit in the programme's role-reversal plot, modality (what level of realism and relevance it assumes) and formal characteristics like how the characters and settings were drawn and where the action takes place. This approach offers both a potentially unthreatening way of tackling problematic issues and an easy way of making connections with comparable texts like *The Cosby Show* and *Eastenders*.

Comics and gender

Another good example from English deals with narrative and gender in comics. Looking at the deep structure of comic strips and at the differences in content and presentation between comics aimed at boys and those aimed at girls involved work on language and images, narrative, audiences and representation. The writing which the students produced shows through parody a clear understanding of narrative formulae in girls' comics.

Magazines and romance

This example is nicely complemented by an account of work on popular romance stories. Two groups of female students studied the codes and conventions of magazine romances, discussed the circumstances in which they read them and articulated their feelings about the contents. They worked partly through photographic exercises which enabled them to grasp some of the ways in which such stories work, without themselves being threatened by intrusion into their own private worlds.

The work raised questions about how producers of such texts envisage and construct audiences and what desires and expectations audiences bring to them. In doing so, it inevitably uncovered ideological agenda and assumptions. In this case, there is a suspicion that the teacher's own agenda (which included raising the status of popular romance and questioning the distinction between 'high' and 'low' culture) may have inflected the work in particular ways which closed off the potential of other approaches. Questions about how far as teachers we can allow (or prevent) our own positions to be engaged, how far we can challenge the 'common sense' positions of students and how far those positions themselves relate to students' media experiences remain extremely difficult ones which this account does not acknowledge.

Newspapers as texts

Other potentially fruitful approaches described in the Statement include the study of newspaper content, style and design. As the example from Acland Burghley School clearly shows, students have much more acute perceptions of the differences between newspapers than we might expect. They are also able to deploy these perceptions in practical activities like the construction of their own newspapers. Such work depends on the broader notions of what texts are and how they can be approached which are suggested by the Cox Report.

Book publishing

Similarly, systematic examination of book covers can extend and enrich more conventional textual analysis in English. Comparative analysis of price, implied readership, language, typography and design can embrace a whole range of different issues like categorization and genre, circulation and distribution, audiences and agencies. This is not so much a matter of finding 'interesting applications of media theory' as the Statement puts it (50) as of applying routine Media Education questions to the exploration of literary texts. The benefits of such an approach are very concrete:

- students are able to use knowledge and experience which they bring from outside the classroom;
- students are able to recognize and discuss the formal characteristics of texts in a more accessible way than with conventional literary ones; and
- students are able to see texts within social and economic contexts, as cultural commodities which have an appeal to real readers and compete with other texts for their attention.

Texts and contexts

The study of texts in their publishing contexts means that we can begin to see them as part of our cultural institutions, rather than in isolation. Using this kind of approach means realizing that the distinction between 'literary texts' and 'non-literary and media texts' in the English Standing Order is both unprincipled and untenable. It is incompatible with the holistic approach recommended by the Cox Report.

Reading and Writing

Much work carried out in English classrooms draws upon media materials and processes. The focus of learning in such contexts is usually what is learnt *through* media work which is central to the aims of English. But some work is also concerned with learning *about* the media. It is important to distinguish between them, not because one approach is any more effective or worthwhile than others, but because they are actually different and therefore lead in different directions. The goals pursued by each approach can therefore best be reached if we have a fuller understanding of the strategies, methods and forms of organization which are appropriate to each approach.

Recent classroom research on new approaches to English teaching has given a very useful indication of the range of such work (Brown et al., 1990). It is not always being done by Media teachers and is far removed from the approaches which groups like the British Film Institute have developed. But it is often a systematic attempt to explore media in practical ways which lead to more understanding of how the media operate in society.

The Leeds study (known as the DEFT Project) was carried out in conjunction with the Training Services Agency as part of an evaluation of initiatives in English teaching under the TVEI umbrella. But it began with a much broader concern with 'English for participation' and therefore suggests a wide range of appropriate models for the development of such work in English. The report argues that 'English has emphasised inward states, private forms of knowing and expressions of the uniqueness of experience (and has neglected) the social dimensions of experience.' But, they suggest, if students are to develop as speakers and writers, they need to 'participate as well as reflect' (Brown et al., 1990: 181).

The approaches studied were therefore selected for their specific emphasis on: *language*, which goes beyond the personal and literary into the more public domain of working in teams, decision-making, persuading people, transactional processes, organising, informing, and helping people; and *content*, which includes experience as contributors to technological and economic processes or other aspects of work experience (Brown et al., 1990: 6–7).

Examples discussed in detail include projects such as a careers case-book, producing a community newspaper, a booklet on work experience, designing and producing promotional materials, writing and performing stories for primary children, working with adults who had learning difficulties, mounting a marketing campaign, investigating the use of technology within a school, conducting a survey of library usage, producing brochures on safety and security in the home, investigating local care facilities and interviewing post-16 students about their work expectations and experiences.

In summarizing their evaluation of these projects, the researchers explained that the best writing they found was when

the writers were looking outwards, engaged in informative not introspective acts, seeking as much to change the world (or their part of it) as to understand it, or themselves, better. (Brown et al., 1990: 182)

Common to most of the projects evaluated was an engagement with *non-literary texts*. These were often of a quite conventional kind, such as formal reports. But what is new about this approach is that the reports were of actual experience. As a result, where more than one individual reports on an experience in the same context detailed comparisons become possible and a critical sharpness is added. The transfer of this kind of alertness to the production and analysis of *media* texts may also then become more likely and more natural.

For example, unlike the well-established routine of devising mock advertisements for non-existent products, producing real promotional materials for actual clients demands that students address relationships between audiences and styles with great care (Brown et al., 1990: 174). Richard Andrews, the DEFT Project's independent evaluator, concludes that the approaches suggested produced not only greater personal involvement and more accomplished writing from students, but also major advances in oral competence. He attributes their increased confidence in interviewing, decision-making and other forms of oral work to a greater range of communication tasks associated with 'real audiences and outcomes'. He also claims that the DEFT project developed imaginative involvement through practical contexts which link easily with conventional literature-based approaches and also that 'Knowledge About Language' was developed through interaction with speakers and writers in quite new social contexts (Brown et al., 1990: 144).

Hart's research on the kinds of media work undertaken by English teachers at Key Stage 4 also shows a wide range of approaches to classroom work and a desire to relate learning to 'real' activities (Hart, 1991, 1992; Hart and Benson, 1992, 1993). The aim of the project was to illuminate some of the continuities and differences in Media teaching styles of a small group of secondary English teachers. We wanted to explore their perception of Media Education in an English context and to discover how they saw Media work relating to the other responsibilities of English Departments. We also tried to document some of the perceived problems and rewards of teaching and learning about the media. We explored teachers' attitudes to Media Education both as a theoretical discipline and as a classroom subject; their aims for their pupils; the experience they brought to the work; the key concepts with which they felt most confident and the sources from which their understanding of these concepts derived; their favoured resources and the ways in which these are used; and their expectations for the future of Media Education.

The range of experience of the eleven teachers interviewed was impressive. Most had wide and varied teaching experience, usually involving subjects other than English, and several had business or industrial backgrounds prior to teaching. Surprisingly, though, there was very little evidence of any professional experience of the media or of active engagement. A possible exception to this is that the three men all had unusually strong interests in music as performers and had varied experiences of the media through this activity.

The teachers were, therefore, generally disposed to accept new challenges and inclined to see English as a subject embracing the whole field of communication. Even so, their involvement with media teaching was sometimes patchy and determined more by accident than by conscious pursuit of a career option. Stepping into the shoes of the teacher who has left to have a baby seems to be the most common means of entry into Media Education.

Eight of the teachers had taught for at least ten years and in some cases for more than twenty. None of these had any extended training in Media Education but had generally approached the subject from an interest in Literature and a shifting awareness of literary theory towards ideas that place reader response and a recognition that readers would benefit from reading a range of texts at the centre of their approach. The other three teachers, two of whom were in their probationary year, had deliberately chosen degree or PGCE courses with a Media or Communications content. All of the teachers saw the need for further training in a subject they recognized as changing in its concepts and methods and all valued the work of county advisers and other training agencies. All but one were attending, assisting with, or seeking courses in Media Education; the single exception believed himself too old to benefit.

Overwhelmingly, these teachers believed that Media Education should be a part of pupils' education throughout their secondary education and possibly before. There was very little anxiety about the subject proliferating into other disciplines and most felt secure about their own contributions to any cross-curricular initiatives. On the other hand, none of the schools concerned had yet developed a school policy for Media Education and in some cases the teachers interviewed proved to be unaware of Media work being done in other departments. Some expressed anxiety about attitudes of colleagues in their own departments and feared some disapproval of what was sometimes seen as the study of ephemera. In at least one of these cases, later enquiries indicated that the fears of isolation and hostility were quite groundless and that more Media work was being done in the English Department than the teacher had believed.

The effects of National Curriculum requirements were still being assessed. Generally, these teachers did not feel that the original Order gave much worthwhile support to Media Education. Although the Order appears to be the first statutory document to link Media Education to English, the tasks prescribed were thought to be so vaguely expressed as to require no change in practice. At the same time, other government statements and the sense of continual change and uncertainty were thought to be holding back rather than encouraging the development of Media Education. The subject seemed most secure where schools had taken a decision in the first years of GCSE to introduce GCSE Media Studies as part of the English programme. Departments that had not been ready for this step were now hesitating because of uncertainty about the emerging changes in GCSE English syllabuses.

Teachers tended to express their aims in terms of helping pupils to make up their own minds by recognizing that media texts are constructions representing particular points of view. There was less certainty about how to achieve these aims. Media Education syllabuses are still evolving in schools and it was difficult to discern any consistent pattern, though there were four clearly identifiable areas of appeal, i.e. audiences, representation, image analysis and reader/viewer response.

While these topics largely derive from literary studies, there seemed to be an increasing wish, in seeking suitable content, to move away as far as possible from traditional English themes. Three of the lessons observed were based on popular music, a surprising number in view of the general lack of attention to this topic in Media teaching literature. In addition, 'life-styles' appeared not only as a lesson but in descriptions of favourite work. Comics, too, received serious attention despite fears of hostility from other English teachers.

Other topics covered were closer to traditional curriculum concerns, e.g. advertising, careers, magazines, news, novels and poetry, but in these areas there was a noticeable marketing orientation and some evidence of co-operation with Business Studies teachers. There was much less reference to the medium of television than had been expected, while, judging from accounts of favourite lessons, interest in cinema seemed to be growing.

One effect of fears of other teachers' negative perceptions of Media Education was a general desire to justify the subject through the validity of the tasks set to pupils. Perhaps more important than National Curriculum requirements was the demand of GCSE English syllabuses that coursework should include work based on non-literary texts. Media Education was often justified for its ability to meet this need and there was a consequent temptation to set assignments that conformed to the essay format. Increasingly, though, essays were being supported by storyboards, posters, collages, television scripts and packages of promotional material. There was, however, some fear that the inclusion of such work in GCSE English folders might jeopardize the chances of the most able pupils to gain the highest grades.

Tasks set inevitably influence the teaching approaches and there was a surprising uniformity in classroom techniques. The preferred lesson pattern of teacher introduction followed by group work leading to a brief plenary session was largely taken from English teaching practice and seemed to operate to some extent as a cascade to ensure that the less motivated group members received support from their peers.

Work tended to be classroom-based with a marked unwillingness in some cases to allow pupils to work unsupervised away from the class situation. This attitude seemed to be behind the commonly expressed reluctance to use technical equipment. Although teachers expressed anxiety about their own expertise with videocameras and computers, it seemed that the problems of supervising groups using such equipment gave more real concern. They often spoke enthusiastically, however, of the benefits of such equipment when used as part of special events such as cross-curricular days involving whole year groups.

Working conditions were often poor, with inadequate space and a lack of perishable resources. Readily accessible storage space was clearly in short supply and there was little room for anything other than wall displays. Teachers spent a great deal of time collecting lesson materials such as magazines and advertisements and compiling packages of teaching materials. Often time seemed to be lacking for considered evaluation of these materials or for sharing them with colleagues, but where this was the accepted practice the quality of the material was usually high.

In one or two schools, English Departments had begun to develop Media Education collections for teachers' use. Knowledge of published resources was, however, patchy and it was clear that teachers never used texts in the sequence suggested by authors nor were they likely to use more than a small part of any book. The common pattern was for individual teachers to have 'private' collections of favourite texts to be used to support their own materials. Moreover, none of the schools seemed to make much use of sets of text-books designed for pupil use.

Most of the teachers spoke enthusiastically of the response of their pupils to Media work. They often expressed surprise at the insights they had been able to gain into their pupils' perceptions and preferred modes of working. Pupils who were difficult to motivate often showed new strengths and the pleasant and purposeful atmosphere in the classroom during Media lessons was several times remarked on.

The teachers believed that their own enthusiasm for teaching had been refreshed by their involvement in Media Education and that the techniques they were learning were infiltrating their other English teaching. These feelings were strongest where teachers had the security of certain support from other members of their departments. Heads of Departments were particularly important here and their involvement in the design of teaching packages was especially beneficial. The sympathetic interest of other senior teachers was also much valued and our teachers were looking forward to a time when there would be leisure to make a long-term appraisal of the place of Media Education in the whole school curriculum.

English teachers have a key role to play in developing Media Education. Much work can be geared to the needs of English departments. But this sometimes means moving into areas which are less familiar to students; for example, a GCSE unit which explores how control of the means of production affects television news begins by establishing what we already knew about how news gets to our screens.

It was clear when teaching this unit at a local sixth form college that the gap between the teacher's expectations and students' real understanding was large. In a discussion about the process by which news is gathered and edited, one student volunteered, in all seriousness, 'Don't they do it in a van?' He knew about mobile broadcasting, but, like many other students, could not begin to describe the sequential processes of news gathering, editing and presentation. Several second year A-level students maintained that representatives of the government personally edited news footage. They knew there was a power structure, but their model of it was crude.

The same class looked at the organization of British broadcasting, quickly establishing that most ITV programmes are made in London. But several students could only explain this by suggesting that otherwise 'too many programmes would have people with funny accents'. The federal structure of ITV and its relationship to C4 (Channel 4) was for them a closed world.

Year 8 and 9 classes in another school found it difficult to make sense of some of the subtler advertisements looked at. Many of them could not answer the basic questions 'who is communicating with whom and why?' The language was often too complex for them to cope with how words and images worked for a specific purpose with an intended audience. They had little understanding of how images are constructed rather than found.

Much has been made in recent literature on Media Education of the value of group work for developing skills of social interaction and expression, but perhaps these benefits should not be taken for granted. Group work is more appropriate for some learning needs than others. Buckingham (1990c) has examined some of the claims made for group work in developing social skills, learning to work under pressure, understanding team structures, providing opportunities for self-reflection and exploring the idea that reading texts is a process of negotiation. He endorses the view that in sharing their pleasure in texts with their peers pupils are helped to develop understanding. The evidence of our lessons, though, suggests that group discussions led by an adult are of a quite different order from those in which pupils are left to their own devices. In the latter circumstance, conversation was often restricted by hierarchical relationships that coded the conversation, and was sometimes characterized by uncertainty about, and an unwillingness to engage with, the task prescribed. When prompted by an adult, though, pupils were much more likely to talk coherently about their perceptions and enthusiasms.

These are difficulties which most English teachers are already well aware of. For this and other reasons already discussed, collaboration with English offers great potential for developing Media Education. Yet, in reality, Media Studies within English and Media Education across the Curriculum are not incompatible. We need both forms, rather than one at the expense of the other. It would be as damaging to confine media work within English as it would to adopt the BFI's cross-curricular model uncritically.

The expertise which English teachers already have in teaching about Language and Literature is a powerful resource. We now need to increase this 'natural' resource with more and better training for teachers at every level. Then we shall be able to help students develop the necessary skills and understanding which will make them sophisticated readers rather than merely functionally literate.

We need not feel too constrained by the limitations of the National Curriculum. We are bound, as teachers, to improve on it where we can and extend it where we cannot. To imagine that teaching and learning will be inhibited by the narrowness of the Standing Order for English is to deny one of the most fundamental principles of Literary and Media Studies, that readers bring meaning to texts. Furthermore, like readers, English teachers will apply the framework of the National Curriculum in their own way. As with media texts, the 'structured absences' are significant: what is omitted or excluded is also worth our attention. Even the latest revision of National Curriculum English presents wide-open spaces for enterprising teachers to explore through Media, Drama and 'English' activities.

8

Bilingual Learners: Community Languages and English

Introduction

The National Curriculum has not been devised with bilingual learners as a central concern, though our Language Charter was deliberately constructed to enable bilingual and monolingual learners to expect equal consideration from schools. In this chapter we consider the implications for the language curriculum of recent discussion on the role of multilingual learners. We also address the need to provide a suitable curriculum for both monolingual and bilingual pupils in a multilingual society. However, the current National Curriculum proposals for language have fragmented this whole area into a series of separate language programmes, with an overwhelmingly dominant place for 'English', indeed for Standard English.

Since 1985, the language curriculum has been affected by several important initiatives with implications for speakers of minority languages. For members of such groups, the Swann Report (DES, 1985) has arguably had a negative influence on the status of community/heritage languages in state schools, while it has promoted the 'mainstreaming' of provision for English as a Second Language (ESL). The Calderdale report, from the Commission for Racial Equality, arguing that separate provision for bilingual students was in effect racist (CRE, 1986) also had a profound influence on policy in this area. It reinforced the already strong tendency for ESL support to be integrated into the curriculum mainstream (see Bourne's review of policies and practices: 1989). However, the 1988 Education Reform Act has had the greatest potential impact on the school language experiences of all children, whether monolingual or bilingual, through its proposals for curriculum, assessment, and the local management of schools. With this bilingual perspective, we shall consider four main aspects of the school language curriculum:

1. the place of children's first/home language(s) in school;

2. access for all children to Standard English;

3. development of children's understanding about language ('Language Awareness' or Knowledge about Language: 'KAL'); and

4. access to modern foreign languages.

First/Home Languages in School

In first and junior schools, only children who speak English at home are assured of continuity between home and early school language experience. The Swann Report (DES, 1985) took the view that the use of other community languages even for early school learning would be ethnically divisive, and based this view on the available research evidence, mainly from overseas. This was interpreted to show that no clear-cut academic benefits derived from bilingual school experience. On this basis, it was proposed that the first language development of bilingual children should be the responsibility of the communities themselves, and not be the responsibility of the school.

It was striking that the same arguments were not applied, even by the Swann Report itself, to the teaching of Welsh in Wales. Several commentators have criticized the arguments used (e.g. Hamers and Blanc, 1989). Anyway, while it is hard to assign cause and effect in educational change, such British research evidence as is available on bilingual provision is certainly not negative (e.g. Fitzpatrick, 1987). There is also evidence that it is possible to run British-style primary classrooms with a mix of bilingual and monolingual children, and respond appropriately to the language needs of both (see, for example, Mitchell et al., 1987). If continuity of development between home and school is a crucial educational advantage, the conclusions in Swann cannot be seen as appropriate for bilingual learners. Certainly, they have inhibited the development of a coherent national policy, even while local initiatives have continued, with or without official support. Where there has been local authority involvement, it has been a hand-to-mouth operation, with limited resourcing (Tansley and Craft, 1984). Some short-term projects have gained national or EC funding (Tosi, 1984; Tansley, 1986), but the impact has been unavoidably small.

Arguably, the lack of strong arguments for bilingual schooling has reinforced the linguistic one-sidedness of the National Curriculum in primary schools. Throughout all the early discussion there was heavy emphasis on attainment in English, to be assessed formally at the age of 7. None of the National Curriculum proposals has attempted to address the needs of young bilingual learners with any sensitivity.

In secondary schools, there have been more GCE/GCSE programmes in a number of community/heritage languages (Broadbent et al., 1983), which was the one form of school provision for these languages positively advocated by Swann. The National Curriculum demands that all children must study one modern foreign language between the ages of 11 to 16, and the Secretary of State has the power to specify a list of languages which may be offered in this particular curriculum slot. In a circular published early in 1989, the Secretary of State identified two lists of languages which could be offered. The first consisted of all the officially recognized languages of the European Community. The second list included a number of other languages of international importance (e.g. Russian and Japanese), plus a number of the most important British community languages. In the first proposals, the two lists had different statuses; a school could offer a language from the second list in National Curriculum time only if it was also offering a language from the first list (so that a choice of languages was available). Although the principle of two separate lists has now been abandoned, the effect of current legislation remains the same: only schools which offer official languages of the European community may offer other languages as alternatives.

While this structure of choice seems unnecessarily discriminatory, it does at least give some recognition in principle to community/heritage languages. But when we consider the pressures on schools and Modern Language Departments, together with the vagueness and generality of a Modern Languages curriculum that aims to describe what is demanded from such a wide range of languages, it is difficult to be optimistic. Establishing substantial commitment to community languages will require a major political effort. What is needed is something at least as flexible as the Welsh provision, with appropriate programmes for those who already have out-of-school fluency in the language (some with and some without fluent literacy), and also for those who are genuine beginners. The latter group may be accommodated by a curriculum appropriate for German or Russian, but the former certainly will not be.

Standard English

The Cox Report on the teaching of English (DES/WO, 1989) reflects the current liberal consensus on good classroom practice. It expects English to be used for a diversity of authentic purposes in the classroom, and the issue of the English needed by bilingual children is specifically discussed. It follows the consensus in recommending mainstreaming and the development of appropriate language awareness for all pupils. But it is scarcely surprising that it is aimed predominantly at a typical native speaker of English, and the expected levels of attainment reflect such expectations. Indeed, it is surprising how little political objection there has been to the implications for non-native speakers of English.

This is perhaps partly because there has been a very substantial debate about the role of spoken Standard English (and indeed it is apparent that non-standard speakers of English may be marginalised in ways that non-native speakers already have been). However, the situation cannot be interpreted in over-crude terms. Many parents of bilingual learners may genuinely want a stronger emphasis on the mechanics of Standard English than they perceive in a generally tolerant classroom tradition, and it is clear that there is a strong populist appeal in the right-wing attacks on English teaching. It is not an unknown experience for liberal advocates of linguistic tolerance to be accused by non-standard-speaking parents of thus betraying their non-standard English speaking children's life-chances.

Nonetheless, the proposals for the assessment of 'Speaking', even in the Cox Report, raise many problems – and developments throughout 1993–4 make it unlikely that there will be much official sympathy for sociolinguistically sensitive attitudes to spoken English. Indeed, it was mainly on the issues of 'appropriate' language use and its social role that the government in 1991–2 first attacked and then banned publication of the LINC (Language in the National Curriculum) materials which they had commissioned. Tim Eggar, writing as the responsible Minister in the *Times Educational Supplement* of 28 June 1991, referred favourably to material on grammar, but claimed 'there is a lot more which is a distraction from the main task of teaching children to write, spell and punctuate correctly. A number of fashionable secondary agendas have pushed into the foreground'. Among these he cites references to 'language and social power' and 'language and culture' – both matters of direct relevance to multilingual communities.

The last thirty years of sociolinguistic research has demonstrated that a wide range of styles and norms for speaking persist even within 'monolingual' English-using society, and that our mode of speaking indicates in very complex ways our social identities and group membership. Skilled adult speakers use spoken language in immensely varied ways. To use a single strand of stylistic development, with the illustrated lecture at the top, as the route and goal for all, as Cox proposed, assumed a degree of consensus and conformity that is grossly out of touch with the variety of natural and effective language use. In fact, though Cox does not actually propose that all children should become active users of spoken Standard English, later pronouncements of National Curriculum Council officials have had no such inhibitions. Anyway, even in Cox, it is hard to see how the highest levels of attainment in the Report can be reached without spoken Standard English. The implications for assessment of the Report's position are also worrying. There is a substantial research literature on teachers' and assessors' own linguistic stereotypes and prejudices affecting judgements of speech (reviewed in Edwards, 1982).

As we reported above, the Calderdale inquiry encouraged the tendency to 'mainstream' ESL provision which was already popular in the mid-1980s. However, there is no substantial research evidence on the most effective types of provision, nor on how most effectively to develop partnerships between ESL and other subject teachers. Teachers are dependent on voluntary groups (such as Hampshire's Multilingual Action Research network: MARN, 1988). The reduction of Section 11 funding after 1994 may reduce the number of experienced teachers, and the effects on ESL support of Local Management of Schools may well be to increase the extent to which bilingual learners risk being marginalized into Special Educational Needs classes even more than they were before.

Language Awareness

As this theme is addressed fully in a separate chapter of this book, the discussion here will be brief. Proponents of education for multicultural diversity have argued for many years that all pupils should develop an appreciation of the variety of languages and dialects. Materials to foster such work were produced during the 1980s for primary schools (Houlton, 1985), and for secondary schools (Raleigh, 1981; Hawkins, 1984), while the National Curriculum has inspired further materials (surveyed in chapter 11 on 'Language Awareness') in the 1990s.

Government policy initiatives have sought to promote a more systematic and explicit study of language in the expectation that the development of such 'knowledge about language' will have a positive impact on childrens' language proficiency. The issue of promoting awareness of language variation has survived as one element in this, even though it has been expressed in rather patronizing terms:

It should be made clear to English-speaking pupils that class-mates whose first language is Bengali or Cantonese . . . have languages quite as systematic and rule-governed as their own. (DES, 1988b, ch. 4, para 3)

While the Cox Report contained extensive and systematic proposals for the study of language variation, they were exclusively concerned with variation within English. Yet the Modern Foreign Languages Working Group (DES/WO, 1990c, 'The Harris Report'), which had also been given a brief to promote 'language awareness', addressed the issue even less than Cox. There is no obvious place where bilingualism has to be addressed as part of the National Curriculum.

Modern Foreign Languages

The National Curriculum proposals make it is likely that for most children, whether monolingual or bilingual, the main experience of second language learning in school will be a five-year programme studying a European language from scratch. (Though we should note that the 'slimmed down' curriculum proposed in the Dearing Review might just possibly allow more space for second foreign languages and increased diversification.) However, the position on choice of language for bilingual learners remains unclear, as we indicated in our discussion of First/Home Languages earlier in this chapter.

The other way in which Modern Languages could benefit multilingual learners, is in its attitude to other cultures. However, although there is agreement on the desirability of cultural sensitivity, satisfactory practice is hard to achieve. Byram quotes a Danish commentary on the images of France presented in textbooks current in the late 1970s:

The learner is presented with a picture of a France populated by unworried and friendly middle class people; they have no economic problems, no housing problems. The learner does not see the French at work: shopping and spare-time occupations preponderate . . . There are no social or political problems; there

are no blacks, no Arabs, no immigrant workers, no unemployment, no minority groups of any kind. To sum up, all the language
course material gives a socially and ideologically one-sided picture of France and the French. (Risager and Andersen, 1978,
quoted in Byram, 1989: 16)

Current British coursebooks on French are not significantly
different in their attitude to culture: they concentrate largely on
French in France, and ignore its status in other parts of the world.
Both for monolingual English, and for multilingual learners, a
stronger cross-cultural perspective would have value as a preparation for Britain in Europe and for Europe in an increasingly
available world. Perhaps if the diversity of provision hinted at by
the languages listed for the National Curriculum were achieved,
a greater awareness of cultural variety would also come (the
complexities of the issue of diversification are discussed more
fully in chapter 10 on 'Other Foreign Languages').

A Possible Strategy

The National Curriculum is being substantially modified. In
such an atmosphere of slimming down, and consequent uncertainty, it is important to be secure on the first principles for
curriculum renewal. The whole of this book is an attempt to sort
out how to operate a coherent and just educational language
policy in the context of the National Curriculum. This brings us
back to the Language Charter outlined in chapter 1. That was an
attempt to formulate principles that applied equally to bilingual
or monolingual learners. Only if we have such principles, can we
produce a rationale for our language teaching that is defensible
for a public education system. But ensuring that this Charter, or
one that is more appropriate as a result of public discussion and
amendment, does indeed become a basis for serious curriculum
development, is a political task. It is possible that the increased
influence of parents and governors, enshrined in the 1988 Education Act, may offer people with multilingual interests a greater
opportunity than in the past to influence the curriculum of the

schools attended by their children and by members of their communities. It is possible, too, that greater interest in diversity in the school system may lead to more schools with overt minority-community control. Even if this does happen, though, schools and communities will need to be sensitive to the requirements of isolated bilingual learners who will have little or no support from their communities because they are too small to have any local political impact. Whatever happens, the tensions between personal language needs, local minority needs, and national needs will not disappear. Some agreed basis for a linguistic agenda will always be necessary. But if either the views of the powerful or the views of the majority (and these two groups are not always the same) are to be responsive to the needs of significant minorities, there will have to be constant and public debate.

Note

This chapter is based on the argument put forward in C. J. Brumfit and R. F. Mitchell, 'Language and cultural diversity'. In A. Fyfe and P. M. E. Figueroa (eds), *Education for Cultural Diversity*. London: Routledge, 1993.

9

The First Foreign Language

This chapter covers the teaching and learning of the first foreign language, reflected for most learners in clause iv of the Language Charter. The first part will give a brief historical overview of the evolution of modern language syllabi and teaching methodology. The second will focus on the learner. The final section will then consider the National Curriculum (NC) in terms of possible methodological innovation. Because the guidelines for National Curriculum proposals are still inexplicit about details for particular languages, the chapter will concentrate on general methodological principles that will inevitably need to be called upon.

Background

There is little doubt that the advent of the NC represents a major boost to the teaching of modern languages (MLs) in British secondary schools, though proposed slimming down of the curriculum may limit the achievement. The structure and design of the syllabus puts them in line with other areas of the curriculum, and they now enjoy the status of being a foundation subject. Although some will regret the failure to extend MLs to primary level (though there are a number of experimental courses attesting to interest in teaching foreign languages to younger learners), it does seem that MLs have come of age. It has not always been the case, however, that this area of the curriculum has promoted such a mood of optimism and expansion, and it is worth considering what has brought about this change.

Firstly, we should not underestimate the significance of the professional lobby. The status gained from having languages as an essential component of the NC is immense, and is a reflection of the hard work carried out by professional bodies over the years in making their case. This has not been easy in a country renowned for its reticence in learning languages other than English. It is not so long ago that learning foreign languages appeared elitist and their presence in the curriculum seemed under threat. It is a tribute to teachers' enthusiasm for and commitment to teaching languages to all abilities and age groups that these fears have largely been allayed. An understanding of the importance of the future role of MLs is also evident in the NC's policy of Languages for All, which ensures that, henceforth, all secondary school pupils will continue with at least one foreign language until the end of compulsory education. The national majority of pupils who in the past chose not to continue with languages after Year 9 will no longer be able to do so. Teaching and motivating all pupils for a further two years, and aiming for realistic and useful levels of linguistic competence, presents a major challenge for all concerned in the teaching of languages. It is, then, this potential expansion in the scale of language teaching which partly explains the present energy and enthusiasm of the foreign language teaching world. The feeling seems to be that at last we have been given the opportunity to show what we can do.

These developments come at an opportune time; and it is appropriate that the introductory year for the NC in Modern Languages should have occurred in 1992, the year of the free market, when issues concerning the future of the European community had a high profile in the popular media. Finally, it seems, the European idea has caught on in Britain. People are increasingly seeing Europe as a potential place of employment or residence. In these cases, languages increase possibilities and facilitate access. With this in mind, more students than ever are opting to study languages at A-level and on undergraduate courses. Languages are seen as buying opportunities, as complementary skills worth the investment of time and effort. The atmosphere is therefore right for a new prominence to be given to teaching and learning foreign languages. Schools are turning toward their neighbours on the continent; for studies with European perspectives, for holidays, trips and exchanges, and for a wider view on the vocational landscape.

There are, then, a number of social, economic and educational factors involved in the apparent surge in interest for learning foreign languages. These also coincide with a particularly interesting time in the development of syllabus design and teaching methodology. It is only a few years ago that language examinations came on single sheets of paper, with a limited number of essay titles, and short prose translation passages. Listening comprehension was tested by teachers reading out dictations in often near phonetic expression of foreign vowels and consonants, and passages recounting bizarre happenings in an idealised world. Older learners remember the classic texts of Whitmarsh and the gothic script of German textbooks. Even the later modern so-called audio-visual approaches of the late 1970s and 80s were often based on cultural stereotypes of misleading simplicity, on animals who could talk, on language that was repetitious and alien to pupils' own world view. How often have we heard people claim not to be able to speak languages 'after having received an English education', or passing O-level but not being able to speak a word of the foreign tongue. The O-level oral exam could be the first time a pupil had actually been required to carry on a conversation with another, other than brief question/answer sessions in class or in short spells with the assistant. CSE was supposed to be an alternative but the emphasis was still on depersonalized language and rote memorization. In the oral exam, candidates were required to remember over 100 questions and answers that covered such things as the height of the Eiffel tower or intricate exchange rate calculations.

GCSE did much to change the situation. Firstly, all teaching and testing give equal weighting to Reading, Writing, Speaking and Listening. Moreover, there is a single grade structure – from A to G – which covers two levels: Basic or General and Extended or Higher. Perhaps the most significant change, however, is in the content of the syllabus. GCSE allots the highest possible prominence to the cultural appropriateness and authenticity of its teaching and testing materials. Pupil-as-tourist or host are key concepts, as is comprehensibility to a 'sympathetic native speaker'. GCSE has shaped the teaching and learning of foreign languages across the entire age range, and has encouraged the appearance of a plethora of course books and supplementary teaching materials containing every kind of cultural artefact and language representation from daily life. So tapes now come with built-in background noise, letters are printed in hard to read hand writing, and pupils are required to research and negotiate themselves through posters, brochures, weather forecasts and the like. In oral exams, they are given roles to play and asked to 'get by', to make themselves understood and to elicit specific pieces of information from their partners. When they write, it is often enough to simply get the message across; with grammatical accuracy and linguistic sophistication being increasingly required only as we ascend grade levels.

Such developments in syllabus design and application have run in parallel with changes in teaching methodology; the latter evolving, partly in response to such changes and partly as a result of our increasing understanding of how languages are best taught and learnt. Applied linguistic research expanded at an enormous pace in the 1970s and 80s. In the USA, researchers in an empirical, psychometric tradition amassed an enormous quantity of data, which they used to suggest that languages are best taught through exposure to and oral work within the foreign language. One now famous writer (Krashen, 1981, 1982) popularized a controversial distinction between acquisition and learning, seeming to claim that objective, conscious learning of language rules and structure had little effect on the actual acquisition of true linguistic competence. He also went further, suggesting that such classroom preoccupations can have a very negative effect on the 'natural' processes of language learning, as they encourage overuse of what he called the 'monitor'; which we might understand as the conscious control of speech accuracy through attempted applications of and corrections to explicit knowledge about language. All of this work emphasized the fundamental, organic process of language learning: we need only to tap into this to become competent learners. In the UK a number of writers went in a similar direction. For the most part these came from a less empirically based tradition. Developments in the teaching of English itself began to stress the importance of pupils' own language (Rosen, 1973), of exploratory talk (Barnes, 1969, 1976) in the acquisition of knowledge and the reduced importance of formal grammar teaching.

In foreign language teaching, too, communication became the buzz-word. We can now see, with a historical perspective, how the popular, audio-visual techniques of the 60s and 70s did not prove to be the answer to language learning and teaching difficulties. These gave way to more direct methods which placed a large emphasis on the contextualized, oral presentation and practice of language structures. At the same time, a number of English writers were developing ideas which we would later designate the Communicative Method or Approach (Widdowson, 1978; Littlewood, 1981; Brumfit, 1984). It is a moot point as to what extent such writers had direct influence on the teaching of foreign languages in the UK. They were often writing for an EFL world. Similarly, it must be said that much of the work in the USA was with adults learning English in universities, or second language contexts. Nevertheless it is true that by the 1980s the academic research mood was communicative.

If ideas which encouraged the active, communicative use of language in foreign language learning were 'in the air', another major influence on our thinking came from the schools themselves; namely the Graded Objectives in Modern Languages (GOML) movement. In this case, the impetus for the idea came from teachers working in the classroom. Taking the principle, perhaps, from another skill based subject, Music, the GOML movement presented the idea of learning languages in a series of graded steps. Tests were criterion-referenced, which is to say pupils passed when they had achieved success in the criteria set for a particular level. Significantly, it was the view that languages could be taught and learnt as a series of small packages. These packages were almost always based on practical, get-by-in language and personal details. The GOML movement had direct influence on the design of GCSE, and in many ways complemented the ideas for writers extolling the virtues of a communicative approach to language learning.

The NC represents the point we have reached in the evolution. We might ask to what extent, and how, a nationally-prescribed syllabus can determine classroom methodology. In one sense the two must interact. It is true that the arrival of the NC stimulated discussion of the aims and objectives of language teaching; what should be taught and how. The NC certainly responds directly to a number of apparent criticisms levelled against GCSE; most noticeably the extra emphases the NC places on the use of the target language in the classroom (and, presumably, in all test materials) and the broader range of topic areas now offered. The report on which the NC was formulated (DES/WO, 1990c) makes it clear that communication is considered to be a guiding principle in future work. 'Learning to use a foreign language,' it states, 'is learning to communicate in this language' (p. 6). Communication is seem as not only an end but a means of achieving this end. 'Communication' and 'Communicative Approach' are ambiguous terms, and it is sometimes unclear exactly what is intended by them methodologically. The examples of good practice offered by the report (pp. 63–7) are useful illustrations, but it is necessary for teachers to generate their own good practice, not merely mimic the successful lessons of others.

A recent concise account of the communicative approach (CILT, 1989) lists ten key principles:

1. Intention to mean
2. Information gap
3. Personalisation
4. Unpredictability
5. Legitimacy
6. Target language use
7. Approach to error
8. Authenticity
9. Speech v. writing
10. Practice v. real language

This is a useful checklist, but it is sometimes difficult to see what the various features add up to in terms of actual lesson planning. Many teachers obviously interpret communicative language as employing as much target language and doing as much oral work as is possible. This also seems to be the mood of the NC. Important questions remain, however, concerning the relevance and appropriateness of such an emphasis, the place of other language skills, and the role of grammar and knowledge about language. Established course books such as *Tricolore* and *Deutsch Heute* are based around a grammar syllabus onto which personalized, cultural orientations have been grafted. More recent publications take a more flexible, often piecemeal, approach to grammar and language structure work, which emphasizes the memorization of pragmatically based language chunks and phrases. The problem of integrating active, oral and communicative work with structural language knowledge is therefore by no means solved. It could well be that the answer does not lie so much in the design of course materials, but rather the organization of the teaching and learning situation. It is a point we shall return to at the end of this chapter.

The Learner

In this section we want firstly to consider the context of language learning for pupils. We shall then focus on the feature of individual differences between learners; in particular, exploring learner strategies.

Learning context

It must be recognized that of all subjects within the school curriculum, foreign languages have not enjoyed great popularity. The archetypical French classroom is one of endless chanting of verbs, incomprehensible grammar explanations and unachievable pronunciations. Mercifully such lessons are largely a thing of the past. Colourful new materials and bright, well-equipped teaching rooms can make the whole experience of learning languages fun and appealing. It would be misleading, however, to claim that this was always the case, or even the norm in all our schools. We must accept that for many pupils languages remain the least favoured of their school studies. Pupils beginning secondary school in Year 7, and studying foreign languages for the first time, almost universally approach them with excitement and enthusiasm. For them it is a new opportunity to discover a fresh outlook on the world and try something from scratch. It is therefore disappointing to see so many drop their language work at the first opportunity. Why has this been the case?

The way the school curriculum is organized often mitigates against success in languages for many pupils. The comparison of language teaching in secondary schools to 'gardening in a gale' (Hawkins, 1981) is now famous; with its picture of the fresh green linguistic shoots so painstakingly cultivated during lessons by the teacher being blasted away by the cold harsh gale of English that greets pupils as soon as they set foot into the corridor. Of course, we cannot keep them in linguistic incubators. This does raise questions concerning the appropriateness of the aims and objectives of secondary school language work. It may be true that the emphasis on grammar explanations and exercises of the past did instill a view of language lessons as abstract and difficult. However, even if we accept the need for maximum exposure to the foreign language as an alternative, the gardening-in-a-gale metaphor highlights the difficulty in arranging sufficient time in most secondary school contexts for this 'natural' process to occur.

Individual differences

It has become a cliché, when discussing pupils with special needs, to assert that *all* pupils have special needs. Of course, that is hardly the intent behind the term, but it does reveal the particular individuality of all pupils. Pupils come with a whole set of individualised personality traits, which will have a determinate effect on how they respond to those early months of foreign language learning. Most noticeably they normally arrive with competence in their first language. Experience and expectations in mother tongue lessons in primary schools may form a basis for their second language learning. Knowledge about language, and what this means in practical terms, will shape their responses to exercises and activities organized in classroom. What is the nature of this knowledge? How conscious is it? And to what extent can it be reinforced and developed in all their language work in secondary school? Some knowledge is simply about organising themselves, their work and scholastic materials.

Good study skills of this sort are notoriously difficult to categorize and teach in any systematic way. We might also ask how many habits and attitudes apply to all subjects across the curriculum and school in general, and how many are specific to language work? Some are quite specific to particular language learning difficulties, as we shall discuss in the section on learner strategies below. These features can be subsumed by pupils' general attitudes toward and expectations of school in general and language learning in particular; for example, cultural stereotypes of European countries – their language and life-styles – are formed by imbibing a wealth of media-based information. The family background also will be determinate in the formation, or not, of prejudice and empathy toward other nations. These affective factors are probably the most influential in determining ultimate success or failure in foreign language learning.

Theoretical Input

One author in the field of individual differences in language learning begins his book on the topic (Skehan, 1989) by observing how much of the thrust of applied linguistic research has tried to discover similarities between learners; in other words, to establish a kind of learning universal. This is understandable enough; if we can ascertain exactly how languages are learnt, then it should be a short step towards designing an appropriate method to actualise the process. Yet, after many years of intensive research, it would appear that such a view is simplistic; learners do not all learn in the same way, there is no one method to language teaching. Skehan's book sets out to group together the various strands of a research tradition into individual differences. The research quoted often involves long and detailed accounts of statistical data analysis. This section is indebted to his work in collecting together others' findings. Here, we shall use some of these findings to link in with actual language teaching methodology and learning, and, in particular, to highlight various aspects of present approaches to language teaching. We shall firstly discuss such features as motivation, aptitude and cognitive learning styles before looking at individual learning strategies.

Motivation

Motivation and success are intimately connected, and whilst motivation is not enough to achieve success in language learning, the opposite would seem to be true; that without motivation, it is probably impossible to acquire competence. The Primary School language project of the 1960s (Burstall, 1974) seemed to flounder partly through lack of motivation on the part of pupils. But what is motivation? The most important work in this area has been carried out by Robert Gardner (Gardner, 1985; Gardner and Lambert, 1972). He defines it as follows:

Motivation = Effort + Desire to achieve a goal + Attitudes

We can see the inverse relationship between these conditions and likely success. But any optimum environment is difficult to pre-plan, based as it is in the general background of learners. Work on diversification (Phillips, 1989) has shown how important attitudes towards certain European nationals are in stimulating commitment to and application to language studies. People's and pupils' motivation for learning languages, then, varies considerably; in some cases, it is for purely instrumental reasons, like the enhancement of job prospects. Yet this is likely to be too long-term for most pupils, and there must be some more immediate pay-off for the effort demanded. The GOML movement addressed the question of motivation head on, by responding to the acute difficulty of maintaining interest and effort in a subject when the main assessment was at the end of five years – the O-level. It might be felt that this is true of any subject, but language competence seems always to be measured against perfect native competence. GOML succeeded in instilling a sense of achievement in the attainment of much more modest levels of proficiency, by rewarding success in small, incremental stages, and thus providing more immediate motivation.

Language learning has also traditionally been characterized by a preoccupation with the correction of error. It is still the belief of many language teachers that their job is to correct mistakes and that without correction learners cannot be expected to learn. Or worse: that learners will adopt incorrect forms into their speech. Yet nothing is likely to have a more negative effect on motivation than for faults to be constantly pointed out. Here, balance is all. A skilled teacher knows how and when correction is appropriate. GOML avoided this over-correction. It also set the pattern of short, achievable steps towards language competence. Certification also occurred at regular, annual intervals. This works where pupils are motivated by academic success, but otherwise there is nothing intrinsically motivating about qualifications. Finally, no matter how much effort goes into parcelling learning into manageable pieces, it is the actual content of learning materials which has a determinate effect on enhancing motivation and consequent success.

Course books and teaching materials have improved enormously over recent years; colour is now common, music is based on disco and pop style, illustration and graphic design is lavish. The content of books places a high premium on authentic information and stories to represent the language, and they frequently use adolescent interests and preoccupations. There is a danger that as this becomes the norm, the positive effects of such factors simply wear off. Similarly, it is all very well for teachers and publishers to pick out interesting features of a country, but this interest often depends on an experience and sensitization which language specialists share, but has yet to come within the world life of pupils. In this case, such representations are simply obscure and alienating. It has become a cliché that pupils spend much of their time ordering meals they will not eat, planning journeys they will not take and making judgements they have yet to formulate in their own language, let alone another foreign one.

There is indeed still much that can be done to improve motivation – trips and exchanges are obvious ways to make the language come alive. It is also important to have lively and attractive teaching exercises and materials. But all of these are only a beginning, in the process of effective language teaching.

Language aptitude

Is there such a thing as language aptitude? If there is, how is it made up? One researcher (Carroll, 1965) lists four components to it:

1. Phonemic coding ability; or the ability to link foreign sounds to symbols – to identify and recall them.

2. Grammatical sensitivity; or the ability to recognize the grammatical function of words in sentences.

3. Inductive language learning ability; or the ability to spot patterns of correspondence and relationship in language material – both syntactically and semantically.

4. Memory and Learning; or the ability to commit language 'information' to memory.

We can clearly see how aptitude in any one or more of these will facilitate language learning. We all know that everyone within normal limits of intelligence can learn a foreign language in the natural environment. But away from this, otherwise extremely intelligent and gifted individuals sometimes have enormous difficulties in acquiring linguistic competence in a formal setting. They just do not 'get it' or are 'no good at languages'. In these cases, their minds do not seem to work *that way*. This has been more formally explored in such research as that of Brown (1987) and Witkin (1962). Based on psychological studies they propose two types of cognitive characteristics: field independence and field dependence, which refer to the ways individuals think about and mentally organize the world. In tests Field Independent (FI) individuals are more able to distinguish features in a field, whilst Field Dependent (FD) individuals do not, but see it holistically. The writers conceptualize that FI individuals are more analytic, more detached and impersonal. FD individuals, on the other hand, are more person orientated, sensitive and emotionally attached. In language learning terms, FDs being more person orientated, will be communicative and conversational. Conversely, FIs will have greater analytic and organising abilities.

The research area is fraught with test design problems and the justification for claims made is debateable. Also, compensatory exercises and activities designed to enhance previously ident-ified aptitude deficiencies of learners, have been disappointing in terms of subsequent improvements in language competence. Still, it is helpful to meditate on these features. It is certainly within the range of the experience of every language teacher that some learners have a better 'ear' for the spoken word than others. This is bound to be of significance if the method being adopted is one that places emphasis on exposure to the oral expression of the language, leaving grammar to be understood on the basis of induction. Similarly, experience would corrob-orate research conclusions that explicit grammar explanations do not 'make sense' for some learners, and therefore cannot be operationalized.

Other research (Wesche, 1981) has drawn the obvious con-clusion from this and shown with some success that matching teaching methodology to learning style can enhance acquisition rate. What is clear from this research on individual differences in language learning is that we are not dealing with a uniform process, and there are social, cultural and psychological factors that have a determinate effect on the outcome of any method-ological approach. It is also evident that many of these factors are beyond the control of individual teachers.

Learner strategies

Let us now look at an area which may be more accessible to influence within a pedagogic framework; namely, learner strategies. Research into this area offers the opportunity of dicovering how language learners actually learn. Many indi-vidual differences are of a deep psychological type; possibilities for effecting change on these are therefore slim. Research that has been carried out in this field has rather suggested that we go against natural learning tendencies at our peril, and learners themselves are often the best judges of how they learn effectively. Strategy use, however, does highlight particular learning habits of pupils and students. If we can identify these in good learners, perhaps we can objectify them and teach them to all.

A strategy might commonly be defined as a intelligent plan or method, or as the art of employing plans towards achieving a goal. A distinction is made in language learning research between communication strategies and learner strategies. A communication strategy is understood as the various ploys, or means, by which individuals exercise some control over discourse. As one author (Bialystok, 1990) insists, they are always interactive. Filler phrases are a good example of a communication strategy. These are means that are used to make space and time within a conversation; for example, repetition and intonation to gain clarification and elucidation, giving definitions as a means to seeking specific vocabulary, etc. These occur in native speaker situations, of course, but we can see how crucial they might be in foreign language discourse as a means of maintaining coherence and cohesion in speech. They are an important source of learning, and it is clear that those adept at employing them will gain much from a communicative type approach to language learning. However, attempts to teach them to students as a means of enhancing learning have not yielded encouraging results. This may be because such strategies are very much dependent on a learner's personality and individual psychology. They arise in spontaneous speech which is almost impossible to bring under conscious control. These strategies are also very unlikely to arise in the prescribed type of role play conversation so ubiquitous in current course books and GCSE-type examinations.

In contrast, learner strategies are defined as the habits and practices adopted by learners in learning a second language. They can include anything that learners do, so it is unsurprising that writers in the field have had such problems categorizing them and presenting them in a systematic manner. Early work

(Stern, 1975) tried to identify the sorts of strategies good language learners use: Planning strategy, Empathetic strategy, Communicative strategy, etc. Later, systematic interviews and questionnaires were used to find out exactly what successful learners do to acquire linguistic competence (Naiman, 1975; Wong-Fillmore, 1979). Again, it was found that learners did a little of everything, as needs be. It must be emphasized that the context of all of this work is crucial. Much of it was carried out in ESL/EFL situations and/or with adults. Where children were studied, it was often in a ESL situations where group dynamics and sociability were all important. In such cases (Wong-Fillmore, 1979), communication strategies are important, and language is acquired slowly as a kind of socio-communicative habit.

Other work (Rubin, 1981) has a different focus, concentrating much more on formal learning situations. Learners are asked to note particular practices in the course of their language studies. Many tens of habits and practices are referred to in work, far too many to be ever able to teach to others. Eventually lists of 'good' habits are drawn up; for example:

- use clues to guess meaning;
- compare native with foreign language;
- ignore word order;
- infer grammatical rule by analogy; and
- look up word in dictionary.

Compared with communication strategies, this type of learner strategy deals with language in a much more analytical, systematic way. Many learner strategies might even be understood as broadly based on more general study skills. In the context of teaching secondary school pupils foreign languages, the following questions become apparent:

- Which of the many strategies identified are applicable to secondary school pupils?
- How can we categorize these strategies?
- Is there a developmental sequence in strategy use and does this vary with age?

- To what extent is it possible to teach these strategies, and which are most appropriate for the various methodological approaches we might use?

We might begin to list such strategies as ways of organizing work, asking for clarification, finding out meaning, monitoring progress, etc. It is possible that these could be taught in an explicit way. They could be systematized and inculcated in learners' learning habits in the course of teaching. They are not so dependent on personality and the spontaneity of speech or real-life situations as communicative strategies. Learners can therefore learn and make themselves use them. In other words, by making the unconscious, automatic habits of the good language learners available to all, we might be making many more good learning practices available to all. Moreover, by using them, learners begin to use language more spontaneously. This enhances the use of communicative strategies, and hence increases the rate of language acquisition. Much work still needs to be done to identify the strategies appropriate for various learners in school, to ascertain which comes first and to what extent these can be systematically taught. Some may be gained through the teacher designing specific work, others may have to be discussed and practised for this purpose as a kind of study skill programme.

Teaching Strategy

At the beginning of this chapter we discussed the general background to recent developments in syllabus design enshrined in the NC, with the particular intention of highlighting the problems thrown up by these changes for actual language learning and teaching activity. We then considered the case of the learner; focusing on individual experiences and differences, and examining learner strategies. We shall now turn to the implications of such aspects of language learning for methodological orientations and innovation within the evolution of classroom practice under the influence of the NC. To summarize the various arguments so far:

- The NC presents us with a challenge to formulate new approaches for teaching modern languages in British secondary schools.
- Past years have seen enormous moves forward in curriculum design and assessment procedures. Many current teaching materials are lively and attractive.
- The model of language learning implicit in the NC is, however, not precise.
- The type of methodology used to teach the NC is also still ill defined, and is often based on euphemisms and bland declarations, but is loosely termed 'communicative'.
- Important questions about the role of grammar can be left unresolved in a simplified, idealized model of communicative language teaching, as can the way to develop generative language use and the significance of pupils' knowledge about language.
- Past developments in foreign language learning and teaching in schools have done much to address issues of motivation, relevance, authenticity, etc. The problem of face validity for pupils remains, as does the question of coping with individual differences in language classrooms.

Faced with the above, it may be useful to list the kind of principles on which language learning and teaching might be based. We would suggest the following:

That language teaching is about speaking and using the language.

That language learning is about 'making sense' – in both productive and receptive senses of the expression.

That language learning should be about the expression of individual identity.

That we should aim as far as possible to teach learners to generate their own language.

That formal grammar explanations may be eschewed but generative language means having structures and patterns that are transformable. It is not enough to have a large list of stock phrases.

That knowledge about language comes about from reflections on language in use.

That pattern seeds can be sown and pupils slowly sensitised to grammatical differences and applications.

That all lessons needs structuring, both organizationally and linguistically, if teaching is to be effective.

The Communicative Approach

Many methods and approaches are evident in use in our schools today. The most recently popular communicative approach has concentrated on oral exposition in the target language. A stereotypic lesson is likely to be composed of oral presentations followed by oral practice by pupils. This would be followed by oral feedback or some kind of writing/reading consolidation exercise. Most of the work makes great use of authentic materials and focuses on the national culture of the country whose language in being studied. Yet experience shows such lessons can also often get reduced to the rote memorization of stock phrases and the creation of a world of make-believe that becomes disconnected from pupils' own experiences. As such it is just as boring and demotivating as any grammar/translation lesson. The NC has partly recognized this by broadening out the areas of experience to include creativity, imagination, the environment, the world of work, communications and technology. Perhaps, then, we can forget the stereotypic role-plays to which we have all become so accustomed. Changes in the topics of the syllabus content are not enough. Real advances in language learning must be about the realization of improved pedagogic action. In the past, we have perhaps been over-reliant on a single approach to language learning throughout all years in the secondary school. Differences from one year to the next have been expressed in terms of topic, grammatical and the functional-notional content of the syllabus. It could well be that a more fundamental rethink needs to be undertaken about the relative emphasis of classroom activities.

Grenfell (1991) has tried to describe the way the orientation of language lessons may evolve in the course of pupils' learning. He describes these as cycles: Introduction, Orientation and Specialisation. The term cycle was employed partly to argue that any one cycle should include components of the other two, that these will cross year boundaries and that the accent for classroom activity will alter as pupils progress. Thus, the very first lessons should aim at getting the message across to learners that language lessons are about speaking and using the language, and that language is another source of individual expression and imagination. This slowly gives way to exercises aimed at raising awareness of learning strategies and sensitization to patterns in language. The latter are seen as sowing the seeds, which may be taken up as explicit grammar rules later in the course. Finally, there is an orientation cycle which directs pupils to the type of final language work and assessment which they will meet. The cycles are very much a way of trying to ground the fundamentals of learning and then slowly integrate the necessary structures and practices for further progress.

Scaffolding Structures

Changes in methodology for teaching the NC can therefore come from established practice. Recent workers on the psychological ideas of Vygotsky have been keen to map out the classroom as an experience of shared understanding between teacher and taught and between pupils; in other words of 'common knowledge' (Edwards and Mercer, 1987). Much is made by them of this shared discourse and of the 'handing over' of knowledge. The necessary 'scaffolding' must be developed as organizational and discoursal structures to support this handing over. These may be contained in the planned activity of a lesson, in the elements of a conversation designed to enhance communicative strategies, or a set of linguistic problems given to help develop the learner strategy of, for example, dictionary use. Such scaffolding structures are crucial in the language classroom. Even an old technique in direct language teaching such as three-stage questioning offers insight into the innate dynamic in these structures. In this case, after oral presentation of, for example, a vocabulary item such 'a dog' through flashcard generated repetition, the sequencing of questioning would proceed as follows:

1. This is a dog, yes or no?
2. This is a dog or a cat?
3. What is this?

This may appear simplistic and naïve. It is surprising, however, with pace, how such a series of vocabulary items can be worked on with energy and dynamism. Of course, it is not particularly progressive nor individualized, and yet it has proven to be popular and successful with generations of teachers and pupils. It is easy to see why, for the teacher can grade the difficulty of the question by the intended response. In 1. just recognition is required on hearing the word and seeing the symbol. In 2. the pupil sees the symbol and hears the word, and has to select (and importantly) say the given word, expression or phrase. In 3. recognition must be followed by remembering the target language expression and its correct pronunciation. If there is a problem, then the next level of difficulty is reverted to until a correct answer is given. This is a good example of how the inner character of a particular language sequence can offer varying degrees of support to the learner.

Autonomy

The NC is, therefore, overly vague about methodology. The communicative approach, as popularly understood, is unlikely to be enough to cope with the flexibility required in future language classrooms. A more cyclic approach, based on varying activities according to learners' development may well offer an improved method. Similarly, much can be gained from a deeper knowledge of classroom structures. However, there is still a need to search for other ways of getting learners in touch with the language and managing their own learning. Present dissatisfactions with existing materials and methods have led some teachers to adopt more autonomous approaches for learners. It is possible that many of the characteristics of good language teaching and learning are realisable through these approaches. How so? The term itself is ambiguous, and might refer to total pupil liberty to set syllabus content and teaching methods, or to more restrained moves to increase choice in limited aspects of the teaching programme. There are two distinct components here; namely autonomous learning and autonomous teaching. By autonomous learning we understand any situation in which pupils can make free choices about what they do and say. An open-ended role-play is, in one sense, autonomous if pupils have the freedom and space to create their own language content and expression. On a more organized level, language learning through various drama exercises and techniques enable pupils to develop their own linguistic independence. Autonomous teaching, on the other hand, is almost a contradiction in terms, but may refer to the organisation of time and space to facilitate pupils' autonomy. We can identify three common models:

1. *The Carousel*: in this case there are a number of separate language activities available at any one time in the classroom; for example, there might be a computer game, a role-play, a listening exercise, some reading to do, etc. Activities which cover different language skills are made available to pupils, and they work through them more or less at their own speed. The autonomy lies in the pace of work and the fact that pupils have to negotiate and solve their own on-the-spot problems. Also, there is the choice of which activities they will do, and the order in which they do them.

2. *The Project*: here a specific topic area is chosen and then a set of activities and exercises devised so that pupils ascertain certain pieces of information they need for the task in hand. This could be planning a trip to Europe, in order to be interviewed for a job, researching something like the listening and viewing habits of fellow pupils and making compari-

sons with a European exchange school. Pupils might work through details at their own pace, and individually make choices about the sort of pieces of information they require and what they are going to do with them.

3. *Guide to Materials*: in this model teachers supply guides for linking various course book chapters along with other material sources. This enables the teacher to select points where pupils make choices about what to do next – pupils can then work at their own pace.

All three standard models provide opportunities for differentiation, and pupils can work at a level appropriate to them. Clearly, some model activities enable pupils to give their own opinions and wishes, whilst others restrict self expression. There is then individualization of pace, topic, expression, activity. This varies between models and from activity to activity. There are important decisions to be made concerning the time that teachers need for the preparation of each of these; a series of exercises based on original authentic source materials is clearly going to take up more preparation time than a guided work sheet. A carousel of activities may take substantial time for organization depending on school and departmental logistics.

There are clearly pros and cons for the different models. Examples of their application in British schools emphasise the importance of finding operational frameworks with which both staff and pupils can feel unthreatened and confident. All of the models presented are, of course, limited in their scope for autonomy. It becomes evident that we are not in an either/or situation, and it is perfectly possible to combine both standard teacher input sessions and more autonomous activities. One project conducted in a group of London schools (Frith and Harris, 1990; Harris and Noyau, 1990) gives an indication of what is involved in moving teachers and pupils into increased group work and limited autonomy. Conclusions would seem to indicate that such work does indeed have a positive effect on motivation and involvement. However, later reflections (Grenfell and Harris, 1992) suggest that more attention needs to be given to the processes of language teaching involved in such approaches. In short, why should autonomy and group work facilitate language learning? Which strategies and practices do pupils need to possess in order to operate in such an environment? Changes in the structural arrangement of lessons are therefore not enough; pupils also need to be trained to operate effectively and efficiently *on their own*. Initially, some consideration has to be given to making the reasons for such arrangements perfectly clear to pupils. Ground rules for activity in the classroom must be set. Leni Dam (Gathercole, 1990) calls them the ten commandments; for example:

- speak as much target language as possible;
- be prepared in every lesson; make sure you know what you are doing; and
- ask three other pupils and use a dictionary before asking the teacher.

Pupils also need to carefully record what they have achieved, what was difficult for them, what they need to work on, how, and the result of the assessment tasks they have carried out. Constant feedback is also necessary in order to ascertain where pupils are at and what they are going to do next. Specific quizzes and questionnaires can be supplied to pupils for them to focus their thought on just what their classroom practice is. It is also possible to start giving pupils the kind of language learning strategies referred to earlier; for example, to practise role-plays pupils might:

- make up a jumble or a jigsaw of the words and then put them back in order;
- listen over and over again to a tape;
- practise with a friend; and then
- act it out using props to make it seem real.

Or, to polish up writing, pupils might:

- use a wordprocessor to draft and redraft a story;
- take a text and substitute own words; and then
- do a gap-fill exercise. (Rendall, quoted by Grenfell and Harris, 1992)

All of these strategies begin to enable pupils to work on their language work without constantly being organized by the teacher. We might start categorising such activities in developmental sequences, making decisions about what should be taught first, which can be made explicit to whom, and how far we can instill such practices through deliberately designed teaching activities. These can start to move learners from learning to acquisition, from controlled to automatic language use, from conscious to unconscious knowledge about language.

Conclusion

It is clear, therefore, that there will be no single language teaching methodology for the NC. Already we have experiments in modularized language learning, as demonstrated in the SEG modular French course. Here, formative rather than summative assessment is used to monitor progress. It may well be that such courses are the answer to a languages for all policy, as some pupils' language competence plateaus out after their initial years of learning. In this case, applied competence becomes rather more important than increased linguistic proficiency.

Real advances in the levels of linguistic competence achievable by pupils, however, will only come about from a better understanding of the processes involved in language use and choice. So that rather than language programmes based on idealised models of notional-functional syllabuses themselves determined by versions of teacher-focused pragmatic usefulness, we have language carefully chosen for its strategic function in terms of what it requires the learner to make of it. We must surely have a more carefully designed language syllabus, align it with the necessary developmentally based learner strategies, and devise ways of allowing learners to set the pace and directions of what comprises a language course. We will then be moving in the direction of having the type of language teaching methodology that is now so clearly on our horizon – one which makes sense in and of the National Curriculum.

10

Other Foreign Languages

Introduction

Our Language Charter refers to competence 'in at least one language other than their own' and the National Curriculum requirement is only for one foreign language. Yet recent years have seen increased interest in diversification of foreign language provision, so some specific discussion of further foreign language work is necessary.

French has been firmly entrenched in British schools for so long now that to loosen its grip has been a slow and difficult process, fraught with problems. Languages in general are now enjoying a high profile in schools, thanks in the main to the National Curriculum, with its policy of Languages for All. However, if 'Languages for All' is not, in practice, to become 'French for All', the need for diversification of the first foreign language has never been more urgent.

Why has French been so dominant?

According to Hadley (1981), 'The dominance of French here is founded, not upon the superiority of the case for that language in linguistic, cultural, political or economic terms, but upon tradition, teacher supply and a geographical proximity of no great importance in our shrinking world.' Historically of course, the languages of religion dominated. Greek, Hebrew and particularly Latin were regarded as the necessary vocational tools of the seventeenth century. It was not until the eighteenth century that French really started to find favour, with the splendour of Louis XIV's reign encouraging an interest in all things French. Following the Revolution in France, French was taught by the educated aristocrats and scholars who had been forced to find refuge in this country. French become the language to speak, for the educated gentleman with diplomatic aspirations, or the high-born lady for whom it was considered a valuable social asset. The nineteenth century saw 'Modern' Languages (i.e. French and by now German too) competing with the established 'Classical' languages, but after World War I, German fell from grace and French took hold. It was taught in the grammar and independent schools and was considered 'good training and contributed to the basic intellectual equipment of the educated classes' (Phillips, 1988). Languages, predominantly French, enjoyed a period of popularity and improved status generally up to the 1960s, helped also by the decline of Latin over this period. But why was French still so dominant?

As Hadley indicated, it is not only tradition but also teacher supply which has guaranteed the position of French for so long. It is seen as appropriate because of geography and cultural contact, but a spiral rapidly develops in which more French in schools means more French graduates, and thus a larger pool of teachers to teach French in schools. And therein lies the problem which has so often thwarted attempts to promote languages other than French in the past. This self-perpetuating cycle, which French has enjoyed for so long, needs to be challenged by the other languages, if they are to flourish.

Other factors have served to strengthen the position of French still further rather than challenge it. The Primary French Project of 1974, for example, had an unexpectedly adverse effect on languages other than French. Instead of enabling learners who had been successful to move into second foreign languages when they reached secondary school, it turned out that the provision of French tuition was so uneven across the feeder primary schools that the secondary schools decided to start French from scratch and delay the start of another language for at least a year or two.

Hadley (1981) also cites as another contributory factor:

> the expansion of language teaching which accompanied the reorganisation of secondary education, with schools opting for French

as FL1, for reasons of safety (i.e. availability of staffing and resources).

Moreover there was the practical problem of how to deal with pupil-transfer across Local Education Authority boundaries, which made it difficult for schools to abandon French altogether as their first foreign language.

So why should a move away from French be so desirable?

The Arguments for Diversification

The economic argument

Those in power are beginning to realize that our complacency regarding language learning in general is costing us valuable export orders, not to mention jobs. As one DES document put it in 1987:

> Nationally, there is a need for people fluent in a range of languages, particularly those of our European trading partners. (DES, 1987: 29)

The following year, when the DES document *Modern Languages in the School Curriculum, a Statement of Policy* appeared, the economic argument was reiterated (DES, 1988):

> We need to establish a richer and more varied pool of linguistic talent among young people which more closely matches the broad needs of international trade and the service industries. The availability of potential recruits with a variety of MFL will encourage employers and others to pay more regard to the precise language qualifications of those they recruit, rather than assuming that only French will be on offer.

The document goes on to warn that:

> the current situation is clearly inappropriate to the needs of a modern trading nation. In trading terms alone, a number of studies suggest that German and French are equally in demand

by exporting companies; and that there is also a strong need for Italian and Spanish. A capability in German or Spanish is useful not only to firms operating in Western Europe but also to those with markets in Eastern Europe and Latin America respectively. On commercial and cultural grounds, priority should be given to the main languages of the European Community.

DES Minister Alan Howarth, speaking at the National Conference of the UK Centre for European Education in November 1990, emphasized the

> need to equip more of our young people with marketable foreign language skills in a wider range of languages. Improved competence in Modern Languages will significantly benefit the UK economically.

The educational/linguistic argument

The dominance of French relates purely 'to tradition and the supply of teachers rather than to any intrinsic advantages possessed by French' (DES, 1987). There is no evidence to suggest that linguistically French has any advantages whatsoever over other languages. Indeed, the Hadley Report (1981), in its conclusion, states categorically that:

> There is nothing in the nature of a language other than French or in its teaching context that makes it either more or less feasible than French as the first foreign language in a secondary school.

As for the relative difficulty of the different languages, the research carried out by OXPROD (1989: 39) found:

> that pupils' responses to the languages were greatly affected by the nature of the language itself. Pupils learning German commented frequently on the close relationship between the way German is spoken and written and on similarities in vocabulary between German and English. Such similarities were not mentioned by French learners, who commented instead on the difficulty of writing French down and the disparity between the written and the spoken language.

The report also points out that:

> While it was found that pupils were most positive about German in all areas examined, it was also very encouraging to see Spanish holding its own against French. It was found that compared with French learners, higher proportions of pupils said they enjoyed learning Spanish, higher proportions found it easy and useful and higher proportions wanted to go to Spain!

Although pupils' experiences are obviously greatly influenced by individual teaching styles, the OXPROD survey of first-year pupils nevertheless concludes

> that beginners respond at least as well to German and Spanish as they do to French so that, in educational terms, the introduction of these languages can only be a positive move! (p. 40)

A year later, when the same pupils were again questioned,

> the languages could be ranked in the order Spanish – German – French. Pupils, particularly boys, were found to be enjoying Spanish and German more than French, to perceive them to be easier than French and to be keener on contact with Spain and Germany than with France. Among the linguistic difficulties mentioned, verbs were common to all languages; French learners also perceived vocabulary, gender and pronunciation as difficulties, and German learners mentioned gender and spelling; Spanish learners were more positive in their comments, mentioning pronunciation and similarity to English as reasons why they found Spanish easy. (OXPROD, 1990: 35)

This second survey is encouraging in its findings for

> it shows pupils to be at least as positive in every respect about German and Spanish as they are about French. (p. 36)

The social and cultural argument

Before the spread of diversification, most pupils' experience of a foreign language and culture was confined to that of France.

Diversification of the first foreign language gives languages a higher profile in school and as a result, pupils' awareness of the language and culture of two, maybe three European countries is raised. It was hoped by the DES (DES/WO, 1988) that it would also help 'to widen cultural horizons for the country as a whole'.

We need to combat pupils' xenophobia so that prejudiced comments such as 'I'm glad I'm not learning German because after what Adolf Hitler did, I wouldn't want anything to do with Germany', and 'I've never liked the French' (cited in OXPROD, 1989) become a thing of the past (see also Phillips, 1989).

Angela Rumbold, talking at the JCLA Conference in 1987, had this to say:

> We are convinced that there would be immense advantages if the other great languages now taught in schools – German, Spanish, Italian and Russian – were on offer to many more pupils. They would widen and enrich the range of cultural experience open to children; offer them a greater variety of linguistic and intellectual challenges and lay a stronger foundation for the later learning of other less common languages.

She went on to conclude:

> There is, therefore, a strong case both economically and on broader educational and cultural grounds, for widening the access to languages other than French in schools.

It is a strong case, indeed – which has been argued vehemently for many years and which has only recently, it seems, been taken seriously in official and political circles.

The Promotion of Languages other than French

The promotion of languages other than French is not a new phenomenon. The battle to erode the dominance of French has been going on since the beginning of the century. Before the First World War, Spanish, Italian and Russian had been the poor relations as far as language learning in this country was concerned.

They were considered neither as intellectually nor as culturally valuable as French or German.

However, as far back as 1929, dissatisfaction with this state of affairs was being voiced by the Board of Education, which recognized that:

> There are in addition strong utilitarian reasons why an opportunity should be given for the learning of Italian and Spanish in select schools and districts having a considerable trade with countries in which those languages are spoken . . .

And added encouragingly:

> . . . The Board would favourably consider any proposal for the introduction of either language into the curriculum. (Board of Education, 1929: 13)

The 1930s and 40s saw that great champion of Spanish, E. Allison Peers, take on the fight to topple French from its seemingly unassailable position. 'Tradition,' he claimed, 'that inexorable dictator, has ordained French for all' (Peers, 1944: 58). Commenting angrily on the fact that in 1939, for example, for every student studying Spanish, there were ten studying German and 72 studying French, he asked:

> Can anyone maintain that such a disproportion serves the best interests either of the pupil or of the community? Dare anyone assert that . . . French is 100 times as important as Spanish? Is it not the duty of anyone who considers the disproportion excessive to do what he can to reduce it? (p. 43)

In 1943, *The Norwood Report, Curriculum and Examinations in Secondary Schools* claimed that both German and Spanish:

> have intrinsic claims comparable with those of French; quite apart from their great political and commercial importance, the languages provide the discipline and the emotional appeal which is demanded from the study of a language as a school subject.

Modern Languages generally expanded over the next two decades. This was particularly so during the 1960s, when the new audio-visual approach was adopted and the introduction of comprehensive education aimed to offer as wide a range of subjects as possible. The 1970s, however, did not live up to expectations. Primary French, as has already been noted, did not enhance provision of languages other than French at secondary level, nor did comprehensive reorganisation sustain a positive influence over the provision of languages.

The Modern Languages Committee of the Schools Council was concerned about the position of languages other than French in secondary schools, and in 1975 set up a working party to examine the situation. It came to the conclusion that:

> the only way in which any impact, limited though it might be, could be made against the dominance of French in the secondary school would be for more schools to introduce a language other than French as first foreign language.

In 1977, HMI carried out a study of 83 comprehensive schools, which marked perhaps the beginning of a definite government policy towards the promotion of languages other than French. It concluded that the learning of foreign languages could be significantly improved by a more rational distribution of opportunities.

The official demand for change gathered momentum, with The Schools Council's exploratory study of *Languages other than French in the secondary school* in 1981, providing further concrete evidence in favour of diversification.

The following year, the Schools Council issued another report, this time with the somewhat alarming title *The Second Foreign Language in Secondary Schools, a question of survival*. In it they pointed out that:

> the second foreign language has not benefited as one might have expected from the years of expansion and affluence in secondary education; in many schools . . . the second language would fail any reasonable test of cost effectiveness.

Foreign Languages in the School Curriculum – A Consultative Paper was published in 1983, and three years later *Foreign Languages in the School Curriculum – A Draft Statement of Policy* appeared. The former reinforced the findings of the Hadley Report two years previously, and kept up the pressure for change by again emphasizing the economic arguments:

> Our links with other European countries make it desirable to study the language and culture of as many of them as is practicable. Industry and commerce need a strong capability in a number of languages, and this needs as wide a base of successful language as it is practicable for the schools to provide.

The Draft Statement of Policy of 1986 pledged the government's commitment to improving Britain's effectiveness as a member of the European Community and pointed out that:

> It is not only the individuals concerned who benefit from being able to communicate with foreigners in their own language. The country too can benefit economically and culturally; opportunities will be opened up in trade, tourism, international relations, science and other fields.

A year later, in 1987, Angela Rumbold put forward the government's position on Diversification at the JCLA Conference, and the DES document *Modern Foreign Languages, 11 to 16* was published. In it the government maintained that 'Languages other than French could be introduced more frequently as first foreign languages, either on their own or as alternatives to French'. This effectively paved the way for the definitive *Statement of Policy* which was to follow (DES/WO, 1988), which went further, by providing practical suggestions on implementation:

> We suggest that, in order to secure diversification in the first foreign language offered, larger schools now offering only French as a first foreign language, should offer two alternative first foreign languages; and smaller schools might break altogether with the tradition of French as a first foreign language, offering some other language in its place, with French normally offered as a second foreign language.

The DES provided financial backing for these proposals, in the form of the award that year of Educational Support Grants to ten

LEAs. The money was to be used by the chosen LEAs to finance pilot projects for Diversification.

The Practical Implications of Diversification

To give a sense of the tensions in diversification, the views of some schools which diversified under one of the pilot projects are outlined below (drawing on Dean, 1990).

Learners, teachers and particularly Heads of Modern Languages Departments, all felt the effects of Diversification. Learners almost universally wished to continue with their languages other than French, and teachers reported strong interest and motivation by learners. For teachers of diversified languages it was not straightforward, however. Even those confident and well qualified in the language concerned (and of course many teachers of French were being asked to use rusty second foreign languages, or even to substantially extend limited competence) had to make adjustments in approach, pace and choice of materials, etc., depending on whether their pupils were studying the language as their first or second foreign language. Teachers commented on the marked difference between those taking the language as their first foreign language, generally in mixed ability groupings, and those taking it as their second foreign language, who are obviously that much more mature in their linguistic skills and generally more able. German and Spanish teachers were having to cope with full, mixed-ability teaching for the first time. They were learning to set realistic goals and to approach the teaching of grammar in a new way. However, many felt the need for guidance on working towards differentiation, particularly on how to cope with pupils with special needs.

One of the problem areas most commonly mentioned by teachers was that of resources. Languages such as German and Spanish have up to now been taught as the second foreign language. As a result, the materials available are pitched relatively high. Teachers have therefore had to adapt these materials and develop their own, in order to cater for the wider range of ability now studying the language as the first foreign language.

Similarly, the opposite situation exists with French. Up to now it has been the first foreign language, but with diversification it is now being taught, for the first time, as the second foreign language. Teachers found that the materials available are pitched too low for second language learners, who in addition, often find them too childish, as the materials were originally designed for younger pupils.

In spite of these difficulties, the general feeling among teachers of diversified languages was overwhelmingly positive; words such as 'thrilling' and 'enthusiastic' were not uncommon. The delight of fluent, well qualified and confident users of languages other than French came through strongly. Others, while happy to teach another language, expressed the need for more In-service education (INSET) to improve fluency, confidence, background knowledge and competence. 'Being able to give classroom commands with confidence in the target language' was a priority.

Observation in the fifteen pilot schools showed that teachers of diversified languages were enthusiastic and positive about the initiative. But the demands were felt to be heavy, as one teacher commented:

> This takes my own time and my holiday time has been used for all my courses . . . I've also done evening classes for two years, so year after year, you begin to feel the pressure.

Another teacher reported:

> I used to teach it in English like everybody else did, and I find now, trying to teach in Spanish, I go to say things and the words aren't there. Words like the Spanish for 'rough book', etc., I just don't know and *I've* got Spanish to degree level!

It seems clear that desirable initiatives succeed only with the goodwill of teachers, and that this goodwill is necessarily dependent on appropriate resourcing. Ensuring that teachers, at any level in the school system, have adequate and up-to-date linguistic knowledge, is a high priority for a serious language curriculum policy.

Staffing has long been considered one of the major obstacles to diversification of foreign language teaching. Surprisingly, although the six Heads of Department interviewed had all experienced staffing problems of one form or another, these were not necessarily attributed to diversification. Indeed, there was some evidence that diversification attracts and retains specialist staff. Altogether, it appeared that not only is it beneficial from the pupils' point of view to have languages other than French on offer, it is also important for staff morale, for existing expertise is then recognized and used to maximum advantage.

The effects of LMS on Modern Languages staffing

With the introduction of Local Management of Schools, whereby schools take responsibility for their own budgets, staffing has become an area where Heads of Departments are now having to make difficult decisions. 'Languages for All' has meant an increase in modern languages class sizes generally, including those at the lower end of the ability range. Diversification has created the need for extra help for such pupils, not just in French but in the diversified languages as well. Thus Heads of Department are grateful for any help that can be obtained from native speakers of the target language (see also Mitchell et al., 1992). Some are actively seeking such native speaker teaching assistants, but of course this is heavily dependent on the state of an individual school's budget, and LMS has reduced the ease with which co-operation between schools for such purposes could be developed.

Schemes of work

All departments were having to review their schemes of work in the light of diversification. The need for a parity of approach and experience between the languages taught was felt to be of crucial importance. Some departments found that devising a simpler course in German or Spanish to suit first foreign language learners was proving easier than devising a faster, more mature course in French to suit second foreign language learners.

As one Head of Department pointed out:

> The fact that we have now got two languages of equal status gives an extra dimension to the language teaching in the school. Now there is a lot of diversity as well as diversification, because we have both languages as first and both languages as second foreign language, so double the amount of input and combinations of work. For every year, it has meant extra challenges – for the first time we are having German as a first language in such and such a year and French as a second language in such and such a year – it has meant complexity of schemes of work.

The impact of the National Curriculum

It is worth stressing as a conclusion to this review of second foreign languages, a comment from within one local authority:

> The position of the second foreign language in the national curriculum is not made any more secure by diversification. Indeed, the paradox of moves towards greater diversity is that there will be larger numbers of pupils leaving school with a qualification in a language other than French, but fewer with more than one language.

There are a number of factors threatening this revival of interest in second foreign languages. Firstly, the time allocation for the second foreign language is constantly in danger of being eroded. One school had had the second language forced back to Year 10, although to her credit, the Head of Department concerned had successfully battled to have a taster course introduced in the summer term of Year 9. Two other schools used to offer a second foreign language to Year 8 pupils, but this had now been pushed back to Year 9.

Three schools, on the other hand, had managed to maintain a Year 8 start for the second foreign language. This, however, had been at the expense of either the first foreign language or other curriculum areas, and other teachers understandably resented this, particularly if the second foreign language was then dropped at the end of Year 9.

In two schools, the second language was competing with Technology and in another it was up against Double Science. The fact that it was a boys' school seems to have contributed to the pressure on the boys to opt for the Double Science rather than the second language.

The later the start of the second foreign language, the less likely pupils are to opt for it, particularly when faced with the dilemma of choosing between a second language and Technology or Science, for example.

There is the added consideration of ensuring pupils end up with a 'balanced' curriculum. Some would argue that for a pupil to take on another language in addition to the one they are already learning, at the expense of a technology subject, for example, would result in an imbalance, although could the same not be said of double science?

Both the *Hadley Report* of 1981 and the DES Document *FL2 in Secondary Schools: a question of survival* a year later argued that the existence of German, Spanish, Italian and Russian as first foreign language in more schools would strengthen their position as second foreign language in others, and added positively that there were certainly sufficient staffing resources in the system to allow for a modest number of initiatives to be undertaken.

The Government's Diversification Project did indeed allow these initiatives to be undertaken. A more recent initiative, entitled 'The Modern Languages Retraining Programme', launched by the DES in January 1992, provided another £200,000 in addition to European Community LINGUA funding, in a further bid to address the problem of teacher supply.

Conclusion

The fact that the second language has not benefited from Diversification is not in itself a cause for alarm. Diversification of the first foreign language was never intended as a support for second foreign languages. What it was intended to do was to arrest the decline and possible extinction of languages other than French. As soon as the National Curriculum requirements for all subjects were known, in the late 1980s, it was obvious that such pressure on the curriculum was likely to put the squeeze on the second language.

Diversification may not have helped any one child to learn more than one language, but what it *has* done is enable more languages to survive. However, there is still a real danger of Modern Languages for All becoming first foreign language for all in Years 10 and 11. To put the second foreign language in with the first foreign language block is not feasible as it would mean mixing pupils in with others who had already spent 100 per cent more time on the language in Key Stage 3. The only chance for a second foreign language is elsewhere. Thus, at option stage, the second foreign language will inevitably find itself competing with other popular subjects which pupils may perceive as more useful in the job market.

The National Curriculum requires all pupils to learn a language up to the age of 16, but which language? If it has to be the language in which they stand to achieve the best result, then again, because of the time allocation to the first language, it is going to be the first foreign language that wins every time.

The situation which is already upon us, whereby the second language becomes barely more than a 'taster' in Years 8 or 9, only to be dropped at the end of Year 9, looks set to continue. Pupils will feel increasingly pressurised to opt for other subjects, often despite their own wishes.

Diversification of the first foreign language has certainly contributed to an immense improvement in the status of languages generally. As the Head of Department in one school, where the Modern Languages Faculty is now the second biggest faculty in the school, put it: 'Nobody questions languages anymore'.

Increasingly nowadays, schools are in the business of Public Relations, and the diversification of foreign languages can certainly enhance the image of a school. A Head of Department, for example, discovered, via the Governors, that:

> Most of the parents who are coming in from the outside and who are on appeals to get their child into the school, are either citing

languages or music as their reason for wanting this school. It is the *choice* of languages in the School that is the big selling factor.

Languages other than French have indeed come a long way, particularly in the last ten years. At least the dominance of French is now being seriously challenged. The question of teacher supply will no doubt continue to prove problematic but the policy-makers, as well as the language teachers, seem to be united in the belief that the way forward lies not only in more young people learning a language, but in more languages being learnt.

11

Language Awareness

Introductory Overview

Clause iii of the Language Charter expects learners 'to develop their knowledge of how language operates in a multilingual society'. This expectation picks up an interest of many teachers during the previous decade, which appeared in various guises. For some, the 'language awareness' movement was the rallying point; others, usually at the upper end of secondary schools, were concerned with linguistics in the classroom; others used the term 'knowledge about language' (KAL). An HMI survey undertaken at this time (DES/WO, 1990a) reported the involvement of up to 10 per cent of all English secondary schools in language awareness work; and this was underwritten by extensive and widespread discussion of the place of language awareness in the school curriculum. It was a combination of ideas emerging from theoretical linguistics and classroom initiatives at grass-roots level (by teachers of both English and Modern Languages) that had led the way in the early seventies; by promoting practical classroom development projects, teachers were concerned to increase children's understanding of language in all its aspects (Donmall, 1985). As well as acknowledging one potentially powerful rationale for the explicit study of language in school, that it might lead directly to the enhancement of language skills, the language awareness movement promoted alternative rationales in addition: enhanced understanding of the human condition, through awareness of the nature of social interaction and of personal identity expressed through language choice, and improved motivation for language (particularly foreign language) learning.

The National Congress on Languages in Education (NCLE), a body set up in 1976 to reflect the interests of professional associations for languages of all kinds, responded to the then current concerns by setting up a working party on language awareness in the early 1980s; the working party offered a succinct (if somewhat nebulous) definition of 'language awareness' as:

> a person's sensitivity to and conscious awareness of the nature of language and its role in human life. (Donmall, 1985: 7)

It was suggested that the teaching of language awareness in schools would involve making explicit the knowledge which pupils *implicitly* possess through their (already vast) experience of language in use, as well as promoting purposeful analysis of language; and that language awareness programmes would have both cognitive and affective aspects:

> developing awareness of pattern, contrast, system, units, categories, rules of language in use and the ability to reflect upon them . . . forming attitudes, awakening and developing attention, sensitivity, curiosity, interest and aesthetic response. (Donmall, 1985: 7)

The move towards incorporating language awareness projects into the language curriculum had not, however, filtered down from above so much as emerged from the 'grass roots'; individual classroom initiatives in the early seventies had moved the whole debate further forward.

To appreciate why this interest in promoting the development of language awareness in schools had arisen, it is necessary to see it in the general context of language teaching in the post-war period, which was characterised overall by the rise of experiential approaches and the marginalisation of traditional grammar teaching, in both English and Modern Languages classrooms. There was a shift away from the strong and explicit focus on the teaching of grammar which had previously characterised the teaching of foreign languages, and an increasing emphasis on learning a second language without the conscious attention paid to form in the long-established grammar-translation method; similarly, in English classrooms, teachers were espousing growth-oriented pedagogic philosophies, where the focus was shifting from a skills-oriented product approach to one where the learning *process* was more important, where children's development was fostered by engaging in activities through language, rather than by decontextualised drills and exercises (see, for example, Dixon, 1967).

However, set alongside the rise in experiential approaches to the teaching of languages in this period were a number of factors that would contribute to the inception of the language awareness movement. It should be noted firstly that the gradual demise of traditional approaches to languages teaching (particularly concerning grammar) caused concern in many quarters, not least from the general public, as the continuing existence of the 'complaint tradition' described for earlier periods testifies (Milroy and Milroy, 1985): complaints about the standard of English (as expressed, for example, in letters in the press) were prevalent, and reflected a lay demand for a return to the formal, prescriptive teaching of grammar. In official circles too, concern was expressed; and the Crowther (1959) Report's call for the 'rethinking of the whole basis of the teaching of linguistics' in schools led to the setting up by the Schools Council, in 1961, of a programme in Linguistics and English Teaching, which eventually led to the publication of *Language in Use*, proclaiming 'a new approach to language for the teacher of English' (Doughty et al., 1971):

> The units aim to develop in pupils and students awareness of what language is and how it is used and, at the same time, to extend their competence in handling the language. (p. 9)

The programme was an ambitious one, which, in a sense, set out to incorporate new developments in linguistics into the English curriculum, although in no way advocating a return to the traditional approach to grammar as formerly practised; under broad headings dealing with the nature and function of language, language and the individual user, and language and society, the intention was to explore and develop the pupils' own knowledge and intuitions regarding language.

The increasing relevance of *socio*linguistics especially, the study of language as it interacts with society, was reflected elsewhere in the growing concern with aspects of language variation such as accent, dialect, audience and style, and the familiarization of teachers with such aspects by leading figures such as James Britton and Harold Rosen (see, for example, Britton, 1970). In parallel with this, there was also an increasing recognition of multilingualism within British society, which was to lead eventually to the case being argued for an explicit study of individual and societal bi- and multi-lingualism being a core element in a multicultural curriculum for all pupils (e.g. The Swann Report, DES, 1985).

Meanwhile, the move from selective to comprehensive secondary schooling from the sixties onward, implying as it did the democratization of access to foreign languages, required some re-orientation on the part of Modern Languages teachers, who found themselves having to rc-think approaches originally designed for the ablest and/or most socially advantaged of their pupils (the 25 per cent who had been admitted to the selective grammar schools). There was concern that teaching programmes were failing those pupils who had not previously had access to learning a foreign language, which the publication of the interim study of the Primary French Project (Burstall et al., 1968) did little to allay.

All these varying factors were shaping influences in the rise of the language awareness movement throughout the seventies and into the following decade, so that, by the mid-1980s, such language work was sufficiently prominent in schools to occasion the HMI survey carried out in 1987–8 (DES/WO, 1990a). What were the main types of work reported by the Inspectorate? At the time of the survey, they found most such work to be concentrated in an area roughly between London, Birmingham and Sheffield; the number of language awareness courses had trebled between 1984 and 1987, with much of the increase in urban, multi-ethnic areas. Almost all the work was carried out by English and Modern Languages teachers; this, together with the fact that it was very much a grass-roots movement, serves to highlight the need perceived by teachers on the ground to implement such courses. Such courses tended, then, to be run within English and MLs departments on borrowed time, generally either in a block (say a term at the beginning of Year 7, intended to lay the foundation for foreign language learning) or strung across the year (with perhaps one lesson a week taken).

Materials used reflected the variety of the shaping influences discussed above: variation in language use, language variety and change, child language acquisition and foreign language learning, multilingualism, the structure of language – these were the topics commonly covered, as exemplified in a small set of topic books widely in use in language awareness projects in the 1980s, the *Language Awareness* series edited by Hawkins (introduced in detail in Hawkins, 1984). The booklets were intended for use with ten to fourteen year olds; they were not intended to be used sequentially, and they aimed to get pupils involved in mini-language projects which would draw on their own implicit knowledge. For example, the booklet *Using Language* (Astley and Hawkins, 1985) looks at aspects of variation according to appropriacy (e.g. writing formally or informally) and function (e.g. greeting, persuading, informing), as well as exploring the issue of dialectal variation (e.g. 'standard' versus 'non-standard' English). Another booklet, *How Language Works* (Jones, 1984), explores the notion of grammar (drawing on pupils' implicit knowledge of their *own* language) as a way of encouraging insight into pattern in order to promote successful learning of the foreign language. The intention could be seen as at least threefold: through sensitive discussion and exploration of such topics with the pupils, teachers hoped, in varying degrees, to enhance linguistic tolerance and understanding; to encourage critical analysis of the role of language in social control (increasingly on the agenda in the English-subject classroom); and to help lay the foundations for successful foreign language learning. There was also, of course, the thorny question of the contribution such language study might make to the development of pupils' language skills; this tended to remain perhaps an implicit and *potential* aim rather than one for which definitive claims could be made.

This intensive focus on language awareness work in the early years of secondary schooling was paralleled further up the age range by the development in the eighties of A-level English language programmes; the London Board first made its syllabus available in 1987, the (then) JMB in 1989 (and, indeed, it was already possible to sit for a paper at AO-level some years earlier, in 1982, set by the Oxford and Cambridge Board). Such programmes are currently flourishing, with around 11 per cent of the London Board's A-level English candidates sitting the language (rather than literature) option in 1993. Typically, such areas as the forms and functions of the English language, language and society, language acquisition, language varieties and language change are common to such syllabuses.

However, the continuing success in general terms of language awareness initiatives of the seventies and eighties cannot be reported in similar terms, at least in their original form; indeed, their demise seems to have been marked, at least in part, by the indictment contained in the HMI survey (DES/WO, 1990a), which reported wide variability in the aims, content and structure of the courses sampled:

> There were positive gains in knowledge, insight and attitudes for some pupils . . . but these were generally too slight to justify the time spent on the course. Many courses . . . were superficial and had no clear rationale for developing the pupils' understanding of language. (DES/WO, 1990a: 16)

The report concluded that language awareness courses had contributed to the debate on how insight into language and effective language learning could be achieved, but suggested that they had outlived their usefulness (at least in their current form), since much of the potential agenda for language awareness work had now been incorporated into the National Curriculum for English. The Report also referred to what was seen as a contributory factor in the lack of success of some 30 per cent of the lessons observed: they referred to teachers' 'lack of expertise' in certain areas, to 'staff insecure in their knowledge' (p. 5). The point had already been made some fifteen years earlier in the Bullock report (DES, 1975): there was a need for training programmes to address teachers' relative lack of expertise and confidence in this whole area (a factor which no doubt had a part to play also in the relatively low uptake of the Schools Council *Language in Use* project mentioned above). The issue would be addressed again in a report already impending as the Inspectorate took themselves into schools in 1987: Kingman (DES, 1988b) was on the horizon.

The Shaping of National Policy

Sir John Kingman was appointed by the government at the beginning of 1987 to 'recommend a model of the English language as a basis for teacher training and professional discussion, and to consider how far and in what ways that model should be made explicit to pupils' (DES, 1988b: 1). Continuing public disquiet about English teaching combined with politicians' concerns with educational standards and with a perceived decline in standards of literacy in particular had led to external pressure on the English teaching profession to take grammar teaching more seriously. A discussion document from the Inspectorate had earlier proposed that a central focus of the English curriculum should be teaching *'about* language' (DES, 1984: 1.6); and there was a tendency among English teachers to see in this official pronouncement the threat of a return to an arid, prescriptive teaching of grammar (see, for example, Allen, 1988). A follow-up publication (DES, 1986) took account of teachers' concerns, and concluded that there was a clear need to settle an agenda as to what might be taught *about* language both to teachers and to pupils; the Kingman Committee was to help set such an agenda.

The Committee's recommendations did in fact call for the reinstatement in the English curriculum of formal language study, but not in the shape many teachers had feared; the proposals were embedded in a wider treatment of language informed by contemporary linguistics, more in the spirit of the fifteen years of language awareness work preceding the Report than of the traditional teaching of grammar. The Kingman model paid scant attention, however, to the sociolinguistic perspective; this was addressed more comprehensively in the wider proposals for English in the National Curriculum itself, in the Cox Report (DES/WO, 1989). The 1988 proposals, although not implemented as they stood, nonetheless fed into the wider debate on the whole issue of language awareness, or what, in the following year, became more commonly known as 'knowledge about language' or 'KAL' (at least within English-teaching circles).

While the English Working Party was debating the contribution of 'knowledge about language' to the shaping of the English curriculum, the Modern Languages (MLs) group was separately busy with its own proposals for the place of 'language awareness' in the foreign language classroom. But parallel with the move towards a more explicit and systematic consideration of the part that language study might play in the English curriculum, the Modern Languages discussions were, conversely, tending to move in a somewhat different direction. Teachers of foreign languages, influenced by the concerns of the 'communicative language teaching' movement (e.g. Brumfit, 1984) with its central focus on promoting message over form in the second language classroom, as well as by the more accessible theories of second language acquisition (e.g. Krashen, 1981), had been gradually shifting towards the promotion within the classroom of more *meaning*-oriented language use (Mitchell, 1988); talk *about* language was coming to be seen as increasingly undesirable.

A closer look at the final recommendations regarding language awareness of the National Curriculum documents for both English and Modern Languages will illustrate the differing approaches. The English Report (DES/WO, 1989) devoted a whole chapter to the consideration of knowledge about language, and, in two further chapters, also separately discussed the linked issues of Standard English and of linguistic terminology; and the statements of attainment included explicit references to the KAL strand across all three profile components (speaking and listening, reading, writing), although only from Level 5 through to Level 10. The Modern Languages Report (DES/WO, 1991), on the other hand, accorded relatively scant attention to the language awareness dimension: the main references occur in a subsection (one of six) of the Programmes of Study entitled 'Developing language learning skills and awareness of language', which deals somewhat summarily with the topic (p. 25). Thus, the Report briefly asserts that pupils should have regular opportunities to learn phrases and short texts by heart; to develop and increase their awareness of differences along the written/spoken and formal/informal dimensions of language; and to use knowledge of linguistic patterns and forms to further the development of their receptive and productive skills in the foreign language. There was little in the way of elaboration. Indeed, in the follow-up 'Non-statutory guidance' (NCC, 1992a), it was overtly surmised that most beginners in the foreign language classroom would bring with them a knowledge about language acquired through their earlier work in English, and Modern Languages teachers were further directed to the final report of the *English* working party for clarification.

The *draft* Modern Languages proposals (DES/WO, 1990b) had contained rather more extensive discussion of the whole language awareness issue, particularly as it related to the understanding of grammar and the development of language learning skills. The question of how far teachers should aim to make learners aware of the structures of the language under study was to some extent addressed, with the report favouring an inductive rather than explicit approach, and with the emphasis firmly on learning the target language through *use*; it was acknowledged that modern languages teaching and learning had suffered in the past from 'extremes of practice' in the treatment of grammar, and it was asserted that:

> Nothing said here should prevent learners from spending as much time as possible on listening to, speaking, reading or writing the target language. (DES/WO, 1990b: 9.22)

In a sense, it might be claimed that the grammar issue was fudged somewhat: the Report made little reference to current theories of second language acquisition, other than a nod in the direction of the notion of 'communicative competence', with awareness of 'rules' deemed most likely to follow on from language in use, rather than to give rise to such use; in this respect, a more implicit and exploratory approach on the part of the learners themselves was posited, rather than the teacher guiding pupils to an explicit awareness of the underlying structures of the target language. Teachers were offered little concrete guidance on the whole issue, however, other than to assume that pupils' acquisition of the target language grammar would largely take care of itself. Elsewhere in the MLs draft report (DES/WO, 1990b: 8.14–8.19), some attention was devoted to the ways in which foreign language study might contribute, in a cross-curricular perspective, to learners' general awareness of language; here there was some evidence of the broader concerns that underlay much of the language awareness work of the seventies and eighties, which were now apparently largely subsumed into the remit of the teacher of English.

The English Working Party, by contrast then, laboured long over the issue: they reiterated the case for including explicit knowledge about language in the English curriculum (positing a link between heightened language awareness and aspects of pupil performance, as well as recognizing the contribution of KAL to learners' understanding of their wider socio-cultural environment); and they re-examined the possibility (rejected by the Kingman Committee) that it should become a separate profile component, concluding for the time being that it should remain integral to the curriculum, rather than be an element 'bolted-on'. (This was at least in part due to a recognition of the inadequacy of teacher training programmes in respect of language issues, although it was primarily justified in terms of KAL being firmly tied to language *in use,* in an attempt no doubt to allay teachers' fears of a return to decontextualised grammar study.)

In the elaboration of the proposals regarding KAL, then, it was suggested that a syllabus for knowledge about language should take account of three main areas: language variation in its broadest sense (how forms match to functions, how styles vary along social and regional dimensions, etc.), language in literature, and language change across time; and specific targets relating to KAL were included in the statements of attainment from Level 5 through to Level 10. Thus, for example, at Level 6 (which an 'average' child might be expected to have reached by around the age of 14), pupils were expected to be able to demonstrate an awareness of the following: in the Speaking and Listening profile component, 'grammatical differences between spoken Standard English and a non-standard variety', and, in the Reading component, 'that words can change in use and meaning over time'; and, at Level 7 in the Writing component, 'what is appropriate and inappropriate language use in written texts'.

In spite of the detailed consideration given to the place of knowledge about language in the English curriculum, it is arguable that the proposals lack overall coherence; it is certainly the case that the Working Party was constrained in its task by the requirement that language learning development, essentially a recursive and cyclical process, be mapped onto a set of ten levels implying a neat, linear progression. (Indeed, this was a specific criticism from the National Association for the Teaching of English (Bain et al., 1989), the professional body of the English teaching profession, in a text otherwise broadly welcoming, albeit cautiously, the overall thrust of the Report.) There is also evidence to suggest that the specific proposals in respect of KAL were difficult for teachers to access and make sense of as a coherent whole, even a member of the Working Party suggesting that the organisation of a possible syllabus for KAL was not made sufficiently explicit in its final Report (Stubbs, 1989). At a plenary address to the NATE annual conference too, a KAL agenda for classrooms was offered in a summary version which was considered 'fuller and more even . . . than the Cox Committee felt able to do', under the broad headings of language and variety, language and society, language acquisition and development, history of languages, and language as system (Richmond, 1991: 12). Elsewhere, in the course of an observational classroom study carried out in the school year 1991–2 (reported in Mitchell, Hooper and Brumfit, 1994), an established Head of English had this to say in interview:

> it is phenomenally difficult, it is actually difficult with many of [the Statements of Attainment] for the three of us Heads of Department [of English] to agree on what it actually means. Now I suspect that a lot of that is quite deliberate, I suspect that – I mean, Cox *did* know, because he said, or the group said, language is not linear, and that there must have been an awful lot of disagreement, and that the English language is actually a very flexible one, and you can leave a lot of wonderful ambiguities. (School 1, 1991)

It is nevertheless possible to seen in the 1989 proposals the potential at least for the development of a coherent teaching programme in respect of language awareness.

Language Awareness and Language Learning: the Contemporary Case

The National Curriculum programmes for language awareness in English and Modern Languages took little apparent account, in their recommendations and rationales for such work, of Vygotskyan perspectives on language development (as well as on development of a broader educational nature). This section will seek to incorporate such perspectives in an attempt briefly to set out a contemporary rationale for language awareness work throughout children's schooling. (Much of what follows draws on the ideas succinctly expressed in Edwards and Mercer, 1987; and Wertsch, 1985.)

Vygotsky (1896–1934) played a leading role in the development of Soviet psychology; it was many years, however, before his ideas became widely available in the west, with the publication of *Thought and Language* (1962) marking the beginnings of a profound and continuing influence on western psychology. Unlike Piaget, whose theories have been widely taken up by educationalists and have strongly influenced British classroom (particularly primary) practice in the past two decades, Vygotsky argued for a theory of intellectual development which acknowledged the central role of interactions in shaping children's understanding: children are inducted into a culture by their interactions with others, primarily through *language*. According to Piaget's view, by contrast, the role of *action* rather than language is of primary importance in the development of children's thinking; the adoption of his theories in an educational context is perhaps best exemplified in the Plowden report, *Children and their Primary Schools* (Plowden, 1967), where children are recognized as the agents of their own learning through discovery and first-hand experience:

The treatment of the subject matter may be summarized in the phrase 'learning by discovery' . . . This involves a great exercise of judgement on the part of the teacher. He will miss the whole point if he tells the children the answers or indicates too readily and completely how the answers may be found . . . Essential elements are enquiry, exploration, and first hand experience. (Plowden, 1967: para. 669)

In Piaget's view, then, the natural development of children's thinking is largely a consequence of their direct involvement with physical reality; language does not play a central role in this process, but is rather seen to follow on from the development of more general, underlying cognitive structures. Vygotsky, however, while acknowledging the importance of physical activity in learning, argues centrally also for the importance of *language* in cognitive development: children's understanding is primarily shaped by talk, and their induction into human culture achieved by the sharing of knowledge through language. Clearly, such a position has crucial implications for the classroom context, where the teacher is responsible for inducting the child into new understandings which cannot be realized through first-hand experience alone. These ideas have been taken up and elaborated by Bruner (e.g. 1985) in the context of formal education in the notions of 'scaffolding' and 'handover', by which learners gradually come to take control of the learning process: the child is enabled to advance by being under the tutelage of an adult or more competent peer, who 'scaffolds' the learning task, until the child achieves conscious control over the new concept (i.e. possesses the tutor's knowledge and/or competence), and 'handover' is successfully effected (Bruner, 1985: 24–5).

It is important to emphasize that the process does not imply a transmission mode of teaching, where bodies of knowledge are simply passed on to the learner who passively receives them; the metaphor of 'scaffolding' is central in stressing the interactive nature of the process, whereby the teacher leads children to new levels of conceptual understanding through a process of guided discovery, in which joint activity and shared conceptions carried by language are the main constituents (Edwards and Mercer, 1987: 86).

The implications of the Vygotskyan perspective for language awareness work are twofold: the suggestion is that learners will benefit from being initiated explicitly and systematically into the conceptual frameworks available to their teachers; and will benefit also, in terms of enhanced conceptual understanding, from opportunities to reflect on both their own, and others', language use. In both cases, the notion of reflectiveness is central. It is argued, then, that a purely experiential (i.e. activity-oriented) view of learning does not take sufficient account of the role that reflection can play in promoting the development of conceptual understanding. This point will be taken up again in the concluding section of this chapter.

Current and Potential Language Awareness Practices

The teacher or student wishing to examine empirical evidence of language awareness practices in languages classrooms would have difficulty in finding relevant research material. The large volume of classroom language research conducted in recent years has concerned itself with language as communication, as social interaction, and as means of cognitive and/or affective growth, as well as means of control; but the question of how language is actually talked *about* in language classrooms by ordinary teachers and pupils has received little attention. A two-year (1991–1993) research study at the University of Southampton (Mitchell, Hooper and Brumfit, 1994) set out to collect such evidence: funded by the Economic and Social Research Council, the 'KAL' project had as one of its aims to document the handling of explicit knowledge about language in classrooms. During the school year 1991/1992 then, a group of English and Modern Languages teachers in three Hampshire secondary schools were observed and audio-recorded over a period of two months during all their lessons with one Year 9 group each (i.e. pupils aged 13–14). In all, three English teachers and four foreign language teachers (of French, German and Spanish) were involved in the study.

The substantial body of data thus gathered (around a hundred hours of classroom activity) was coded according to the broad area of knowledge about language being addressed, under five headings very similar to those proposed by Richmond (1991: see above), as well as by the level of language (e.g. word, paragraph, whole text), the degree of planning (along a preplanned to responsive continuum), and the strategies employed by the teacher in dealing with such topics; and an individual 'KAL profile' was built up for each of the seven teachers. How were these teachers dealing with language awareness topics on a day-to-day basis in their classrooms in a period of intense debate concerning such practices?

In a sense, and unsurprisingly perhaps, the teachers' observed classroom practices in respect of knowledge about language seemed as yet largely unaffected by the very recent official pronouncements; it was clear, however, that English teachers, in particular, were engaged in some serious re-thinking of current KAL practices, and, indeed, broadly agreed in welcoming the requirement to clarify and systematise approaches to KAL within their Departments. One English Department, for example, was in the process of jointly constructing discrete KAL modules for years 7 to 9, in order to ensure coverage of topics previously not accorded a very high profile, such as child language acquisition, and accent and dialect. It was perhaps a typical feature of the English teachers' thinking, however, that such a separate focus would gradually diminish in favour of the re-absorption of such topics into the overall curriculum, so that they would eventually arise more naturally (and systematically) out of and alongside ongoing work.

The language awareness practices observed in the English classrooms tended to fall largely into the (perhaps somewhat traditional) areas of language variation and language development. Within the broad area of language genres, then, one teacher, for example, devoted some time to the explicit discussion with her pupils of stylistic devices in poetry as a prelude to small-group discussion and readings of a range of poems selected by the pupils from among a wide choice of texts brought in by both the teacher and themselves; the pupils were later asked to write their own poems. In another school, another teacher, in a series of lessons centred around a class novel, took the language of story-telling as an explicit and intermittent focus, and, in working towards the writing of a narrative piece by the pupils, spent one lesson focusing in on a brief extract from a Dickens novel chosen partly for its rich descriptive detail. Such practices (in respect of their language awareness dimensions, at least) seemed to reflect a dual rationale: the enhancement of pupils' encounters with, and response to, literature; and heightened sensitivity to the ways in which texts are put together, which would feed through into more effective language performance.

Within the area of language development too, an obvious rationale for explicit KAL work was its potential contribution to improved pupil performance. A third teacher, for example, spent several lessons on a project which (within the broader context of encouraging pupils' extensive reading) was aimed at developing pupils' oral skills: pairs of pupils were video-recorded while interviewing each other about a book each had recently read, and subsequent teacher-led discussion centred on the characteristics of such talk, and the development of criteria for making it more effective. Such KAL-related talk was not the exclusive preserve of the English-subject classrooms (where, indeed, it was seen less often than might have been expected); in the Modern Languages classrooms too, there was some evidence of language discussion with a developmental focus. Another teacher, for example, unusually among the foreign language teacher sample, regularly invited pupil reflection (in English) on language learning strategies; pupils were asked, at the end of (some) French lessons, what new vocabulary they thought they had learned and by what means they had learnt it, and were invited to reflect explicitly on the usefulness of a range of conscious learning strategies. One teacher's French lessons also evidenced an explicit focus on strategies for dealing with unfamiliar vocabulary, though this was of a less consciously systematic and more intermittent nature.

Classroom talk about language variation along the dialectal and multilingual dimensions was very largely absent from the lessons observed; it surfaced mainly in the English-subject classroom of a teacher who taught one substantial planned episode on contrasts between 'slang' and Standard English, and referred in passing elsewhere to accent/dialect variation, and associated language attitudes. She also referred intermittently to the bilingualism of a minority of pupils, with the apparent aim, confirmed in interview, of raising the profile and status of their mother tongue in the school. The over-arching rationale for such language awareness work might be perceived as the fostering of pluralist attitudes through explicit classroom discussion; that it only tended to occur in the more urban school with a substantial minority intake of bilingual pupils was perhaps unexceptional, though it might have been considered an advantage for it to be a regular part of classroom discourse in the more monolingual schools too.

Within the Modern Languages classrooms across all three schools, the language awareness work which featured most prominently – not unsurprisingly, perhaps – fell in the area of language as system. A majority of the teachers seemed to have made a strategic commitment to building up with their pupils, over time, an overt reference model of the target language system (or, rather, of selected aspects of the grammar). Thus, a teacher devoted regular lesson time to planned explicit discussion (in English) of particular features of the target grammar, such as the perfect tense or the formation of adverbs in French; teacher explanation and/or rule-giving (with a principled commitment to the use of appropriate linguistic terminology) would be followed by a practice phase, during which pupils would 'apply' the rules in the production of oral and written examples. This firmly deductive approach contrasts strongly with the inductive approach favoured in another's (Spanish beginners') classroom, where a structure would be seen in use before being 'signposted' by the teacher; thus, for example, the definite and indefinite article system ('el/la', 'the', and 'un/una', 'a, an') in use in an episode centering on the topic of asking the way would be drawn to the pupils' attention (in Spanish), 'There's an important difference – what is it, and why?', and this might lead to a brief oral or written practice phase contextualized within the overall topic. Nonetheless, the principle remained broadly the same: whether an inductive or deductive approach was preferred, the grammar was generally a guiding focus in the classroom teaching of the target language, although the degree to which this was shared with the *pupils* varied very widely along an explicit/implicit continuum.

One teacher was somewhat exceptional in dealing with sentence structure at a fairly abstract level, teaching explicitly the concepts of subject, verb and complement through a variety of action games, in which the pupils, allocated to groups representing the building-blocks of a sentence, were asked to make up a number of French examples of the particular feature (subject, verb, etc.) assigned them, before combining with members of other groups to form complete sentences. It was notable that the activity was recalled and commented on very favourably by some of the pupils several months after the observed lessons, in the course of discussion tasks run by the research team; for example:

> [Pupil 1] And it helps build your confidence where . . . before the teacher said to us, now try and write your sentence . . . /[P2] Couldn't/[P1] And we found that we could only write a couple of words in a sentence. Then she showed us how to use the sentence-building sort of thing and . . . we was writing really long sentences . . . about . . . we could make them up about twenty words long . . . in French. So that was pretty good.

What emerges clearly from this (albeit brief and limited) survey is that pupils in English and Modern Languages classrooms were receiving largely divergent messages in the KAL area. In the foreign language classrooms, attention was largely focused on language as system at the sentence level or below; while in the English classrooms, attention was focused at the level of whole texts, and on the distinctive characteristics of language genres, literary and non-literary.

This divergence was also reflected in materials published in response to National Curriculum requirements in the area of language awareness. On the Modern Languages side, writers' and publishers' energies were taken up with producing new course materials competing for the vast post-National Curriculum market; and, given the relative lack of emphasis accorded in the MLs documentation to the development of awareness of language, the new materials evidenced little in return. Indeed (and taking French as an example), the one major secondary coursebook which made a point of incorporating a variety of language awareness topics throughout, under the regular heading 'Point Langue', had been conceived well before the requirements of the National Curriculum were made public: by 1993, *Arc-en-ciel* stood apart from the other coursebooks mentioned in its systematic and relatively broad coverage of language awareness matters. Thus, in Stage 1 (Miller and Roselman, 1988), the regular 'Point Langue' feature appeared 29 times, demonstrating a preference for grammatical points, certainly, but going beyond this concern to touch on other areas such as questions of appropriacy and slang, bi- and multilingualism, and dictionary use. In Stage 3 (Miller et al., 1990), it ventured further afield, with language-learning strategies, variations in French around the world, word-borrowings and suchlike peppering the familiar grammatical territory of perfect and imperfect tenses.

By contrast, other major French courses, with one notable exception, chose not to make language awareness a noticeable feature, except (and even then, not very explicitly) in the traditional grammar area: here the coursebooks varied in their treatment between short summaries throughout dealing with particular points or a fuller summary at the back, and sometimes both (although language structure generally was accorded a rather low profile, at least as far as making it explicit to pupils was concerned). On the whole, though, the treatment of language awareness topics was very sparse, with only the occasional brief foray (in *Avantage* (McNab and Barrabe, 1992), for example) into non-grammatical areas. The exception was *Auto* (Buckby and Huntley, 1992), which deliberately implemented an attempt to raise awareness of language-learning strategies in a regular section headed 'Autonomie'; a further feature, under the title 'Du nouveau', dealt briefly with language awareness topics such as pronunciation rules, spelling patterns, and pictures and symbols used in other cultures.

Even where course materials *did* raise language awareness topics, however, the general tendency was to treat them in a fairly patchy and superficial fashion, offering snippets of information with occasional follow-up questions or activities. In this respect, the authors of *Auto* (Buckby and Huntley, 1992) were at an advantage in choosing to concentrate largely on one aspect of language awareness, reflection on the language-learning process, for they were thus able more easily to integrate and develop the selected aspect in a coherent fashion, offering suggestions throughout for pupils to reflect on (and share) their own strategies for learning.

The picture with regard to *English* was very different: the National Curriculum gave rise to an outpouring of print relating specifically to knowledge about language. The publications that appeared between 1990 and 1993 could broadly be classified under two types: those that sought to provide a coherent rationale for knowledge about language in the English curriculum as a backdrop to suggestions for, or exemplars of, the implementation of KAL in the classroom; and those which aimed to supply materials for actual classroom use. The former tended to be weightier and more thoughtful on the whole; though less immediately useful in the short term, they gave pause for thought, stated what was already being done, and done well, in English (and primary) classrooms, and looked to ways in which such practices might be systematized and extended in keeping with the demands of the National Curriculum. Haynes (1992) and Keen (1992), for example, provided useful explorations of what was primarily a text-based approach to language awareness and language study, the one at primary and the other at secondary level. The use of texts both spoken and written, literary and non-literary, was seen as pivotal in the development of pupils' language awareness, as too was the recognition (and incorporation) of children's own experience and (implicit) knowledge and understanding of language.

Of those publications which set out to provide ready-made classroom materials, Seely's *Language Live!* (1991), for pupils at Key Stages 3 and 4, might be seen as representative of the best in this field: the lively and colourful format utilized a wide variety of accessible texts and text extracts to explore a whole range of language knowledge, from dialect and Standard English through grammar, appropriacy, language change and so on. The incorporation of transcribed interview extracts (available on accompanying audio-cassettes) from real 'ordinary people' (p. 5) provided a welcome and useful stimulus too to the discussion of language attitudes. However, the materials thus devised might still be seen as crystallizing teachers' fears in an approach which tended to remain, despite its best intentions, somewhat de-contextualised; perhaps inevitably, teachers might reject the wholesale use of such materials, preferring to dip in occasionally for useful bits and pieces, but generally working within the more coherent framework suggested by Keen (1992), and drawing, for their language reflections and explorations, on the evidence to hand, in the texts their pupils were studying and drafting, and in the children's own experiences and ideas. Nonetheless, such materials tended to provide a broader coverage of language awareness topics, in systematic fashion, than had perhaps traditionally been espoused in pre-National Curriculum English-subject classrooms.

Valiant attempts were even made to resurrect the spectre of 'grammar' in versions which acknowledged the advances made in linguistic theory since the days of parsing and clause analysis; a notable (if somewhat singular) example was a book aimed at English (and primary) teachers entitled *Teaching Grammar* (Hudson, 1992). After a discussion of grammatical ideas, its author, an academic linguist, set out suggestions for ten 'grammar lessons' which ran through all the National Curriculum levels, covering such topics as ambiguity, tense, and subjects, verbs and dialects. Set somewhat apart from other KAL publications in both tone and purpose, it seemed more likely to be a book for inducting teachers into current ideas on grammar rather than providing any readily usable ideas for classroom practice (but perhaps nonetheless useful for that).

Finally, it should be noted that publications arising from the Language in the National Curriculum (LINC) Project formed a significant proportion of the language awareness materials aimed at the English-teaching profession. This was a government-funded in-service teacher training project intended to address the language issues raised in the Kingman and Cox Reports: the project would produce materials and run training activities over its three-year lifespan (1989–92). Two key publications which emerged from the project were the LINC Reader *Knowledge about Language and the Curriculum* (Carter, 1990) and

Looking into Language: Classroom Approaches to Knowledge about Language (Bain et al., 1992). These two accessible volumes neatly complemented one another, the one comprising a collection of articles discussing key issues in the teaching of language, the other a varied selection of classroom evidence illustrating approaches to the development of children's KAL across the age range 5–16. However, it was a mark of the political sensitivity of the whole language awareness issue during this period that the bulk of the materials produced, which were meant to provide a detailed and comprehensive overview of approaches to KAL and to go some way to addressing the lack of teachers' expertise and confidence in the language field, were not allowed to be published: the government withheld permission. Ministerial hostility to the materials reflected the continuing disagreements over rival definitions of 'knowledge about language', and, more fundamentally, over alternative rationales for its inclusion in the curriculum. Press commentaries around the LINC controversy reflected the continuing popular belief that explicit grammar instruction is essential to ensure accurate mastery of (especially written) Standard English, a view which was essentially that evidenced in the government's refusal to permit publication of the materials produced.

Conclusion

It will be clear that the question of the place of language awareness work in schools continues to be fraught with controversy, of which the story of the LINC project is but a recent reminder. The continuing tensions between professional and lay opinion are reflected in the 1993–4 debate over the National Curriculum for English, which was subjected to further proposals for revision (NCC, 1992b) when still barely in place, in part at least because its specifications on language work did not conform to the government's view of the importance of explicit grammar instruction and of conformity to Standard English usage. Languages teachers (and those in initial training) are meanwhile faced with the need to develop a coherent professional position on the language awareness debate, a position which will allow them to remain in sympathetic and constructive dialogue with a public concerned about such issues as literacy standards and access to Standard English. These are, indeed, very natural concerns for parents who commit their children to teachers' charge.

It is part of the argument advanced in this chapter that teachers, in working out their position on the language awareness question, should give due thought to the Vygotskyan perspective outlined above, which suggests the importance of reflective practice in promoting the development of learners' conceptual understandings. Perhaps the most surprising feature of the classrooms observed in the course of the research study described above was the relative infrequency of episodes aimed at sharing teachers' conceptual frameworks and learning theories with their pupils; yet this may well be an aspect of central importance in a language awareness programme, providing an over-arching justification for such work. It will not be easy for language teachers to develop a coherent position on this issue in the prevailing climate of controversy and disagreement, yet it is vital that they do so.

Part III

Language after Sixteen

12

Language after Sixteen

Although the Language Charter outlined in chapter 1 is aimed at school education, it has implications beyond school. Aspects of the curriculum that have been described in the previous chapters are clearly intended as a preparation for life after compulsory education. In the case of mother tongue teaching an important aim will be to develop the complex language skills that are necessary to live, to study and to work in late twentieth century society, and indeed well into the twenty-first century. Another aim will be to develop the critical skills inherent in the study of the media and of literature. Because there will be continued exposure to language in all its forms beyond compulsory education it is likely that these skills will continue to develop, whether in further or higher education, in the workplace, or simply through leisure activities, some of which of course involve far more sophisticated use of language than others.

In the case of the foreign language curriculum it can certainly not be assumed that an adequate level of proficiency in the various language skills will have been attained by the end of compulsory education. However, there should be a firm basis for further work in higher education or possibly for developing more specific work-related language and language skills. Again, it may be that through the increased opportunities that exist for continued exposure to the foreign language there could be further development of foreign language skills, either by natural second language acquisition processes or by conscious independent language learning outside of any formal educational or training context. There is little evidence that this happens in more than a small minority of cases, but these cases are certainly significant and could repay further study.

English Mother Tongue after Sixteen

English in education

Traditionally, the teaching of English after age 16 focused almost exclusively upon English literature, and the aim of English teachers at A-level and beyond was to foster an appreciation of English literature based on an understanding of the context in which it was written and increasingly also on the reader's personal response. This is certainly a worthwhile aim, and the study of English literature has been seen as a way into the study of culture in the English speaking world. It was assumed that language skills were adequately mastered by age 16 and that the continued study of language beyond this stage was either unnecessary or uninteresting. In recent years, though, there has been a growing realisation that language skills are in many cases not fully mastered by the end of compulsory education, and that language is an interesting object of study in its own right. There has therefore been a certain shift towards theoretical language study and the development of advanced practical language or communication skills. Our emphasis in this chapter will be on the study of language, which is probably not so well known or documented as the more established study of literature post-16. We shall consider some of the developments that have taken place in vocational courses such as the new GNVQs, A-level syllabuses in English Language and Communication Studies, and degree level work in Linguistics and, particularly in the newer universities, Communication Skills. These latter courses, normally run alongside specialist courses in other subject areas, are reminiscent of the long-standing Freshman Composition tradition in the USA.

A-level syllabuses

There are two examining boards which currently have Advanced Level English Language syllabuses, and both of these were set up in the early 1980s. The London Board actually started with a single paper, *Varieties of English*, offered as a paper within the English Literature A-Level course (Freeborn, 1992). By the mid

1980s, though, this had grown into a full A-level syllabus in English Language, with aims more advanced but not at all dissimilar from those of the Kingman Inquiry Report (DES, 1988b), now substantially incorporated into National Curriculum discussion, though diminishing in the content of the Curriculum with each revision. The Northern Examinations and Assessment Board (formerly Joint Matriculation Board) syllabus is perhaps a little closer to the better established English literature syllabus, with some critical response to literary material being required and with an assessed coursework portfolio including some original writing.

Both of the syllabuses require students to develop their knowledge about language in a systematic way, thus building on the National Curriculum: 'Knowledge about language should be an integral part of work in English, not a separate body of language to be added on to the traditional English curriculum' (DES/WO, 1989). Both syllabuses require students to learn about the forms of the English language, the processes of communication and comprehension, and to have some understanding of historical and geographical variation within English. At this level it is unlikely that such study contributes significantly to the development of students' language competence, but language is viewed as a worthy object of human study in its own right: 'It is just as important to teach about our language environment as about our physical environment, or about the structure of English as about the structure of the atom' (DES, 1988b). Although more practical and essentially eclectic in approach, the study of English language at A-level clearly bears a strong resemblance to, and is at least in part derived from, the academic study of Linguistics, which of course cannot be undertaken until the student enters higher education. This is perhaps one reason why A-level English Language is only offered in a minority of schools and colleges, as Linguistics is not a subject with which many English teachers feel particularly at ease.

A-level Communication Studies has a slightly longer history than A-level English Language, dating back to 1976 in the case of the Associated Examining Board syllabus. This syllabus, as described by Neill (1984), has involved an investigation of the development of communications, theory of communication, means of communication and mass communications, and there was also a Use of English paper, presented in the form of a case study. Students were required to develop their writing, particularly their argumentative writing skills, and the ability to write in a number of different registers for a number of different audiences. This course also involved an individual project, with an oral examination based on the project. Thus, although language is not the focus of study, developing language skills is a very important part of the course, perhaps to a greater extent, at least overtly, than in the English Language A-level courses we have just been discussing.

Although courses like the AEB Communication Studies described above may have a vocational thread running through them (Limb, 1986: 16), A-level syllabuses are still generally directed at the more 'academic' students, and whilst the Government, against all the best advice (e.g. Department of Education and Science, 1988a), insists on maintaining the narrow focus that A-levels represent, it is likely that the courses we have been describing will be taken almost exclusively by students whose interests are in the humanities, including the social sciences. In a broader sixth-form curriculum English Language or Communication Studies, or perhaps a resuscitated Use of English paper, could have a considerable appeal for students whose major interest is in the sciences but who wish to maintain a spread of interests or to develop further their knowledge about and use of English.

Vocational further education courses

This is already happening with the more 'vocational' post-16 courses. The City and Guilds and BTEC examination courses are mostly being subsumed within the NVQ and GNVQ framework, but the integrated approach and the focus on the transactional that have characterized them in the past seem to be remaining much the same. Typical performance criteria for writing might be (for Communication Level 3):

1. the fullness and accuracy of information included is appropriate to the purpose and needs of the audience;

2. documents are legible;

3. grammar, punctuation and spelling follow standard conventions; and

4. the format used is appropriate to the purpose of the material and information is ordered appropriately to maximize audience understanding. (*BTEC GNVQ Core Skills Levels* 1–5, Issue 1, July 1993)

The focus is very much on the use of language and the conventions of written English rather than on the study of language as such, and there is little in the way of critical response or evaluation. The emphasis is on practical concrete situations and there is not very much to stimulate the imagination, though at this level the subject matter might include 'a letter on a sensitive issue' or 'summarizing a complex document'.

Lecturers in Communication in Further Education colleges tend to work very closely with the main subject tutors, and the teaching of communication, along with 'application of number' and 'information technology' is integrated within the main subject of study. The planning that goes on must be similar in many ways to what takes place in primary education, where integration of the various skill areas has been established as the norm for a number of years. The expert in communication has an important role at the planning stage, to ensure that the various language and communication skills are included in the syllabus design. Thereafter, it is arguable that much of the work can be done by the subject specialists themselves, though there can be little doubt that the best results are achieved when the subject specialist and the communication expert work closely together and where the teaching of communication is skilfully integrated, so that the Lecturer in Communication has a regular teaching role which is perceived to be relevant by the students.

Higher education

As far as higher education is concerned, the older universities tend to divide English language between the study of English, which is primarily concerned with English literature and cultural studies, and the more recent but now reasonably well established study of Linguistics, looking at language from a more 'scientific' point of view, but with the emphasis very often on theoretical models rather than on practical linguistic description. Linguistics is of course a subject with a number of different branches, and most Linguistics courses would include some study of phonetics and phonology; morphology and syntax; discourse analysis, pragmatics and semantics; sociolinguistics; psycholinguistics, including language acquisition; historical linguistics; applied linguistics; and so on. Linguistics is a popular subject in combined honours degrees, and is often taken alongside a modern language, English, philosophy or psychology. However, it is still perfectly possible to take a degree in English without studying any of these branches of Linguistics. Thus, English graduates, who in many cases become teachers of English, may end up teaching 'language' in our schools on the basis of three years of full-time literary study and with very little expertise in the area which they are required to teach (Brumfit, 1990; 1993). This situation is likely to deteriorate if PGCE subject teaching is replaced more and more by practical experience in schools.

Alongside courses in English and Linguistics, a number of courses in Communication Studies have been developed, mostly in the newer universities. These sometimes include practical courses in linguistic description, but the emphasis is usually on the media and other forms of mass communication. Although they are often quite separate from courses in English, they do in fact have a certain amount in common with many English courses, in that both are a form of cultural studies, and many English courses now contain elements of media or film studies alongside the more traditional literary studies.

The North American tradition of 'Freshman Composition' has not generally found much support in the older universities in the UK, although a number of newer universities and a few of the older ones do run courses in communication skills. There is certainly a need for such courses, and many colleagues, particularly but by no means exclusively in science and engineering departments, complain that their students lack the linguistic and organizational skills necessary to write adequate reports and the presentation skills to give an adequate oral presentation. Traditionally, these were skills that it was assumed would be 'picked up' during the first year at university, if they had not already been mastered at school. However, lecturers in science and engineering departments now seem to have a less sanguine attitude, and there is a recognised need for some sort of teaching of communication skills. The sort of provision which many universities make for overseas students (Dudley-Evans, 1984; Blue, 1993) could be of great value to home students too. On the other hand, the current debate in the USA about freshman composition, where there is a perceived need for lecturers in the relevant departments (rather than in the English department) to induct students into the disciplinary culture, including giving some instruction in how to write within that disciplinary culture, is also relevant to British higher education (see Bazerman, 1988; Lindemann, 1993; Swales, 1990). The humanistic 'liberal studies' approach which used to be typical of communication skills courses is no longer seen to be appropriate, and if such courses are taught by a 'language' or 'communications' expert, that person must also be able to show familiarity with the topics and the concepts which the students are dealing with and which they are having to talk and write about.

Overall, it is perhaps disappointing that there is so little linking between the language and literature strands in post-16 education in English. Indeed, it could be claimed that there is a definite polarisation into two camps. On the one hand, there is the English Literature A-level, leading in many cases to university studies in English literature or cultural studies. On the other hand, there are A-levels in English Language and in Communication Studies, leading in many cases to opportunities to study Communication Studies or Linguistics in higher education. Drawing on the 'language' side, and at the more 'vocational' end of the spectrum, courses in communication in both further and higher education aim to help students develop their language skills without studying either language or literature as such. The approach is a very instrumental one, similar to that which has been developing in much modern foreign language teaching.

English at work

It is perhaps the recognition that many 16-year olds do not have a very sophisticated command of language that has led to the development of Communication units, along with other Core Skills, in GNVQ qualifications. These are also being made available as free-standing awards, independent of the GNVQ. They are clearly work-related, and it is claimed that they 'recognise skills which are essential to a person's achievement in many areas of work . . .' (City and Guilds, 1993: 4). Of course, a very wide variety of linguistic demands is made on people in the workplace, but it is probably the case that the majority of jobs now involve higher levels of literacy and oracy than ever before. Understanding detailed, often complex instructions, both oral and written, is an important aspect of many jobs, and the ability to communicate is also highly valued. The late twentieth-century revolution in the field of information technology has undoubtedly added to the communicative demands of working life, and for many people this is also spilling over into leisure or 'non-work' activities.

Coleman (1989) has usefully distinguished three kinds of work. The first type, *work which is defined by language*, is becoming increasingly important in our post-industrial society. It includes all those work activities which would not exist without language, either because they would be unnecessary and perhaps even unimaginable (e.g. language teaching, translation) or, and this probably accounts for much paid employment today, because they simply could not take place without the medium of language (e.g. journalism, the work of a solicitor or barrister, telephone marketing). In Coleman's second type of work, language is seen as *important but not defining*. A florist, for example, could probably perform many functions of the job without using language, but placing and receiving orders, discussing different kinds of flower arrangements, giving instructions on how to water, where to put flowers or plants, etc. are greatly facilitated by the use of language, and florists are of course expected to be competent language users. Coleman's final category is *work in which language is incidental*, and two of his examples are boxing and burglary. The number of legal openings in work of this kind are likely to be fairly limited, although certain types of factory work or agricultural work could possibly fit into this category rather than the second. Although it may be possible to perform some work tasks without using language, 'it is difficult to think of any work activity in which language might not have an incidental role, as a way of lightening the burden of that work, as a means of expediting the work, or as a motivation for performing the work in the first place' (Coleman, 1989: 125–6). Indeed, no sophisticated division of labour could operate in society without language (Bloomfield, 1933: 24).

The boundaries between Coleman's categories are not clear-cut, and the linguistic demands of a job can change, often quite radically, over a period of time. There are some cases where these demands have been reduced, particularly in some branches of retailing, where the drive towards self-service outlets has made it possible to shop and to work in a shop without really communicating at all. On the whole, though, the tendency seems to be for the communicative demands of most types of job to increase with time, so that the young people of today generally need greater communication skills than their parents did.

Another factor that needs to be considered is that there are probably more non-native speakers using English at work now than ever before. The work of Jupp and Hodlin (1975) and others in helping immigrant workers with some of the basic transactional language skills still goes on, but the emphasis now tends to be on a rather more general approach to 'empowerment' in the workplace, where language no longer necessarily assumes pride of place. At the same time, English has firmly established its place as the international language of business, information technology and much of science and engineering, so that English is often used as the *lingua franca* even in situations where none of the participants has English as their mother tongue. This gives native speakers a certain advantage, but as we shall see later there are no grounds for complacency as regards our knowledge of foreign languages. Nor should the importance of English as an international language lead us to assume that native speakers have an adequate mastery even of English to operate effectively in an international context. The communicative demands and skills of interpretation that are involved in interacting with non-native speakers from a variety of language backgrounds can be far greater than what many people are used to, and this is something which formal education rarely prepares us for.

English and leisure

Just as English has become the language of international business, so it is the *lingua franca* of tourism, and it is often difficult for the British tourist to find opportunities to practise speaking languages other than English. This certainly has its benefits, but it means that English speakers have to be fairly skilled at understanding imperfect pronunciation, unusual collocation, incorrect grammar and non-native discourse structure. It also means that English-speaking tourists may fail to enter fully into or to gain a full appreciation of other cultures. What is true of tourism may be true of a number of other leisure activities too. Certainly in the field of international sport English seems to dominate, and it is possible to go to the cinema almost anywhere in the world and see films in their English versions.

The distinction between work and leisure is often blurred nowadays, particularly as unemployment has become so widespread in the western world. If one takes activities like gardening or decorating, for example, it is clear that one person's paid work is another person's leisure, and with the changes that are taking place in the nature of work people are increasingly looking for opportunities for creativity or productivity in their leisure activities.

In the same way as Coleman distinguishes three types of work, so we can distinguish three types of leisure activity (or unpaid activity). We think firstly of *leisure activity which is defined by language*. This includes all those activities which could not take place without language (e.g. reading, the cinema, the theatre, listening to the radio, crosswords, foreign language learning). In our second type of leisure activity language is seen as *important but not defining*. In many cases an important part of the activity is socializing, and although it is possible to imagine the activity taking place without the use of language, this might almost defeat the object of the activity. Examples of this kind of activity might include eating out, drinking in the pub, computer games, spectator sports (with subsequent discussion of the match), watching television, some participative sports, e.g. squash. In the third category, *leisure activities in which language is incidental*, we might place, for example, listening to classical music, disco dancing, and some participative sports, e.g. swimming. Whilst most of these activities involve both speaking and understanding the spoken language, only a few involve reading and even fewer necessitate writing. Reading is undoubtedly an important leisure activity for very many people, as is revealed, for example, by sales of newspapers, but writing, although a necessary part of living in the late 20th century, with all the forms that need to be filled in, letters to be written, etc., is a skill that is perhaps more commonly associated with school and with work than with leisure.

Foreign Languages after Sixteen

Foreign languages in education

In the same way as the teaching of English after age 16 traditionally focused on literature, so the traditional emphasis in post-16 foreign language teaching was also on literature, with some concession to the fact that high level language skills had still to be mastered, particularly in the sixth form but also to some extent in higher education. As with English, there has been a move away from this traditional emphasis, and there is now very much more interest in developing language skills at the more advanced levels, both for instrumental and for educational reasons, as well as in studying the foreign culture through non-literary sources such as film, newspapers, politics, history, and so on. We shall consider some of the developments that have taken place in A-level syllabuses, in vocational courses such as GNVQs and FLAW, and in degree level work.

A-level syllabuses

The move away from literature in A-level foreign language syllabuses has been in evidence for some years, but the trend is
probably accelerating in the light of changes in pre-16 language
teaching. Many sixth-form teachers would agree with Rees
(1992) that students who have obtained good grades in their
GCSE courses are 'able to cope well with gist comprehension,
usually impressively fluent orally in relation to the old O-level
norm, and bubbling with enthusiasm and confidence'. But many
would also endorse her view that students have 'a more limited
command of *structure*'. Rees reports how the future, conditional
and pluperfect forms in French now have to be taught from
scratch. She also reports her finding that a clear majority of her
post-GCSE students 'had read nothing longer than, at best, four
or five paragraphs of continuous text in French'. Given this background, it is not surprising that the transition to an A-level with
literature would appear particularly daunting for many students. Even the non-literary A-level syllabus entails reading
fairly long contemporary texts with quite a wide range of often
unfamiliar vocabulary. The National Curriculum does attempt to
give weight to the written language, and two of the four profile
components relate to using and responding to written language
(DES/WO, 1990c). However, the current emphases in many
GCSE classrooms on spoken rather than written language and
on fluency rather than accuracy have brought a number of real
benefits, especially for less able linguists, which many teachers
will not wish to lose. The GCSE course has much to commend it
for many of the pupils for whom it is designed. It simply leaves
a certain amount to be desired as a preparation for A-level, and
A-level syllabuses will probably need to be modified still further
in future.

Many A-level courses already involve a mixed-skill methodology, organized on a topic-by-topic basis, where the 'cultural
dimension is further enhanced by the use of authentic materials
in reading and listening exercises, ensuring that students have a
broad exposure to the contemporary society' (Pickering, 1992: 2).
There is a new emphasis on communicative skills and on the use

of the target language in the classroom, and grammar, although still considered important by many teachers at this level, tends to be emphasized less than used to be the case. Where it is taught, it is often taught in context, arising out of the topic work, rather than in isolation as something to be learned. The same is, of course, true of vocabulary learning. And while this approach probably results in fairly motivated students, who are relatively at ease orally in the foreign language, they may have problems with their reading and writing skills and also with their study skills if they go on to study languages in higher education.

Vocational further education courses

Since the 1970s, if not earlier, there has been a concern to make language teaching relevant to the needs of adult learners. This is seen most clearly in the work of the Council of Europe (e.g. Richterich and Chancerel, 1977; van Ek and Alexander, 1975). The concern is exemplified in a number of practically oriented 'vocational' language courses, such as those offered under the auspices of BTEC, FLAW and the more recent NVQs and GNVQs, which draw upon the National Language Standards of the Languages Lead Body. The aim in all of these courses is to teach language skills which are relevant to the world of work, and the emphasis is often on developing fairly basic transactional skills, although provision is also made for higher level language skills.

The Business and Technician Education Council (BTEC) was established in 1983 and immediately recognized the importance of languages for the future economic performance of the country. BTEC approves centres to offer vocationally relevant language courses alongside other vocational studies or, for part-time students, alongside work. The aims of BTEC-devised units are:

* to develop the ability and confidence to use the language in vocational situations;
* to enable students to assess their levels of competence, so they can judge if assistance is required for a task involving language skills;

- to develop common skills and vocational competence through language assignments closely related to students' other studies or work; and
- to foster the ability and confidence to engage in further language learning at work or elsewhere. (BTEC, 1987: 6–7)

The emphasis in BTEC foreign language courses is on effective performance of practical, realistic tasks such as leaving messages in the foreign language on telephone answering machines or responding orally in English to a request for clarification of material written in the foreign language. 'Effective communication is more important than linguistic accuracy or grammatical correctness, and this should be emphasized to encourage confidence in using the language' (BTEC, 1987: 11). This is, of course, sound advice, but from talking informally to teachers who are involved in teaching BTEC language programmes one gains the impression that students at this level are not always being sufficiently challenged by the demands of the course, and that the levels of achievement would only be comparable in many cases to the lower to middle range attainment levels of the National Curriculum.

The Foreign Languages at Work (FLAW) scheme was also established in 1983, by the London Chamber of Commerce and Industry Examinations Board. This scheme developed out of the LCCI's own research into the language use of non-linguists in commercial and industrial firms (LCCI, 1972, cited by Austin, 1991) and also out of a report prepared by a British Overseas Trade Board Study Group working under the chairmanship of HRH the Duke of Kent (BOTB, 1979). Concern was expressed in the BOTB report about the small proportion of students, many of whom perform well in their foreign language courses at school, who continue their language studies after the age of 16. The FLAW scheme was designed to encourage students to continue their language study alongside other subjects, and FLAW courses are intended to cater for the needs of these 'non-specialist' students. The title of the scheme indicates on the one hand that students are expected to put their linguistic knowledge 'to work' and on the other hand that courses should 'reflect the actual uses made of foreign languages *in the world of work*' (LCCI, 1992: 5).

Foreign Languages at Work is an imaginative scheme which enables different centres to tailor their courses to the needs of their students, or of local companies, subject to the agreement of the course consultant. Courses can therefore take place at a variety of levels, and course proposals can be submitted for any language, including English as a foreign language. The minimum period of tuition is 50 hours, but courses can last for as long as desired beyond this minimum. The emphasis in all FLAW courses is on listening and speaking. Whilst reading is considered 'indispensable for reinforcing these skills and for expanding registers' (LCCI, 1992: 7), writing is an optional element. Students are internally assessed on a minimum of 10 skill areas chosen from a list of 17. These include giving instructions, obtaining and giving information, using the telephone, informal conversation, reading correspondence, etc. Students are graded at performance levels 1 to 5, with the main criterion being the *'usability* of the end-product' (LCCI, 1992: 10). In other words, how well can the student understand and convey meaning? In addition to the grades given for each skill area, the course report form which students receive at the end of the course includes a detailed teacher's statement. This contains a description of the course followed and an appraisal of the student, drawing attention to particular strengths and describing the uses the student could be expected to make of the language.

Finally, no discussion of vocational language courses could be complete without a mention of the work of the Languages Lead Body. Four claims are made for the system which they have devised:

- New National Language Standards and a framework for vocational qualifications have been established which reflect the needs of business and commerce.
- The new system is based on what people can do rather than on what they know.
- For providers of language training the standards will become the backbone for new vocational courses and qualifications which have national recognition and meet employers' needs.
- Employers will be able to evaluate the skills of their staff more accurately, and will find the standards an aid to recruit-

ment, appraisals and job descriptions. Individuals will be able to use the standards to provide proof of their competence in a real work environment. (Languages Lead Body, 1993a: 1)

There are five levels of achievement, and at each level there are a number of statements of what students should be able to do using each of the four language skills. For example, for Level 3 Speaking students should be able to:

- give and seek instructions and guidance to fulfil key work tasks; and
- contribute to routine business discussions; seek and respond to opinion on a variety of matters; deliver prepared presentations.

For each of these four elements there are a number of performance criteria. For example, for 'contribute to routine business discussions' the following performance criteria are listed:

- language is selected to communicate clearly in predictable contexts;
- language used is sufficiently clear and precise to be understood by others;
- language used is appropriate to one's role and relationship to others; language used is appropriate to the context of the discussion and level of formality required;
- where necessary, appropriate action is taken to clarify meaning; and
- conversations are conducted in a manner that respects the social and cultural norms of the context. (Languages Lead Body, 1993b: 3, 29, 31)

The Standards Framework is primarily an aid to assessment of language competence. If one considers the descriptors above, it would seem that different assessors could apply them to students at quite different levels, and it may be that a great deal of assessor training will be needed to achieve a measure of standardisation. As well as facilitating the assessment of language competence, it is also claimed that the framework can be used to 'act as an operational guide to the design, development and delivery of training programmes and materials' (Languages Lead Body, 1993a: 3). It can also be used for needs analysis and for setting targets. The standards grew out of 'an intense 18-month period of fieldwork, research and consultation with employers and experts in the language field' (Languages Lead Body, 1993a: 11). No details of this fieldwork, research and consultation are given in the publications that we have been able to obtain. It is astonishing, though, that despite the eminence of many members of the Languages Lead Body, there seems to be either an ignorance or a dismissal of existing qualifications and theoretical work on needs analysis, syllabus design and the assessment of language proficiency. No mention is made, for example, of the pioneering work of the Council of Europe (e.g. Richterich and Chancerel, 1977; van Ek and Alexander, 1975), of Wilkins (1976) or of Munby (1978), or of the important developments that have taken place since these works were published. One could have expected some reference, for example, to the National Curriculum document *Modern Foreign Languages for Ages 11 to 16* (DES/WO, 1990c).

Although they are for the moment relatively untried, the National Language Standards are likely to be widely used in the future. They have been approved by the NCVQ as providing units which can be used in conjunction with occupational and sectoral NVQs, and are being used to develop the optional language units for GNVQs. They have also been adopted for a number of company language training schemes and are being considered by a number of awarding bodies. It will be very interesting to see how effective they are when there is the opportunity to carry out a proper evaluation in the future.

Higher education

As with many disciplines, a modern language can be studied either for a single honours or a combined honours degree. Grauberg (1990: 15) comments on the striking increase in the number of students taking combined degrees, and although the numbers taking single honours degrees have remained relatively stable over the last 25 years or so, there has been an enormous growth in the numbers taking a foreign language as part of a degree, either as a combined honours degree or as a minor component of a degree in another subject. Combinations of two languages have remained very popular, as have the traditional Arts combinations of a language with English, music, philosophy, and so on. But more and more students are keen to study a language in combination with non-Arts subjects such as economics, politics, accounting, business studies, and even mathematics, engineering and oceanography, to name but a few.

The traditional focus on the literature of the target countries still exists in some university courses, but it is now the exception rather than the norm. Alongside the literary tradition, courses have developed with a major emphasis on cultural studies, area studies, and applied language studies. In nearly all of these courses language now plays an important role. Indeed, it has been described as 'the only principle of coherence' within modern language courses (Evans, 1988: 173). Language may be the only element which is common to all modern language degree courses, but many modern linguists would argue for the centrality of other areas such as the history, politics, economics and culture (including philosophy, artistic and literary traditions) of the countries concerned. Evans goes on to claim that 'the language, which is the principle of coherence of the discipline, is something which is best learned outside the frame of the discipline' (Evans, 1988: 173). It is true that time spent in the relevant countries is of great importance to language learning, and most courses insist on students spending a substantial period of time abroad, either in a university, as a language assistant in a school, or on some kind of work placement. However, language teaching in many British universities, not least the newer universities, is now treated extremely seriously. Whilst most university departments would not wish to discard the traditional emphasis on linguistic accuracy, there is a new emphasis on fluency and on helping students to achieve communicative competence (Rigby and Burgess, 1991: 15). Rigby and Burgess quote Robert Jackson, former parliamentary Under Secretary of State for Education, speaking in March 1990:

... we shall need not necessarily more specialised modern linguists, but many, many more people in a wide range of jobs and professions ... To bring this about more and more courses that are taken at all levels in further and higher education should include a modern foreign language element ... What is clear, however, is that the emphasis is going to have to move even further away from the traditional single honours language and literature degree to degrees covering more than one language, and with greater emphasis on the history, culture and society of those who speak them.

In many ways this is just what has been happening in the last few years. Certainly, more and more courses in higher education include a foreign language element. This element is often provided by a language centre, which may be separate from the modern language departments, although the best practice is generally to be found in the institutions where there is close collaboration. In some cases this collaboration also extends to EFL units, and there is a great deal to be learnt from the way in which these units, now quite widespread in universities, have developed courses for overseas students, who are also generally non-specialist linguists. Rigby and Burgess (1991: 19) suggest that there are four main ways in which non-specialist linguists can pursue their language studies in higher education:

formal voluntary 'language for all' schemes where language tuition is available as of right for any student, or member of staff, who wants it;

self study schemes;

optional or elective courses available within the structure of a degree course in another discipline (e.g. chemistry, economics, engineering, law, mathematics);

prescribed courses forming a compulsory part of a degree course in another discipline (e.g. history of art, Caribbean studies, European history, chemistry).

The state of flux that exists in modern languages teaching in higher education inevitably gives rise to a certain amount of tension, and some university departments and individual members of departments have been more willing to adapt than others. Generally speaking, though, one gains the impression that modern linguists in universities are responding positively to the challenges that are presenting themselves and that they are rather enjoying the new prestige that languages have been given by the integrated European Union, even if this does mean in some cases that they are now responsible for a considerable amount of 'service' language teaching.

Foreign languages in the world of work

Much of what we said earlier about English at work applies also to foreign languages. Of course, the hegemony of English in the workplace may mean a reduced role for modern languages. There are conflicting views about this. We reproduce below two of the statements reported by Rigby and Burgess (1991: 8):

> It is possible to be a civilised and educated person while speaking and understanding only English . . . Only a few of us need to be competent in foreign languages – for diplomacy, marketing, teaching and other specialised purposes. (Chairman of the National Advisory Body for Public Sector Higher Education (NAB), October 1988)

This is a view which is not atypical of the stereotyped insular British attitude towards foreign language learning, which is still remarkably widespread, although fewer people are prepared to articulate it than used to be the case. Even the Chairman of NAB recognized the importance of foreign languages for specialised activities such as marketing though, and it is perhaps worth remembering that marketing can directly or indirectly involve a very large number of people in an organization. The other quotation represents what many would feel to be a more enlightened view, more in touch with the reality of our position in the European Union at the end of the twentieth century:

Competence in modern foreign languages is an imperative. It is critical to our ability to establish and maintain effective trading and cultural links with other countries. We simply must extend the ability of our young people to speak foreign languages. (John MacGregor, former Secretary of State for Education, October 1990)

If companies can employ staff who are already competent in the languages they are required to operate in, this obviously reduces their training budgets. However, many companies have come to accept that staff have to be given time and resources either to learn a language from scratch or to improve a language of which they already have some knowledge. This may be particularly important where a company is developing contacts with new markets, for example, where a greater diversity of languages may be required than is usually provided in school or even in higher education. Because time is at a premium companies are often not interested in general language courses but wish their staff to follow courses in language for specific purposes (LSP). This often involves language course providers in undertaking a fairly extensive needs analysis to ascertain the circumstances in which the foreign language will be required by a particular member of staff and to try to predict as far as possible the forms of the language that will be needed. Whilst this is relatively straightforward for occupations where language is tightly prescribed, such as air traffic controllers, it is much more difficult for occupations such as marketing. Quite often a compromise solution is arrived at, where the language course will attempt to simulate the working environment but there will also be some scope for developing more general language.

Adults needing a foreign language for their work often find it difficult because of the demands of their job to attend a language course on a regular basis. Language learners in such circumstances are often able to exercise a high degree of autonomy in their learning, and they may make use of course books, audio cassettes, even video cassettes and computer-assisted language learning packages. This may be through institutional self-access language resources centres or through purchasing some of the self-directed language learning materials that are available.

Foreign languages and leisure

Foreign language learning has become a very popular leisure activity, and many adult education centres run a wide range of courses in different languages and at different levels. There has been a considerable diversification of provision as more and more people go on holiday to more adventurous destinations. Autonomous language learning also plays an important role for those who wish to learn a foreign language for leisure purposes. In the early stages this may need to be in the form of more structured language learning materials, but at the more advanced levels it may be simply through exposure to the foreign language.

There is no doubt that there is a great deal of interest in both learning and using foreign languages. For some this will be in order to make contact with people from the foreign countries, often by visiting them. For others, it may be more as a way of gaining access to the culture of the country, possibly by reading but more often by listening to the radio, watching films or through other artistic forms. Apart from the cinema and film clubs a number of foreign language films are now shown in their original versions on television, and in many parts of the country it is now possible to have access to foreign television stations via satellite or cable television. The fact that different leisure pursuits involve differing amounts of language use means that it is possible to start using the foreign language in activities where the communicative demands are not too great and gradually to progress to more linguistically demanding leisure pursuits in the foreign language.

Conclusion

There is clearly a great deal of interest in both English mother tongue and modern foreign languages post-16, whether it be in education, at work or for leisure purposes. At this level as in compulsory schooling, there has been a great deal of debate about standards. Our finding is that on the whole standards are quite high, but that young people tend to have different skills from those that their parents may have possessed. In both mother tongue and foreign language work there is an emphasis on language in use, and this means that time is spent developing language skills for basic communication, with the accent on fluency rather than accuracy. There is little doubt that accuracy has suffered, but there can be little doubt either that standards of communicative competence are generally higher than they used to be.

The interest and enthusiasm that exist within the field and the many exciting possibilities that are opening up, especially in the field of vocational further education, mean that there could be a very exciting future for language work in post-16 education. And the communicative demands that are made upon the young people of today mean that they may have many more opportunities for practising and improving their language skills, both mother tongue and foreign language, outside of formal education, in the workplace and through their leisure pursuits.

Bibliography

Allen, D. 1988: *English, Whose English?* Sheffield: NATE for NAAE.

Applebee, A. N. 1978: *The Child's Concept of Story: Ages Two to Seventeen.* Chicago: Chicago University Press.

Astley, H. and Hawkins, E. 1985: *Using Language.* Cambridge: Cambridge University Press.

Austin, M. 1991: 'An overview of recent developments in modern languages teaching', in Stevens, 1991.

Bain, R., Bibby, B. and Walton, S. 1989: *National Curriculum in English for ages 5 to 16: Summary and Commentary.* Sheffield: NATE.

Bain, R., Fitzgerald, B. and Taylor, M. (eds) 1992: *Looking into Language: Classroom Approaches to KAL.* London: Hodder & Stoughton.

Barnes, D., Britton, J. and Rosen, H. 1969: *Language, the Learner and the School.* Harmondsworth: Penguin.

Barnes, D. 1976: *From Communication to Curriculum.* Harmondsworth: Penguin.

Bazalgette, C. (ed.) 1989: *Primary Media Education: a Curriculum Statement.* London: BFI.

Bazerman, C. 1988: *Shaping Written Knowledge: The Genre and Activity of the Experimental Article in Science.* Madison, Wis.: University of Wisconsin Press.

Beard, R. 1993: *Teaching Literacy, Balancing Perspectives.* London: Hodder & Stoughton.

Beed, P. L., Hawkins, E. M. and Roller, C. M. 1991: 'Moving learners toward independence: the power of scaffolded instruction', *The Reading Teacher*, 44, 9.

Benton, M. and Fox, G. 1985: *Teaching Literature 9–14.* Oxford: Oxford University Press.

Benton, M. et al. 1988: *Young Readers Responding to Poems.* London: Routledge.

Bialystok, E. 1990: *Communication Strategies: A Psychological Analysis of Second Language Use.* Oxford: Basil Blackwell.

Black, A. 1991: 'Interview with Ken Taylor', *Drama Magazine*, July.

Bloomfield, L. 1933: *Language*. London: George Allen and Unwin.

Blue, G. M. (ed.) 1993: *Language, Learning and Success: Studying through English*. Basingstoke: Macmillan.

Board of Education. 1929: *Modern Languages: Memorandum on Teaching and Organisation in Secondary Schools*. London: HMSO.

Bourne, J. 1989: *Moving into the Mainstream*. Windsor: NFER-Nelson.

Bowker, J. (ed.) 1991: *Secondary Media Education: a Curriculum Statement*. London: BFI.

Boylan, J. 1990: 'National drama: the final solution?' *London Drama*, March.

Britton, J. 1970: *Language and Learning*. London: Penguin.

Broadbent, J. et al. 1983: *Assessment in a Multicultural Society: Community Languages at 16 +*. York: Longman for Schools Council.

Brown, A. L. 1982: 'Learning how to learn from reading' in Langer and Smith-Burke, 1982, pp. 26–54.

Brown, A. L. and Palincsar, A. S. 1987: 'Reciprocal teaching of comprehension strategies: a natural history of one program for enhancing learning', in Day and Borkowski, 1987, pp. 81–132.

Brown, H. D. 1987: *Principles of Language Learning and Teaching*. Englewood Cliffs, N.J.: Prentice-Hall.

Brown, J. et al. 1990: *Developing English for TVEI*. Leeds: Leeds University.

Brumfit, C. J. 1984: *Communicative Methodology in Language Teaching*. Cambridge: Cambridge University Press.

Brumfit, C. J. 1985: 'Summary of comments on language in *Education for All*', in Brumfit, Ellis and Levine, 1985, pp. 199–206.

Brumfit, C. J. 1989: 'Towards a language policy for multilingual secondary schools', keynote lecture to CILT/European Community Pilot Project Seminar, London, September 1986, published in Geach, 1989.

Brumfit, C. J. 1990: Inaugural Lecture: 'Is language education or is education language?', *CLE Working Papers* 1, Southampton: University of Southampton Centre for Language in Education.

Brumfit, C. J. 1993: *Advanced Language Training for English Teachers, Briefing Document no. 3*, Southampton: University of Southampton Centre for Language in Education.

Brumfit, C. J., Ellis, R. and Levine, J. (eds) 1985: *English as a Second Language in the United Kingdom*. Oxford: Pergamon.

Bruner, J. 1985: 'Vygotsky: a historical and conceptual perspective', in Wertsch, 1985, pp. 21–34.

BTEC. 1987: *Foreign Languages: Guidance and Unit Specifications*. London: Business and Technician Education Council.

Buckby, M. and Huntley, T. 1992: *Auto: Pupil's Book 1*. London: Collins.

Buckingham, D. 1990a: 'English and Media Studies: Making the Difference', *English Magazine*, 23 (Summer).

Buckingham, D. 1990b: 'English and Media Studies: Getting Together', *English Magazine*, 24 (Autumn).

Buckingham, D. (ed.) 1990c: *Watching Media Learning*. London: Falmer.

Bulman, L. 1985: *Teaching Language and Study Skills in Secondary Science*. London, Heinemann.

Burstall, C. 1968: *French from Eight*. Slough: NFER.

Burstall, C. et al. 1974: *Primary French in the Balance*. Slough: NFER.

Byram, M. 1989: *Cultural Studies in Foreign Language Education*. Clevedon: Multilingual Matters.

Campione, J. C. and Armbruster, B. B. 1985: 'Acquiring information from texts: an analysis of four approaches', in Segal, Chippman and Glaser, 1985, pp. 317–59.

Carroll, J. 1965: 'The prediction of success in foreign language training', in Glaser, 1965.

Carter, R. A. (ed.) 1990: *Knowledge about Language and the Curriculum: The LINC Reader*. London: Hodder & Stoughton.

Cermak, L. S. and Craik, F. I. M. (eds) 1979: *Levels of Processing in Human Memory*. Hillsdale, N.J.: Lawrence Erlbaum.

CILT. 1989: *Information Sheet No. 12*. London: CILT.

City and Guilds. 1993: *GNVQ Specifications: Core Skills*. London: City and Guilds of London Institute.

Clark, J. and Goode, T. 1991: 'On a road to nowhere', *The Drama Magazine*, July.

Clay, M. M. 1985: *The Early Detection of Reading Difficulties*. London: Heinemann.

Clay, M. M. 1991: *Becoming Literate*. London: Heinemann.

Coleman, H. 1989: 'The present and the future of work', in Coleman (ed.), 1989.

Coleman, H. (ed.) 1989: *Working with Language: A Multidisciplinary Consideration of Language Use in Work Contexts*, Berlin: Mouton de Gruyter.

Commission for Racial Equality. 1986: *Teaching English as a Second Language: Report of a Formal Investigation in Calderdale LEA*. London: CRE.

Cooper, C. R. (ed.) 1985: *Researching Response to Literature and the Teaching of Literature*. Norwood N.J.: Ablex.

Cox, C. B. 1991: *Cox on Cox. An English Curriculum for the 1990s*. London: Hodder & Stoughton.

Crowther, G. 1959: *15 to 18: Report of the Central Advisory Council for*

Education. London: HMSO.

Currie, L. A. 1993: 'English language 5–14, novel studies and the development of metacomprehension skills', *Support for Learning*, 8, 1.

Davies, F. 1990: 'Reading in the National Curriculum', in Harris and Wilkinson, 1990, pp. 61–95.

Day, C. and Norman, J. L. (eds) 1983: *Issues in Educational Drama*. London: Falmer.

Day, J. D. and Borkowski, J. G. (eds) 1987: *Intelligence and Exceptionality: New Directions for Theory, Assessment and Instructional Practices*. Norwood, N.J.: Ablex.

Dean, S. 1990: *Education Support Grant Project: 'Diversification of the First Foreign Language'*. Hampshire County Council, mimeo.

Department of Education and Science. 1975: *A Language for Life* (The Bullock Report). London: HMSO.

Department of Education and Science. 1977: *Modern Languages in Comprehensive Schools*. London, HMSO.

Department of Education and Science/Welsh Office. 1983: *Foreign Languages in the School Curriculum: a consultative paper*. London: DES/WO.

Department of Education and Science. 1984: *English 5–16. Curriculum Matters*, 1. London: HMSO.

Department of Education and Science. 1985: *Education for All* (The Swann Report). London: HMSO.

Department of Education and Science. 1986: *English from 5–16, The Responses to Curriculum Matters 1*. London: HMSO.

Department of Education and Science/Welsh Office. 1986: *Foreign Languages in the School Curriculum: a draft statement of policy*. London: DES/WO.

Department of Education and Science. 1987: *Modern Foreign Languages 11 to 16* Curriculum Matters 8. London: HMSO.

Department of Education and Science. 1988a: *Advancing A Levels: Report of a Committee appointed by the Secretary of State for Education and Science and the Secretary of State for Wales* (The Higginson Report). London: HMSO.

Department of Education and Science. 1988b: *Report of the Committee of Inquiry into the Teaching of English Language* (The Kingman Report). London: HMSO.

Department of Education and Science/Welsh Office. 1988: *Languages in the School Curriculum: a Statement of Policy*. London: DES/WO.

Department of Education and Science. 1989: *Drama from 5–16*. Curriculum Matters 17. London: HMSO.

Department of Education and Science/Welsh Office. 1989: *English for*

Ages 5 to 16 (The Cox Report). London: DES.

Department of Education and Science/Welsh Office. 1990a: *A Survey of Language Awareness and Foreign Language Taster Courses*. London: HMSO.

Department of Education and Science/Welsh Office. 1990b: *National Curriculum Modern Foreign Languages Working Group: Initial Advice*. Darlington: DES.

Department of Education and Science/Welsh Office. 1990c: *Modern Foreign Languages for ages 11 to 16*. London: HMSO.

Department of Education and Science/Welsh Office. 1990d: *English in the National Curriculum (No. 2)*. London: HMSO.

Department of Education and Science. 1991: *Drama in the National Curriculum, Wall Chart*. York: National Curriculum Council.

Department of Education and Science/Welsh Office. 1991: *Modern Foreign Languages in the National Curriculum*. London: HMSO.

Department for Education. 1993a: *English for ages 5–16 (1993)* London: National Curriculum Council/HMSO.

Department for Education. 1993b: *English for Ages 5–16, Proposals for the Revised Order*. London: Department for Education.

Dias, P. and Hayhoe, M. 1988: *Developing Response to Poetry*. Milton Keynes: Open University Press.

Diller, K. (ed.) 1981: *Individual Differences and Universals in Language Learning Aptitude*. Rowley, Mass.: Newbury House.

Dixon, J. 1967: *Growth through English*. Oxford: Oxford University Press.

Donaldson, M. 1978: *Children's Minds*. Glasgow: Fontana.

Donmall, B. G. (ed.) 1985: *Language Awareness: NCLE Reports and Papers 6*. London: CILT.

Doughty, P., Pearce, J. and Thornton, G. 1971: *Language in Use*. London: Edward Arnold.

Dudley-Evans, T. 1984: 'The team teaching of writing skills', in Williams, Swales and Kirkman, 1984, pp. 123–34.

Durkin, K. (ed.) 1986: *Language Development in the School Years*. London: Croom Helm.

Dweck, C. S. and Leggett, E. L. 1988: 'A Social-cognitive approach to motivation and personality', *Psychological Review*, 95: 256–73.

Eco, U. 1992: *Interpretation and Overinterpretation*. Cambridge: Cambridge University Press.

Edwards, D. and Mercer, N. 1986: 'Context and continuity: classroom discourse and the development of shared knowledge', in Durkin, 1986.

Edwards, D. and Mercer, N. 1987: *Common Knowledge*. London: Routledge.

Edwards, J. 1982: 'Language attitudes and their implications among English speakers', in Ryan and Giles, 1982, pp. 20–33.

Ek, J. A. van and Alexander, L. G. 1975: *Systems Development in Adult Language Learning: The Threshold Level in a European Unit/credit System for Modern Language Learning by Adults.* Strasbourg: Council of Europe.

Evans, C. 1988: *Language People: The Experience of Teaching and Learning Modern Languages in British Universities.* Milton Keynes: Open University Press.

Fillmore, C. et al. (eds) 1979: *Individual Differences in Language Ability and Language Behaviour.* New York: Academic Press.

Fish, S. 1980: *Is There a Text in this Class? The Authority of Interpretive Communities.* Cambridge, Mass.: Harvard University Press.

Fisher, M. 1964: *Intent Upon Reading.* Leicester: Brockhampton Press.

Fitzpatrick, F. 1987: *The Open Door.* Clevedon: Multilingual Matters.

Freeborn, D. 1992: 'A Levels in English language: a personal view', *British Association for Applied Linguistics Newsletter* 2: 20–5.

Freund, E. 1987: *The Return of the Reader.* London: Methuen.

Frith, A. and Harris, V. 1990: 'Group work in the modern languages classroom', *Language Learning Journal*, 1: 71–4.

Gardner, R. 1985: *Social Psychology and Second Language Learning: The Role of Attitudes and Motivation.* London: Edward Arnold.

Gardner, R. and Lambert, W. 1972: *Attitudes and Motivation in Second Language Learning.* Rowley, Mass.: Newbury House.

Gathercole, G. (ed.) 1990: *Autonomy in Language Learning.* London: CILT.

Geach, J. (ed.) 1989: *Coherence in Diversity.* London: CILT.

Glaser, R. (ed.) 1965: *Training, Research and Education.* New York: Wiley.

Grauberg, W. 1990: *Language Teaching in the UK – 21 Years On*, Southampton: University of Southampton Language Centre.

Grenfell, M. 1991: 'Communication: sense and nonsense', *Language Learning Journal*, 3: 6–8.

Grenfell, M. and Harris, V. 1992: *Learner Strategies in the Secondary School Classroom.* University of Southampton: *Centre for Language in Education, Occasional Paper* No. 8.

Hadley, C. G. et al. 1981: *Languages other than French in the Secondary School.* London: Schools Council.

Hamers, J. F. and Blanc, M. 1989: *Bilinguality and Bilingualism.* Cambridge: Cambridge University Press.

Harding, D. W. 1962: 'Psychological processes in the reading of fiction', *British Journal of Aesthetics*, 2, 2: 133–47.

Hardy, B. 1975: *Tellers and Listeners. The Narrative Imagination.* London:

Athlone Press.

Harris, J. and Wilkinson, J. (eds) 1990: *A Guide to English Language in the National Curriculum*. Cheltenham: Stanley Thornes.

Harris, V. and Noyau, G. 1990: 'Collaborative learning: taking the first steps', in Gathercole, 1990.

Hart, A. 1991: *Understanding the Media*. London: Routledge.

Hart, A. 1992: Mis-reading English', *English Magazine*, 26 (Spring).

Hart, A. and Benson, A. 1992/1993: *Models of Media Education Parts 1 and 2*. Southampton University: *Centre for Language in Education Occasional Papers* 11 and 12.

Hawkins, E. 1981: *Modern Languages in the Curriculum*. Cambridge: Cambridge University Press.

Hawkins, E. 1984: *Awareness of Language: An Introduction*. Cambridge: Cambridge University Press.

Haynes, J. 1992: *A Sense of Words: Knowledge about Language in the Primary School*. London: Hodder & Stoughton.

Hollindale, P. 1972: 'Why have things gone wrong?' *The Use of English*, 23, 4: 334–6.

Hornbrook, D. 1989: *Education and Dramatic Art*. Oxford: Blackwell.

Hornbrook, D. 1991: *Education in Drama: Casting the Dramatic Curriculum*. London: Falmer.

Houlton, D. 1985: *All Our Languages*. London: Edward Arnold.

Hudson, R. A. 1992: *Teaching Grammar: A Guide for the National Curriculum*. Oxford: Blackwell.

Inglis, F. 1981: *The Promise of Happiness*. Cambridge: Cambridge University Press.

Iser, W. 1978: *The Act of Reading: a Theory of Aesthetic Response*. London: Routledge.

Jefferson, A. and Robey, D. 1986: *Modern Literary Theory* (2nd edn). London: Batsford.

Jenkins, J. J. 1979: 'Four points to remember: a tetrahedral model of memory experiments', in Cermak and Craik, 1979.

Jones, B. 1984: *How Language Works*. Cambridge: Cambridge University Press.

Jupp, T. C. and Hodlin, S. 1975: *Industrial English: An Example of Theory and Practice in Functional Language Teaching for Elementary Learners*. London: Heinemann.

Keen, J. 1992: *Language and the English Curriculum*. Buckingham: Open University Press.

Kermode, F. 1990: *An Appetite for Poetry*. London: Fontana.

Krashen, S. 1981: *Second Language Acquisition and Second Language Learning*. Oxford: Pergamon.

Krashen, S. 1982: *Principles and Practice in Second Language Acquisition.* Oxford: Pergamon.

Kundera, M. 1988: *The Art of the Novel.* London: Faber.

Langer, J. and Smith-Burke, T. (eds) 1982: *Reader Meets Author, Bridging the Gap: A Psycholinguistic Perspective.* Newark: International Reading Association, Dell Publishing.

Languages Lead Body. 1993a: *Introduction to the National Language Standards.* London: Languages Lead Body.

Languages Lead Body. 1993b: *National Language Standards: Breaking the Language Barrier across the World of Work.* London: Languages Lead Body.

Leavis, F. R. 1936: *Revaluation.* London: Chatto and Windus.

Leavis, F. R. 1948: *The Great Tradition.* London: Chatto and Windus.

Limb, A. G. (ed.) 1986: *Language and Languages 16–19, NCLE Papers and Reports 7,* London: CILT.

Lindemann, E. 1993: 'Freshman composition: no place for literature', *College English,* 55, 3: 311–16.

Littlewood, W. 1981: *Communicative Language Teaching.* Cambridge: Cambridge University Press.

London Chamber of Commerce and Industry (LCCI). 1992: *Foreign Languages at Work 1992–93.* London: LCCI.

Lunzer, E. and Gardner, K. 1984: *Learning from the Written Word.* Edinburgh: Oliver & Boyd.

McNab, R. and Barrabe, F. 1992: *Avantage, Pupil's Book 1.* Oxford: Heinemann.

Markless, S. and Morrison, J. 1992: *Enhancing Information Skills in Further Education,* British Library Research Paper Series, no. 99.

Mathieson, M. 1975: *The Preachers of Culture.* London: Allen & Unwin.

Meek, M. 1982: *Learning to Read.* London: The Bodley Head.

Meek, M. 1988: *How Texts Teach What Readers Learn.* Stroud: The Thimble Press.

Miller, A. and Roselman, L. 1988: *Arc-en-ciel, Pupil's Book 1.* London: Mary Glasgow Publications.

Miller, A., Roselman, L. and Bougard, M. 1990: *Arc-en-ciel, Pupil's Book 3.* London: Mary Glasgow Publications.

Milroy, J. and Milroy, L. 1985: *Authority in Language* London: Routledge & Kegan Paul.

Mitchell, R. F. 1988: *Communicative Language Teaching in Practice.* London: CILT.

Mitchell, R. F. 1991: 'Multilingualism in British schools: future policy directions', *British Studies in Applied Linguistics 6, Language and Nation.* London: BAAL/CILT, pp. 107–116.

Mitchell, R. F., Hooper, J. V. and Brumfit, C. J. 1994: *Final Report: 'Knowledge about Language', Language Learning, and the National Curriculum*. University of Southampton: *Centre for Language in Education Occasional Papers*, 20.

Mitchell, R., McIntyre, D., Mclennan, S. and Mcdonald, M. 1987: *Report of an Independent Evaluation of the Western Isles' Bilingual Education Project*. Department of Education, University of Stirling.

Mitchell, R., Martin, C. and Grenfell, M. 1992: *Evaluation of The Basingstoke Primary Schools Language Awareness Project: 1990–91*. Southampton University: *Centre for Language in Education Occasional Papers* 7.

Munby, J. 1978: *Communicative Syllabus Design: A Sociolinguistic Model for Defining the Content of Purpose-specific Language Programmes*, Cambridge: Cambridge University Press.

Naiman, N. et al. 1978: *The Good Language Learner*. Toronto: Ontario Institute for Studies in Education.

National Curriculum Council. 1991a: *Art for Ages 5 to 14*. York: NCC.

National Curriculum Council. 1991b: *Music for Ages 5 to 14*. York: NCC.

National Curriculum Council. 1992a: *Modern Foreign Languages Non-statutory Guidance*. York: NCC.

National Curriculum Council. 1992b: *National Curriculum English: The Case for Revising the Order*. York: NCC.

Neelands, J. 1984: *Making Sense of Drama*. London: Heinemann.

Neelands, J. 1990: *Structuring Drama Work*. Cambridge: Cambridge University Press.

Neill, D. 1984: 'Testing communication studies at A-Level', in Williams, Swales and Kirkman, 1984, pp. 169–79.

Norwood Report. 1943: *Curriculum and Examinations in Secondary Schools*. London: HMSO.

O'Neill, C. 1983: 'Content or essence: the place of drama in the curriculum', in Day and Norman, 1983.

OXPROD. 1989: *Occasional Paper 3*. Oxford University Department of Education.

OXPROD. 1990: *Occasional Paper 5*. Oxford University Department of Education.

Paris, S. G., Wasik, B. A. and Van der Westhuizen, G. 1988: 'Meta-metacognitions: a review of research on metacognition and reading', in *Dialogues in Literacy, 37th Yearbook of the National Reading Conference*. Chicago: National Reading Conference.

Peers, E. A. 1944: *Spanish Now*. London: Methuen.

Phillips, D. 1988: *Languages in Schools: From Complacency to Conviction*. London: CILT.

Phillips, D. (ed.) 1989: *Which Language?: Diversification and the National Curriculum*. London: Hodder & Stoughton.

Phillips, D. and Stencel, V. 1983: *The Second Foreign Language*. London: Hodder & Stoughton.

Pickering, R. 1992: *Planning and Resourcing A Level French: A Handbook for Teachers*. London: CILT.

Plowden Report. 1967: *Children and their Primary Schools*. London: Central Advisory Council for Education.

Protherough, R. 1983: *Developing Response to Fiction*. Milton Keynes: Open University Press.

Protherough, R., Atkinson, J. and Fawcett, J. 1989: *The Effective Teaching of English*. Harlow: Longman.

Raleigh, M. 1981: *The Languages Book*. London: ILEA English Centre.

Rees, P. 1992: 'Reading in French – GCSE to A level', *Perspectives on Reading, CLE Working Papers* 2. University of Southampton: Centre for Language in Education, pp. 78–98.

Richards, I. A. 1929: *Practical Criticism*. London: Routledge.

Richmond, J. 1991: 'Politics, Reading and Knowledge about Language', *NATE News*, April, pp. 7–14.

Richterich, R. and Chancerel, J.-L. 1977: *Identifying the Needs of Adults Learning a Foreign Language*. Strasbourg: Council of Europe.

Rigby, G. and Burgess, R. G. 1991: *Language Teaching in Higher Education: A Discussion Document*. Sheffield: Employment Department.

Rorty, R. 1992: 'The pragmatist's progress', in Eco, 1992.

Rosen, C. and Rosen, H. 1973: *The Language of Primary School Children*. Harmondsworth: Penguin.

Rosenblatt, L. 1938/70: *Literature as Exploration*. New York: Modern Languages Association.

Rosenblatt, L. 1978: *The Reader, The Text, The Poem: The Transactional Theory of the Literary Work*. Carbondale: Southern Illinois University Press.

Rosenblatt, L. 1985: 'The transactional theory of the literary work: implications for research', in Cooper, 1985.

Rubin, J. 1981: 'Study of Cognitive Processes in Second Language Learning'. *Applied Linguistics*, 2: 117–31.

Ryan, E. B. and Giles, H. (eds) 1982: *Attitudes towards Language Variation*. London: Edward Arnold.

Sampson, G. 1946, 'A boy and his books', in *Seven Essays*. London: Cambridge University Press.

Scholes, R. 1985: *Textual Power: Literary Theory and the Teaching of English*. New Haven: Yale University Press.

Schools Council. 1981: *Languages Other than French in Secondary Schools*.

London: Schools Council.

Schools Council. 1982: *The Second Foreign Language in Secondary Schools: a question of survival*. London: Schools Council.

Seely, J. 1991: *Language Live!* Oxford: Heinemann.

Segal, J., Chippman, S. F. and Glaser, R. (eds) 1985: *Thinking and Learning Skills: Relating Instruction to Research*, vol. 1. Hillsdale, N.J.: Lawrence Erlbaum.

Skehan, P. 1989: *Individual Differences in Second Language Learning*. London: Edward Arnold.

Smith, F. 1982: *Understanding Reading* (3rd edn). London: Holt, Rinehart & Winston.

Stern, H. 1975: 'What can we learn from the good language learner?' *Canadian Modern Language Review*, 31: 304–18.

Stevens A. (ed.) 1991: *Languages for the World of Work*, London: CILT.

Stubbs, M. 1989: 'The state of English in the English state: reflections on the Cox Report', *Language in Education*, 3, 4: 235–50.

Swales, J. 1990: *Genre Analysis: English in Academic and Research Settings*. Cambridge: Cambridge University Press.

Tansley, P. 1986: *Community Languages in Primary Education*. Windsor: NFER/Nelson.

Tansley, P. and Craft, A. 1984: 'Mother tongue teaching and support: a Schools Council enquiry', *Journal of Multilingual and Multicultural Development*, 5, 5: 367–85.

Tosi, A. 1984: *Immigration and Bilingual Education*. Oxford: Pergamon.

Tucker, N. 1981: *The Child and the Book*. Cambridge: Cambridge University Press.

Vygotsky, L. S. 1962: *Thought and Language*. Cambridge, Mass.: MIT Press.

Welsh Office. 1989: *Welsh for Ages 5 to 16*. Cardiff: Welsh Office.

Wertsch, J. V. (ed.) 1985: *Culture, Communication and Cognition: Vygotskian Perspectives*. New York: Cambridge University Press.

Wesche, M. 1981: 'Language aptitude measures in streaming, matching students with methods, and diagnosis of learning problems', in Diller, 1981.

Whitehead, F. et al. 1977: *Children and their Books*. London: Macmillan.

Widdowson, H. G. 1978: *Teaching Language as Communication*. Oxford: Oxford University Press.

Widdowson, P. (ed.) 1982: *Rereading English*. London: Methuen.

Wilkins, D. A. 1976: *Notional Syllabuses*. London: Oxford University Press.

Williams, R., Swales, J. and Kirkman, J. (eds) 1984: *Common Ground: Shared Interests in ESP and Communication Studies*, Oxford: Pergamon.

Witkin, H. 1962, *Psychological Differentiation*. New York: Wiley.

Wolf, T. 1980: 'Reading reconsidered', in Wolf, McQuillan and Radwin, 1980.

Wolf, T., McQuillan, M. and Radwin, E. (eds) 1980: *Thought & Language, Language & Reading*. Cambridge Mass.: Harvard Educational Review.

Wong-Fillmore, L. 1979: 'Individual differences in second language acquisition', in Fillmore et al. 1979, pp. 203–28.

Wood, D., Bruner, J. and Ross, G. 1976: 'The role of thinking in problem solving'. *J. of Child Psychiatry*, 17: 89–100.

Further Reading

Chapter 1   Language in the curriculum

Brumfit, C. J. 1989: 'Towards a language policy for multilingual second-ary schools', in J. Geach (ed.) 1989: *Coherence in Diversity*. London: CILT, pp. 7–19.

Chapter 2   The National Curriculum as a language policy

Bourne, J. 1989: *Moving into the Mainstream*. Windsor: NFER-Nelson.

Department of Education and Science. 1985: *Education for All* (The Swann Report). London: HMSO.

Department of Education and Science. 1988: *Report of the Committee of Inquiry into the Teaching of the English Language* (The Kingman Report). London: HMSO.

Department of Education and Science/Welsh Office. 1989: *English for Ages 5 to 16* (The Cox Report). London: DES.

Department of Education and Science/Welsh Office. 1990b: *National Curriculum Modern Foreign Language Working Group: Initial Advice*. Darlington: DES.

Department of Education and Science/Welsh Office. 1990d: *English in the National Curriculum (No. 2)*. London: HMSO.

Department of Education and Science/Welsh Office. 1991: *Modern Foreign Languages in the National Curriculum* (The Harris Report). London: HMSO.

Chapter 3   English teaching: language, literacy and learning

Dixon, J. 1967: *Growth through English*. Oxford: Oxford University Press.

Mathieson, M. 1975: *The Preachers of Culture*. London: Allen & Unwin.

Protherough, R., Atkinson, J. and Fawcett, J. 1989: *The Effective Teaching of English*. Harlow: Longman.

Chapter 4 Reading to learn

Beard, R. 1993: *Teaching Literacy, Balancing Perspectives*. London: Hodder & Stoughton.
Clay, Marie M. 1991: *Becoming Literate*. London: Heinemann.
Donaldson, M. 1978: *Children's Minds*. Glasgow: Fontana.
Lunzer, E. and Gardner, K. 1984: *Learning from the Written Word*. Edinburgh: Oliver & Boyd.

Chapter 5 Literature teaching and the National Curriculum

Benton, M. and Fox, G. 1985: *Teaching Literature 9–14*. Oxford: Oxford University Press.
Freund, E. 1987: *The Return of the Reader*. London: Methuen.

Chapter 6 Drama in education

Day, C. and Norman, J. L. (eds) 1983: *Issues in Educational Drama*. London: Falmer.
Hornbrook, D. 1991: *Education in Drama: Casting the Dramatic Curriculum*. London: Falmer.
Neelands, J. 1990: *Structuring Drama Work*. Cambridge: Cambridge University Press.

Chapter 7 Media education and the secondary English curriculum

Hart, A. 1991: *Understanding the Media*. London: Routledge.

Chapter 8 Bilingual learners: community languages and English

Bourne, J. 1989: *Moving into the Mainstream*. Windsor: NFER-Nelson.

Brumfit, C. J. 1985: 'Summary of comments on language in *Education for All*', in Brumfit, Ellis and Levine, 1985: 199–206.
Raleigh, M. 1981: *The Languages Book*. London: ILEA English Centre.

Chapter 9   The first foreign language

Department of Education and Science. 1990: *Modern Languages for 11 to 16*. London: HMSO.
Department of Education and Science. 1991: *Modern Languages in the National Curriculum*. London: HMSO.
Grenfell, M. 1991: Communication: Sense and Nonsense. *Language Learning Journal*, no. 3: 6–8.
Hawkins, E. 1981: *Modern Languages in the Curriculum*. Cambridge: Cambridge University Press.
Skehan, P. 1989: *Individual Differences in Second Language Learning*. London: Edward Arnold.

Chapter 10   Other foreign languages

Hadley, C. G. et al. 1981: *Languages other than French in the Secondary School*. London: Schools Council.
Phillips, D. and Stencel, V. 1983: *The Second Foreign Language*. London: Hodder & Stoughton.

Chapter 11   Language awareness

Bain, R., Fitzgerald, B. and Taylor, M. (eds) 1992: *Looking into Language: Classroom Approaches to KAL*. London: Hodder & Stoughton.
Carter, R. A. (ed.) 1990: *Knowledge about Language and the Curriculum: The LINC Reader*. London: Hodder & Stoughton.
Department of Education and Science. 1988: *Report of the Committee of Inquiry into the Teaching of English Language* (The Kingman Report). London: HMSO.
Donmall, B. G. (ed.) 1985: *Language Awareness: NCLE Reports and Papers 6*. London: CILT.
Edwards, D. and Mercer, N. 1987: *Common Knowledge*. London: Routledge.
Hawkins, E. 1984: *Awareness of Language: An Introduction*. Cambridge: Cambridge University Press.

Mitchell, R. F., Hooper, J. V. and Brumfit, C. J. 1994: *Final Report: 'Knowledge about Language', Language Learning, and the National Curriculum*. University of Southampton: *Centre for Language in Education Occasional Papers*, 20.

Chapter 12   Language after sixteen

Blue, G. M. (ed.) 1993: *Language, Learning and Success: Studying through English*. Basingstoke: Macmillan.

Coleman, H. 1989: 'The present and the future of work', in H. Coleman (ed.) *Working with Language: A multidisciplinary consideration of language use in work contexts*. Berlin: Mouton de Gruyter.

Department of Education and Science. 1988: *Advancing A Levels: Report of a Committee appointed by the Secretary of State for Education and Science and the Secretary of State for Wales* (The Higginson Report). London: HMSO.

Ek, J. A. van and Alexander, L. G. 1975: *Systems Development in Adult Language Learning: The Threshold Level in a European unit/credit system for modern language learning by adults*. Strasbourg: Council of Europe.

Languages Lead Body. 1993: *Introduction to the National Language Standards*. London: Languages Lead Body.

Index